KT-232-950

Betrayed

61 051 667

By the same author

Helpless: A True Short Story

Trapped: The Terrifying True Story
of a Secret World of Abuse

A Small Boy's Cry

Two More Sleeps

CALDERDALE LIBRARIES	
Bertrams	13/02/2015
362.733LEW	£7.99
BB	CPO328

Betrayed

ROSIE LEWIS

One girl's struggle
to escape a cruel
life defined by
family honour

Certain details in this story, including names, places and dates,
have been changed to protect the family's privacy.

HarperElement
An imprint of HarperCollins*Publishers*
1 London Bridge Street
London SE1 9GF

www.harpercollins.co.uk

First published by HarperElement 2015

1 3 5 7 9 10 8 6 4 2

© Rosie Lewis 2015

Rosie Lewis asserts the moral right to
be identified as the author of this work

A catalogue record of this book is
available from the British Library

PB ISBN 978-0-00-754180-5
EB ISBN 978-0-00-754181-2

Printed and bound in Great Britain by
Clays Ltd, St Ives plc

All rights reserved. No part of this publication may be
reproduced, stored in a retrieval system, or transmitted,
in any form or by any means, electronic, mechanical,
photocopying, recording or otherwise, without the prior
written permission of the publishers.

MIX
Paper from
responsible sources
FSC **FSC™ C007454**
www.fsc.org

FSC™ is a non-profit international organisation established to promote
the responsible management of the world's forests. Products carrying the
FSC label are independently certified to assure consumers that they come
from forests that are managed to meet the social, economic and
ecological needs of present and future generations,
and other controlled sources.

Find out more about HarperCollins and the environment at
www.harpercollins.co.uk/green

Prologue

Moonlight shrouded a robed figure as he entered the unlit hallway, his silhouette fading with a gentle clunk as the double lock was secured behind him. Nine-year-old Zadie watched the stranger's arrival through a narrow gap in the banisters, a chill prickling across the top of her scalp at the sight of the black leather bag clutched in his hand. The realisation of what was inside made her heart pound so hard that she imagined it might squeeze through her ribs and escape from her chest.

Shivering as she crouched on her haunches, her eyes ferreted the shadows for Nadeen. There was no sign of her sister but she could just make out her father as he crossed the hall beneath her, his sandalled feet echoing on the bare floorboards. The late-night visitor followed; a thin, upright sort of man with a thick beard and greying, straggly hair; nothing like the monster who had stalked her dreams. Sensing nervousness in the way her father moved, Zadie felt another hammering inside her chest. Ripples pulsed upwards, teasing her throat into a cough.

She clamped a hand over her mouth to muffle the sound, hardly able to believe that the rumours she had feared since she was a little girl were about to merge with reality. Her stomach lurched, bile fizzing at the back of her throat. Tempted to run directly back to her bedroom, she straightened and was about to turn when muffled sobs from the back room rooted her feet to the floor.

'Please, Papa. I don't need an injection, please.'

Zadie squeezed her hands flat against her ears to try and block out her sister's pleading. Closing her eyes, she was gripped by the sudden image of a woman drifting through the air in front of her. As always, as soon as she tried to reach out for the comfort she knew she'd find there, the grainy presence vanished, sounds of a struggle from downstairs chasing it away.

Zadie whimpered and ran back to her bedroom, slumping down onto her mattress and pulling her pillow over her head. An hour before first light she fell into a troubled sleep but was soon woken by a shuffling noise outside the door. Nadeen walked slowly into the room, tears rolling down her cheeks. As the 12-year-old rolled tentatively into the bed opposite her own, her legs bound tightly together with bandages, Zadie could see tell-tale spots of red on the back of her sister's linen nightdress. Silently she crossed the room, reaching out to stroke Nadeen's back.

Zadie sighed with relief as dawn approached and the male members of the household left for morning prayers.

Chapter 1

'Do you think she'll be like Phoebe was when she first came?' my son Jamie called out from his bedroom.

I couldn't help but smile at the hesitancy in his tone as I swept from room to room, checking there were fresh towels in the bathroom and grabbing a floral duvet set from the airing cupboard. Nine-year-old Phoebe had stayed with us for almost a year before moving on to a long-term carer. The friendly, kind and bubbly girl we said goodbye to was unrecognisable from the angry whirlwind we had first met. Our house seemed so much emptier without her presence and, despite her leaving months earlier and other children staying with us meanwhile, we still missed her. But the first few weeks of Phoebe's stay had been challenging for all of us, especially so for Jamie.

From the moment she arrived Phoebe had fixated on him so that, whenever she was confused or upset, Jamie would be the one who got a wet finger shoved into his ear or a plate thrown at him. As she settled and learnt to trust us we witnessed some dramatic changes in her behaviour, so much so that our motivation to foster had grown even stronger, but the traumatic start had left Jamie chary of new arrivals.

'No, I doubt it,' I said, though my words sounded hollow. I actually had no idea what Zadie Hassan would be like. In a hurried telephone conversation with her social worker late that afternoon, I had been told that the 13-year-old was from a Muslim family who had never come to the attention of social services before, and so information was sketchy. Of Asian heritage, Zadie had been found by two patrolling police officers early that morning, sheltering in a shop doorway in a central northern shopping centre. Apparently she had pleaded with officers not to take her home, begging as if her life depended on it. She had seemed so genuinely terrified that the officers took her straight to the police station and alerted social services.

At 13, Zadie was outside of our approved age range, but she had spent most of the day waiting at the local authority offices, listening as social workers phoned agency after agency, trying to match her with Muslim foster carers. By the time the decision was reached to settle her with a white British family it was almost 5 p.m. and the poor girl was exhausted. Strictly speaking, our family was only approved to take children from 0 to 11, leaving a gap of at least two years between any child coming into our home and my own youngest, Jamie, who was just 13. But when an ideal match isn't possible and a child urgently needs a warm bed to sleep in, social workers are usually prepared to bend the rules.

A gap of two years is recommended between looked-after and birth children so that the family dynamics are roughly unchanged. If disrupted, resentment against the foster child can build to a point where the placement breaks down. Some fostered children have been so badly abused in their own homes that they find it difficult to witness the positive environment when they arrive in a foster home and seek to sabotage the relationships between family members, so it's important to maintain the original pecking order.

Preparing children for family life when they have had little experience of boundaries or parental discipline takes time and patience. Even getting them to sit at the table at meal times can seem like an insurmountable task, in the beginning. I wondered whether we would experience any behavioural issues with Zadie. If so, we would have to brace ourselves to get through the first few weeks while she adjusted to our house rules and boundaries.

I had cared for teenagers before and emerged unscathed so I wasn't *too* worried about Zadie's age. What concerned me more was her culture. Would she feel comfortable living with people who didn't share her faith? I wondered. My own parents were Christian and, having grown up in a house where one adult was more devout than the other, I had witnessed first-hand the problems that differing religious views can cause. My father was so determined to prevent any of his children drifting away from the Church that he would only allow us to mix with families who shared his faith. Such a sheltered existence left me wary of outsiders when I was Zadie's age. It took years for me to realise that people didn't necessarily need to be religious to have a good heart. I wondered whether Zadie might feel as guarded as I had. If so, she might well feel awkward around us, frightened even.

Armed with clean linen and towels, I went through to make up Zadie's bed. It was almost 6 p.m. but the bright, early May sunshine was still streaming through the window, giving the magnolia walls a cheery glow. I was pleased Zadie would have the room in our house that got the most sun during the day; she needed to recover from the nights spent sleeping outside.

I wondered whether there was anything about the place that Zadie's parents might disapprove of, certain that they would have concerns about her staying in an environment so far removed from her own. The last thing I wanted was for Zadie to feel uncomfortable in what was to be her home.

My 16-year-old daughter Emily, still dressed in her school uniform, was already bustling around the room with accessories she thought Zadie might like. As if reading my thoughts, she plucked a book from the shelf beside the bed and handed it to me. It was a children's illustrated Bible. 'I don't think she'll be needing that, Mum,' she said.

'No, you're right,' I said, grimacing. 'Help me scout around and see if there's anything else we should move, would you, Ems?'

Emily nodded, kneeling in front of the bookshelf and running her index finger along the spines. 'There's a Muslim girl in my class, Mum. Aisha. She has, like, a special room to go and pray in. She's never allowed to skip prayers *and* she sometimes has to miss lessons to do it. Muslims have to wash their feet and everything before they pray.'

Betrayed

'And they're not allowed to fart,' Jamie piped up from his bedroom. 'Or they have to start all over again.'

Emily rolled her eyes. 'He's so gross, Mum.'

I could hear Jamie snickering to himself. Leaning out of the bedroom door, I called down the hall, 'How did you discover that then, Jamie?'

'Rohan told me. But I'm not sure if he was lying or not.'

Typical of my son to retain that particular nugget of information, I thought, although, to be fair, it was the sort of thing that captured the imagination of 13-year-old boys. There were actually quite a few Muslim pupils at Jamie's school so he shouldn't have been too ignorant about the faith. In fact, one of his friends from primary school had been Muslim. I remembered Jamie going to Tariq's house for tea one day after school. He must have been about six or seven at the time and the little rascal had cleared his plate, yet at home he had been such a picky eater. When I asked Tariq's mother how she managed such a feat she volunteered to show me how to cook chicken shorba with keema naans. I had taken her up on the offer, so at least I was confident about cooking a traditional meal for Zadie, although it was probably gross stereotyping to assume that she even liked spicy food.

Emily broke my chain of thought, handing me another pile of books – the Harry Potter series. 'Goodness, all of these have to go as well?'

'Honestly, Mum. Muslims are *so* strict. There's no way Zadie would be allowed to read these. Aisha is the only one in our class who hasn't seen the films. I feel really sorry for her.'

'Hmmm,' I said, my mind racing again. Emily had sparked a memory of myself as a child, coming home from school in an excited state and telling my parents about our assembly that morning. It had been close to the end of term and teachers had arranged for a magician to come into our school to perform a show for the children. My father was furious and complained to the school; to him, magic meant sorcery – a violation of the first of the Ten Commandments. He feared that through magic there was a risk of me being seduced by the occult. After that, whenever a story or topic involving magic came up, my teacher would ask me to leave the room. I think my classmates felt sorry for me at the time. I bit my lip. 'Strict isn't necessarily bad, Ems,' I said, bending to rest the heavy pile of books on the carpet in the hall. 'Look at your grandfather and how devout he is, but we weren't unhappy growing up.' I fanned my fingers and swept my hands through the air in front of me. 'And see how I've turned out?'

Emily curled her upper lip. 'Exactly. See what I mean?'

I gave her a mock stern look.

She grinned. 'I'm just *so* glad we're not that religious, Mum. It'd be awful.'

'I think you're generalising, Em. Faith can be a positive thing. And Muslims are no different to anyone else. All religions have their extremists but on the whole people just want get on with their lives and do the best they can, don't they?'

She looked doubtful. 'I don't see how anyone can be happy with all those rules. I bet that's why Zadie ran away. Her parents were wa-a-ay too strict.'

'We don't know that at all,' I said, shaking the pillows and moving the duvet so I could get on with making up the bed. 'We hardly know anything about them.' But what Emily had said really got me thinking. So many questions ran through my mind. Had Zadie rebelled against her faith, or would she still need a special area for prayers? And what about visiting the mosque? I wondered as I manoeuvred the pillows into freshly washed cases. If Zadie wanted to worship in a particular way, then, as a foster carer, I had to honour her beliefs and provide her with whatever she needed to maintain her faith.

Still, whatever hurdles we had to get over, a feeling of excitement ran through me. It wasn't unusual for me to feel apprehensive before meeting a new, temporary member of the family. If I was to take the best care I could of Zadie then there was certainly a lot I had to learn. I got the sense that this placement would open my eyes to a way of life very different to my own but I was looking forward to the challenge. I resolved to do a bit of research on Google if I had time before Zadie arrived. But preparing the room had to be a priority.

Both Emily and I loved the build-up of getting everything ready, and making the child's own special place look welcoming was a practical way of doing something positive for them before they'd even arrived. Usually I would make an effort to find out what interested the child, tailoring the room so that it was unique to them, although often that wasn't possible.

Several years earlier I had been expecting a boy of 10 who was coming into care as an emergency. During the initial phone call with his social worker, she had mentioned that Chester had a passion for motorbikes. With an hour to spare before he arrived I dashed to the shops and bought some models to put on the shelf in his room. When I took him up to show him where he'd be sleeping he got emotional, burying his face in his sleeve. I assumed he was upset because he was missing home so I left him upstairs to have a few words with his social worker. When she came down she told me that Chester was overcome at the sight of the motorbikes. He told me later, 'It was the nicest thing anyone ever done for me, Rosie.'

I think Chester was moved more by the fact that I had taken the time to think about what might be important to him rather than the items themselves. It really is amazing how something so seemingly insignificant can mean so much to someone when they come from a place where kind gestures are in short supply. Since then I've always tried to bear Chester's reaction in mind.

When the room was ready I went downstairs and logged on to the computer to see what I could find out about Islam. My mind strayed to a hot day months earlier when I went to watch one of Jamie's cricket matches. I remembered being surprised to see that some of the school's star cricketers were watching the match from the sidelines. One of the parents told me that some of the boys weren't allowed to join in as it was Ramadan and they couldn't drink anything, not even water. Even medicine wasn't permitted. Before that day I had assumed that fasting during the month of Ramadan meant not eating solid food. I never imagined that fluids were to be avoided as well. To be honest, I didn't even know when Ramadan would next fall, although I knew it migrated throughout the seasons; something to do with the Islamic calendar.

Wikipedia offered the most condensed information so I printed the pages and took them to the living room to read. Emily was already on the sofa. 'I wonder if Zadie will have her face covered, Mum.'

'Yes, I was thinking the same. What does Aisha wear to school?'

'One of those headscarves, but it has to be in school colours.'

From what I had just read, it seemed that Muslims placed great store in the concept of 'haya' – dressing decently and wearing nothing that accentuates the body shape. I couldn't help but wonder what Muslims must think of some of the local girls tumbling out of nightclubs at the end of a Saturday-night session. I supposed Emily might have been right about Zadie rebelling against her own culture. It was possible she would turn up dressed in T-shirt and jeans. What seemed almost certain was that she would only eat halal meat, but I knew that was easy enough to get hold of these days; I had seen a whole section in our local supermarket. The rest would depend, I guessed, on just how strict the family were. I scanned my eyes over the print-out, my stomach rolling with anticipation.

'A car's just pulled up outside, Mum,' Jamie shouted as he hurtled down the stairs.

Chapter 2

'Hello, my lovely. Come on in.'

Zadie was smaller than I had expected. Standing aside to welcome her into our hall, I remember her height being the first thing I registered about her. Strange, really, considering that she was cloaked from head to foot in a black robe. But she barely reached my shoulders and I was surprised because, being only a few inches over five foot myself, I'm usually dwarfed by anyone over the age of 10.

'Peggy Fletcher,' Zadie's social worker said as she followed Zadie in. A heavy-set woman in her fifties, she released a light musky scent into the air as she removed her coat, her chest reacting to the effort with a small wheeze. She was wearing a navy-coloured blouse with three-quarter length sleeves that pinched into her flesh, leaving red welts behind on her skin. Her short grey hair and scrubbed, make-up-free skin gave her a stern appearance.

'Nice to meet you, Peggy,' I said, momentarily flummoxed. I had planned to shake her hand but instead of reciprocating she slipped her coat over my outstretched arm. For a second I swivelled on my foot, one way and then the other, not sure what to do with it. Peggy snatched the coat from me with a sigh, draping it over the newel post at the bottom of the stairs. 'There. Now, shall we go through?' she asked, pushing the glasses she wore further up her nose and gesturing down the hall.

'Yes, please do,' I said, already appreciating Peggy's directness. As I followed them I could hear the social worker's loud breaths, raspy as if she'd jogged all the way from the council offices. When we reached the living room I gestured for them both to take a seat, certain that Peggy probably would have made herself comfortable, invited or not. Zadie hovered in the doorway, one shoulder hitched higher than the other to support a rucksack. Her head was lowered, her slender hands running over and over themselves as if she was trying to rub Vaseline into her fingers. I noticed that the headscarf fell behind her at an angle from the top of her head and guessed that she must have long hair, caught up in a large bun.

'I've heard your name before, Rosie, doing the rounds,' Peggy said as she leaned back into the sofa, her face red with exertion. 'It's nice to finally put a face to a name.'

'Oh dear, sounds ominous,' I said. It was a predictable reply but my mind was distracted by Zadie. She looked so uncomfortable, still standing at the threshold of the room. 'Would you like to sit down, Zadie?'

She dipped her head politely, obediently taking a seat about a foot away from Peggy on the sofa, though she perched on the very edge nearest the door. I got the sense that she wanted to be as far removed from us as possible. Close up I could see signs of wear on her robe. It was badly creased, tatty at the hem and hung shapelessly from her shoulders. The cardigan she wore, threads trailing from the cuffs, was missing a couple of buttons. She sat with one foot tucked neatly behind the other, her dark hands resting in a pile on her lap. There were sores all over them but it was difficult to get a good look because she kept tugging at her sleeves with her fingers, pulling them down over her knuckles. It was as if she were trying to make herself disappear.

'Not at all,' Peggy said after a pause.

I smiled appreciatively, although I knew that generally I was considered to be what local authorities needed their carers to be – a safe pair of hands. 'Would either of you like a drink before we get started?' I asked, wondering for a moment where Emily and Jamie had got to. They were nowhere to be seen. They hadn't passed us in the hallway so I guessed they must have slipped quietly into the garden. It was unusual for them not to crowd around a new house guest, but they were getting older now and probably sensitive enough to make themselves scarce.

'Nothing for me, thanks. I've done nothing but drink tea and make phone calls today. I'll be up all night if I have anything else.' Peggy tucked her fingers into her armpits as she spoke, as if trying to warm them, her palms at rest on the top of her breasts. I got the feeling this was not a woman to be messed with and found myself hoping that Peggy would be more supportive than Phoebe's social worker had been. Back then I had felt as if I was a lone voice, battling against the system as well as Phoebe's traumatic past, something that happened with dispiriting regularity.

'Zadie?'

She looked up with a start and shook her head. It was the first time I managed to get a good look at her face. Even without the softening effect of hair, Zadie was clearly very pretty. Her lips were full, although cracked and sore. The horizontal line of the hijab slicing across her forehead seemed to accentuate the large molasses eyes below, her dark-olive, unblemished skin luminous against the harsh black material. With delicate features and thick dark eyelashes, it was the perfect face for framing with a headscarf.

I'm not sure why but I was hugely relieved to see that most of her face was visible. I think I would have been a little intimidated by the anonymity of a face veil. In the first few weeks of a new placement there are many hurdles a foster carer has to overcome in order to gain trust from the troubled child. Children that have been hurt often erect invisible walls around themselves as a defence mechanism. Sometimes it can take weeks to dismantle the barriers and 'reach' the child behind and I think that a face veil would have been yet another stumbling block to overcome.

I certainly didn't need to be a body-language expert to work out that Zadie was nervous; her knees were bobbing up and down and, though the nails on her restless fingers were already short, she kept raising them to her lips, nibbling at the edges. But she may as well have been wearing a full veil for all the clues her expression gave away. It was impenetrable, neither happy nor sad, just devoid of all trace of emotion. I guessed she was probably completely drained.

'So, Zadie. You've had a bit of a day of it, haven't you?'

She nodded, her large brown eyes meeting mine for a brief moment before she cast them downwards. My eyes followed hers and for the first time I noticed that the Wiki pages were still on the floor where I'd left them before answering the door. I crossed the room and sat down in the armchair, letting a moment pass before discreetly nudging the papers underneath.

Peggy swung her bulky knees around to face the teenager. 'Yes, she's been a very silly girl, haven't you?' The social worker peered over the top of her glasses and spoke in a loud, patronisingly slow voice. 'Hmmm? Dangerous, wasn't it? Wandering around the town at that time of night.'

Zadie nodded her head in avid agreement, her face no longer a blank canvas but dotted with blotches of red. My heart went out to her and I felt the muscles in my jaw clenching. Besides feeling sorry for Zadie, I was irked by the way Peggy was talking to her, as if she had learning difficulties or something.

'Never mind. I've got a comfortable bed ready for you,' I said gently. 'I'll show you in a minute.'

Zadie nodded and gave me a grateful half-smile before looking away.

Peggy turned around again, puffing with the effort of shifting in her seat. 'Anything could have happened,' she said, her voice pitched a little softer as she spoke to me. 'Probably a lad involved somewhere along the line, I shouldn't wonder.'

Zadie glanced at me then hung her head to the floor, her shoulders hunched over.

'Ran away from home two days ago, so she says. Slept around the back of Cannons Leisure Centre on the Sunday night. And then in a shop doorway last night, didn't you?' she shouted at Zadie. 'Thank goodness the police found her before ...' Peggy sighed and closed her eyes. 'Well, doesn't bear thinking about, does it?'

The social worker then lowered her voice to a normal level, though I got the feeling she would rate it as a whisper. 'The family didn't report her missing but I spoke to the father on the telephone this afternoon. He feels that Zadie has brought shame on the family by running away ...'

Zadie blinked at that body blow, her eyes flitting between the ceiling, the fireplace and the window. A chink appeared in her expression and I got the feeling that tears weren't too far away. It was an insensitive thing to say in front of her and I felt my hackles rising again. Children are drawn to their birth parents with inexorable power, no matter what wrong has been done to them, and most, whatever appearances may suggest, genuinely want to please their mother and father. Being a social worker, Peggy must have known that her words were going to hurt.

'So you're not going to do anything like that again, are you, hmmm?' Peggy spoke loudly again, as some people do to foreigners. It then struck me that Zadie might not actually be able to understand or speak English very well.

Zadie shook her head again, her face covered in blotches. My heart went out to her. I scanned my brain, trying to come up with a simple, neutral question to help her relax. Settling back into the cushions, I asked, 'So, which school do you go to, honey?'

'I don't ...' she whispered, the blotches spreading to her neck. Her voice was nasal and thick with a cold, her eyes red rimmed. It wasn't unusual for children to arrive in foster care unwell; prolonged abuse or neglect wears down resistance, leaving youngsters susceptible to all sorts of bugs and viruses.

'Oh.' I looked from Zadie to Peggy and back again. 'No?'

'I don't know anything about the family,' Peggy jumped in, 'but I do know that many Muslim parents worry about lax discipline in schools and the effect on their daughters. It's not unusual for Muslim girls to miss out on secondary education, even in this day ...'

'I used to go,' Zadie cut in. I sensed a defensive tone, as if she were sticking up for her parents. 'Until a few months ago, but Papa felt that it wasn't ...' Her voice grew quieter with each word that she spoke, as if she'd run out of confidence before she could complete the sentence. Though her voice was barely audible, she spoke so eloquently that it really was ridiculous the way Peggy had raised her voice.

I nodded several times, trying to encourage Zadie to continue.

'The parents from our local mosque drew up plans for a free school. Papa would have allowed me to go there but approval for the application has been delayed and ...'

I cocked my ear, straining to make out what she was saying. Both Peggy and I watched, waiting to see if she was going to say any more. When she didn't I smiled and nodded. 'Shall I find a school place for Zadie while she's here?' I asked quickly. The social worker was still staring at Zadie and I imagined her to be the sort of person to bellow something like: *Speak up, girl! No need to be bashful!* Besides, it seemed a shame to me. Zadie was clearly an intelligent girl. For her to miss out on an education at such a critical age didn't seem right at all.

I noticed a frisson of interest from Zadie. Her head turned sharply towards me, a flicker of hope stirring in her smoky eyes. Peggy's jaw dropped as if she was shocked to the core by my question. There was a pause and then she recovered, shaking her head. 'Oh no, Rosie, I don't think so. Not just at the minute.' She lowered her voice again, leaning towards me. 'Things are a little sensitive. We have to tread carefully on this one. The father is not best pleased about her staying with a non-Muslim family as it is. Best not to rock the boat until we know where we stand.'

I prickled. If Zadie was in 'care', then we should be looking after her best interests, but I realised it was probably far too early to worry about it. She could be back with her parents before the end of the week, I thought. It seemed that Peggy actually had no idea why Zadie was too frightened to go home.

Peggy echoed my own thoughts, saying, 'We need to gather more information before we make a decision.'

'You might only be here for a few days, Zadie,' Peggy said in another hammering tone. 'We'll get you back with your family soon, mmm? Would you like that?'

Zadie's jaw tensed minutely, enough to tell me that home was the last place she wanted to be. The subtle change in the teenager's expression seemed to drift right over Peggy's head. 'Good,' she nodded, tapping the papers on her knee. 'We'll see what can be arranged. Meantime, do you know much about Zadie's culture, Rosie?'

I nodded. 'A little,' I said, unconsciously slipping my feet back to the rim of the chair where the printout from Wikipedia was nestling. 'Though I'm sure you won't mind filling me in on what I need to know, will you, Zadie?' I asked, smiling.

Again she nodded, whispering a polite, 'Yes.'

Peggy flexed one of her stout legs and groaned, rubbing the knee. There were red welts on each ankle to match those on her forearms, where her black socks had cut into her skin. 'I'm so swollen after sitting down all day,' she groaned, hoicking one of her legs up with cupped hands and resting her ankle on the knee of the other one. 'I called around all the specialist fostering agencies but every placement was filled. As you probably know, Rosie, we prefer a cultural match if at all possible, but there's a massive shortage of Muslim fostering families at the moment,' she said, her breathing jagged as she rubbed away at her ankle. 'There's been such a surge of Muslim children being taken into care but nothing like the same number of specialist carers coming forward.'

At that moment Emily and Jamie walked in from the garden, probably unable to contain their curiosity any longer. 'Ah, here they are. Emily, Jamie, this is Zadie.'

Zadie forced a stiff smile then lowered her head, shrinking back further into the sofa.

'Hi, Zadie,' they chorused, Emily lifting her hand in a little wave.

'And this is Peggy.'

Peggy's jaw dropped again as if she was shocked by their appearance. Seconds later it was back in its usual position. Her default expression seemed to be a scowl while her brain assimilated a response giving the impression that she was furious with what she had just seen or heard. 'These yours, are they?' she asked. The social worker had a way of depersonalising everything, reducing everyone to inanimate objects.

'Yes. Emily is 16 and Jamie's just turned 13.'

'How do you feel about having someone else about the place, taking up your mum's time?' Peggy asked, talking in the same loud voice she used with Zadie. Emily raised her eyebrows. Jamie glanced sideways at Zadie. I think they both felt as sorry for her as I did, although I didn't think for a second that Peggy meant to sound callous. There was a kindness in her slightly hooded eyes that remained while the rest of her face contorted; she was probably just one of those people who spoke her mind before processing it fully, I thought. Still, it was unlikely to make Zadie feel any better about staying with us. One thing I realised, though, was that Peggy was using the same tone with my own children as she had with Zadie. It must have been her way of communicating with all youngsters. Many of the social workers I had met were awkward around children, strange considering their line of work, although there were exceptions. My supervising social worker, Des, for example, was amazing with youngsters, immediately putting them at ease. But then again he was comfortable in his own skin and I think children responded well to his natural warmth.

'It's cool,' Emily said, bestowing a shy smile. 'Want to come and see your room, Zadie?'

Peggy frowned, her lips stretching to a thin line. 'That's a good idea,' she boomed after a moment, her tone once again incongruous with the look on her face. I had a feeling it was a habit that would take a bit of time to get used to. With a hand at the side of each hip she pushed down on the sofa and rocked forwards, once, twice, until she had enough momentum to heave herself up. 'Lead the way, young lady,' she told Emily, shooing her along with her hand. 'Come on, Zadie. We'll take a wander to check your room and then I'll be off.'

Jamie flopped himself down on the sofa while Peggy bundled Emily and Zadie into the hall, her leg creaking rebelliously as she wheezed along. Emily led the way upstairs. Zadie followed in silence, her robe billowing outwards so that the hem brushed each stair as she climbed. Peggy huffed her way up next, chivvying Zadie along with impatient little noises in her throat. Each stair groaned under the weight of her heavy footfall.

In the room, Peggy pulled the duvet back from the bed and pressed her flat palm all over the mattress, a standard check that all social workers are supposed to carry out each time they visit the foster home. It was a routine put in place ever since it had come to light that some rogue foster carers had put children down to sleep on sheets of MDF, with no mattress or even padding on top.

'Everything OK with the room, Peggy?' I asked.

The social worker straightened and glanced around, her mouth contorted. Emily looked crestfallen. 'It's absolutely lovely, Rosie,' she said after a moment, her face softening into a smile. 'Do you like it?' she boomed, turning to Zadie.

Zadie nodded, rewarding Emily with her own shy smile.

Leaving Zadie to settle in and unpack the few items she had in her rucksack, I went back downstairs with Peggy to go through the placement agreement. Half an hour later, as I said goodbye to the social worker, I was already of the opinion that Zadie had ran away because she was at 'that age' and was testing the boundaries, perhaps resenting the strict rules her parents had in place at home. Having to leave school was probably the final straw, I thought. In my head I had it all worked out.

But, as often happens when fostering, my initial assumptions couldn't have been more wrong.

Chapter 3

Soon after the arrival of a new placement the structure of daily life kicks in and normality replaces those first few hours of awkwardness and polite small talk – a relief, I think, for everyone. Except that in Zadie's case, without school, the only routine to her day was the observance of five obligatory prayers.

The day after her arrival I was woken by the sound of running water. I opened my eyes to a faint orange glow from the street lamps outside my bedroom window. Blinking, I checked the time on my phone; it was just after 5 a.m. I knew it must have been Zadie using the bathroom as Emily was a hibernator, always reluctant to leave her bed in the mornings, and though Jamie still tended to get up early he was drawn by the lure of his Xbox rather than any wish to have a shower.

I yawned, threw my duvet back and pulled on my long dressing gown. It wasn't until I had almost reached the bathroom that I realised Zadie was probably preparing herself for dawn prayers. Having taken my Wiki papers to bed, I knew that Muslims were expected to perform wudu before praying, a ritual washing of the hands, feet, face, arms to the elbow and feet.

'Are you OK, Zadie?' I whispered, tapping quietly on the closed door.

'Yes, sorry,' she said quickly. 'I didn't mean to wake you.'

'It's all right, honey. Not to worry. As long as you're OK.' Our whispered exchange was the longest conversation we'd had since Peggy had left the previous evening. Zadie had politely declined when I invited her to join us for something to eat, asking whether I minded if she went straight to bed. I knew she must have been exhausted so of course I told her it was fine, but I worried that she might have been staying out of the way because she felt unwelcome.

Leaving Zadie to get on with her prayers, I went back to bed for an hour but was too alert to go back to sleep. Lying awake on top of the duvet, I listened to the swirling sound of the sink emptying and then the whoosh as the taps went on again. When she finally finished washing I pictured the teenager up in her room bowing, prostrating and then sitting to face Mecca in Saudi Arabia. I couldn't help but admire her self-discipline. With no adults persuading her, she had still managed to get herself up before dawn. Whatever the problems at home, it was unlikely, I thought, to be a case of the needle on her ethical compass swinging too far in the wrong direction.

At the more civilised hour of 7 a.m, we all sat around the breakfast table. Zadie, dressed in a black robe and baggy cardigan that looked far too big for her, hung her head in silence. Emily, though friendly, tended to be a bit more reserved when older children first came to stay and so I was missing the noisy banter that usually flew between her and Jamie. If Zadie was a toddler, Emily would have been clowning around and trying to make her giggle, but since she was close to her own age she merely threw the odd smile her way and studied her cereal with unusual interest. I tried to behave naturally and let them all get on with it. Children generally hate being thrown together and time usually smoothes the jagged edges.

Sure enough, after a minute or two Emily looked Zadie's way. 'You were up early,' she said as she buttered some toast.

Zadie nodded, lowering her gaze.

'Do you have to get up early to pray?' Jamie asked before ramming another spoonful of cereal into his mouth. He always seemed to eat as if he was expecting a famine.

'Yes,' she whispered, her gaze lingering on Jamie for a second or two before darting back to the table. It was a penetrative look, as if trying to detect whether he had been mocking her. The flash of suspicion in her eyes reminded me that there was a real person beneath the head scarf.

'And is it true that you're not allowed to –'

'J-amie,' I said warningly. 'Shall we save the interrogation for another day?'

He shrugged and blew out a huff of breath so that his lips vibrated noisily. Zadie looked up again, her dark eyes sweeping over us. I think she must have recognised Jamie's interest as simple curiosity because the frozen angle of her shoulders seemed to soften a little. She continued to watch both Emily and Jamie whenever their attention drifted from her but, as is often the way with teenagers until the ice is broken, as soon as they made an effort to include her she averted her gaze, overcome by a sudden urge to examine the back of her hands.

'Not very hungry this morning, Zadie?' I asked. Her toast, though she had cut each slice into neat little squares and arranged them in lines across her plate, remained uneaten.

She looked at me warily. 'No,' she whispered. 'Sorry. It's very nice though. Thank you.'

'You should try to eat something, honey. How about some cereal?'

She gave her head a tiny shake.

'When was the last time you ate?' I pressed. Even though her skin was coffee-coloured there was a pallor to it that I hadn't noticed the previous evening. She looked awfully washed out.

'It's OK. I'll …' She picked up a tiny square of toast and took a tentative nibble. With her free hand she rearranged the left-over pieces of toast until there was an equal distance between each of them. Her fingers trembled as she worked and I could tell that Jamie had noticed too. He sat transfixed and was about to open his mouth when Emily, always quick to be kind, whacked him on the shoulder. 'Come on, you. We'll be late.'

I mouthed a thank you to Emily as she pushed her chair back. Straightening two fingers, she aimed them at the back of Jamie's head and crooked her thumb as if firing a gun. I suppressed a grin and she rolled her eyes in his

25

direction. The usual chaotic build-up to leaving the house then commenced, with Jamie emptying the cupboard under the stairs, trying to find his trainers for PE. Halfway through the search he decided it would be a good time to start printing his geography homework.

'May I leave the table please, Rosie?' Zadie asked.

'Of course,' I said, groaning at Jamie as he switched the computer on.

Zadie began piling the bowls on top of one another. 'Don't worry about that, honey. I'll do it.'

She spoke so softly that I had no idea what she had said, but she continued to collect the crockery and then pottered off to the kitchen. Leaving Jamie to sort the printer out, I took up where he had left off in the hallway. Within 30 seconds I had the trainers in my hands. 'Oh, Jamie,' I groaned again, aware of the sound of running water in the kitchen. Five minutes later Emily called out to Zadie from the hall. 'See you later, Zadie.'

There was a barely audible reply from the direction of the kitchen.

'Actually, Mum, I think I might stay off today as well,' Jamie said, beginning to slip his blazer from his shoulders.

'Oh no you don't,' I said, straightening his tie and flattening his sleep-rumpled hair with the palm of my hand. He gave me a look of disbelief. 'Mum, I like being groomed as much as the next man but I think I can get myself dressed, thanks all the same.'

'Fair enough,' I said. Jamie was teetering on the cusp of adolescence and I was still getting used to the transition as well as the tone of sarcasm that threaded all of our recent conversations. 'Now, have you got everything, honey?'

'Yep,' he said, offhandish, driving home the fact that I was meddling in something I had no business with. 'See you later.'

'Sure? Packed lunch? PE kit?'

'Y-e-sss, Mum,' he said with a long-suffering sigh. 'Bye, Mum. See you, Zadie.'

I stood at the front gate and watched until Emily and Jamie rounded the corner at the end of the road, then closed and locked the door, quite pleased at the prospect of having some time alone with Zadie. With just the two of us around I was hoping that she might open up a little and give me some idea of the problems that led her to run away.

Dropping my keys on the table in the hall, I walked through to the kitchen. Zadie was standing at the sink with the sleeves of her black robe rolled up tightly to the elbow, her forearms submerged beneath the washing-up water. Our breakfast bowls were all washed, propped over in a neat line on the draining board, each dessert spoon resting neatly beside it. 'Zadie, you don't have to do that, honey. Let me ...'

'OK,' she whispered, though her hands remained where they were for a few moments, as if reluctant to leave the sanctuary of the water.

'What do you usually do during the day?'

She lifted her hands from the sink and then turned on the tap to wash them. Squirting some liquid soap into her palms, she scrubbed between each knuckle, a few tiny bubbles escaping and floating above her head. After rinsing off the soap she stretched over the sink and released another generous blob of soap into her palm. It was a delaying tactic that wasn't going to work for ever. When she reached for the soap a third time I handed her a towel.

She took the hint, holding her hands in mid-air for a moment as if not convinced they were clean. 'I clean the house,' she said softly, wiping her hands and then hurriedly pulling her sleeves down to cover her arms. 'Put a wash on and prepare the meals. When the work is done Papa lets me read and …'

I pursed my lips, trying not to grimace. Sometimes as a foster carer it is difficult to hide personal feelings about a child's home environment but, whatever my opinion, Zadie had the right for her relatives' lifestyle to be respected. Children in care often have to cope with hearing negative comments about their parents, either from friends or their families, teachers, sometimes even social workers and foster carers. I have always made an effort not to judge but I still couldn't help feeling that a day filled with housework and reading was a lonely, unfulfilling existence for someone so young. We certainly had enough books in our house to keep Zadie occupied as both Emily and I were avid readers, but I wasn't sure that what we had was appropriate and, anyway, it all seemed a bit depressing to me. 'Well, while you're here, how about we make a bit of a routine to the day? You can have a look around and see if there's anything you fancy reading and we'll go to the library later in the week so you can choose some books for yourself.'

She nodded. 'I'd like that, thank you,' she said, her gaze fixed somewhere between my ear and the wall behind me.

'And this afternoon we'll go for a walk,' I said. One thing I was certain of – staying cooped up in the house all day wasn't healthy for anyone. It would be good for Zadie to get some fresh air, particularly as she was looking so peaky.

There was a flicker of anxiety in her eyes. 'What time will we be going?'

'After lunch probably. Is that all right?'

'I'm supposed to pray after …'

'That's OK. We'll go after that. Now, would you like to use the computer while I get this place cleaned up?'

For the first time since we'd met, her face creased into a genuine smile, the light in her eyes transforming her solemn face. It was often that way at the beginning of a placement; a child may seem untouchable, almost beyond reach, but then it's as if they suddenly emerge from their trance, ready to engage in family life.

'It's all set up, honey. You know where it is, don't you? In the dining room?'

'Yes, yes. Thank you, Rosie,' she whispered, backing away from me in a half bow and vanishing from the room. It was the most animated I had seen her.

As I was pulling on a pair of yellow rubber gloves the phone rang, a skirl that shattered the silence and gave me a jolt. I hadn't realised I was feeling quite so tense. I think it was my strength of desire to put Zadie at her ease that was making me feel anxious, though I knew it probably wasn't helping matters.

It was Peggy.

'The brother has been in touch. He wants contact so I've arranged for him to come to you tomorrow afternoon if that's OK?'

That was it. No, 'Hello, Rosie' or 'How are you?' but I was happy to dispense with small talk. Despite her sledge-hammer approach, there was something about Peggy that I liked.

'Should the family know where we live?'

'Zadie's only with you under a Section 20. There are no identifiable risk factors so it's absolutely fine.'

Since Zadie was in care under a Section 20, voluntary care order, her parents retained full parental rights. Under law, they could have demanded that she be returned home to them. If social services suspected that Zadie was in immediate danger, social workers would have to apply to the courts for an interim care order.

A picture of Zadie's face when Peggy had spoken about reuniting her with her family swept itself into my mind. I had noticed since then that Zadie was expert at presenting a benign expression, so her inability to hide the shadow that crossed her features at the mention of her family left me feeling concerned. 'We know nothing about Zadie's family yet, Peggy.' I paused, biting my lip. 'Or have you already disclosed where we live?'

'No, certainly not. I wouldn't do that without checking with you first.'

'Then I'd really rather keep my address confidential for the moment.'

Peggy sighed. 'Well, that's awkward. There's absolutely no capacity to facilitate contact at a centre at the moment.'

'In the community then?' I offered. 'I'm happy to supervise contact,' I continued, 'but not at my home. I'd feel much more comfortable on neutral ground until we know exactly what we're dealing with.'

'Very well,' she replied, a little stiffly. 'Have you managed to find anything out yet? The brother says that the father is willing to forgive Zadie and my manager is pushing for us to mediate between them and try to get her settled back home as soon as possible. There's only so long we can hold on to her.'

'Forgive her for what?' I asked with incredulity.

'Well, for shaming him by running away, so it would seem.'

'She's frightened, Peggy.'

'I think so, yes. But you need to find out why as soon as you can. As I say, we have no grounds to keep her in foster care unless she gives us something to go on. The family aren't at all happy with the placement so you'll have to bear that in mind when you meet the brother. Lots of diplomacy needed.'

Biting my lip to suppress a scoff, I muffled an 'OK' in agreement.

Peggy called back ten minutes later to confirm that she had spoken to Chit Hassan and that he would meet us at a local beauty spot, the Lavender Fields, at 2 p.m. the next day. The social worker then trilled a hasty goodbye and I headed for the dining room to give Zadie the news. Our house has an open-plan living, dining and kitchen area, with just a few columns dividing the space, so I could see Zadie's back as she sat at the desk. She was leaning so close to the computer screen that her headscarf almost touched it and there was something about the intensity of her posture that stopped me in my tracks. I was too far away to identify what site she was looking at but I could see that her fingers were trembling as she scrolled the cursor down the screen.

'Hi, honey. That was Peggy.'

Zadie spun around, her eyes wide. Her mouth began working at the edges as though she was trying to conjure a response but then she dropped her gaze and swung back to the screen. Making a few hasty clicks, she leaned back and let out a soft breath.

'Everything all right?' I asked, trying to muster a light tone to overcome the awkward moment. The words jarred in my throat and came out strained. It was a redundant question anyway; the wisps of unease snaking through the air between us told my senses that everything was definitely not 'all right'.

'Yes,' she whispered, though her jaw was set at a tight angle. It was as though her mask had temporarily slipped.

'You look ...' I paused, grappling for the right word. 'You look ...' *Guilty*, I thought, taking in her downturned eyes and the two pink spots on her cheeks. 'Anxious ...' I said.

'No, I'm fine, really,' she said. Her expression was suddenly indecipherable; the mask firmly back in place.

'Peggy said that your brother Chit would like to see you.' I paused to let the information sink in. Zadie watched me silently, waiting. 'We're meeting him tomorrow, at the Lavender Fields.'

Betrayed

She released the mouse and let her hand fall softly into her lap where her other hand was waiting. With her fingers concertinaed, she squeezed them together until the pads went white, though her face remained impassive. Again, there was no sign of any emotion, happy or otherwise.

'Are you pleased about that?'

'Yes, thank you, Rosie.' She nodded, but suddenly her eyebrows furrowed. She jumped up and darted from the room, her hand clamped tightly over her mouth. My mind raced. Something had clearly upset her. Was it what she had been reading online? Or perhaps the news about her brother? Small sounds from the bathroom drew me to the foot of the stairs. With my head cocked, I frowned in concentration. Zadie was retching. I turned, intending to fetch a glass of water from the kitchen, but it seemed that my feet had other plans. They were already taking me back to the dining room.

At the computer I perched on the edge of the swivel chair. My eyes drifted back to the stairs as my hand hovered over the mouse. Zadie deserved for her privacy to be respected, I told myself, but then again something had upset her and I needed to find out what it was. It was unlikely that Zadie herself would open up and tell me why. Stupidly, I had forgotten to give her an internet safety lecture before allowing her online. If something untoward happened, it would be my responsibility. With my mind made up, somehow I managed to shut my ears to her gasps long enough run the cursor over the screen.

My breathing became raspy as I checked the recent history. Leaning over the desk as Zadie had done a few minutes earlier, I selected the web address at the top of the page. At first I was faced with a blank white page but then colours began to appear. I squinted as an image flickered to life in front of me. I gasped and jerked back, dropping the mouse as if it was on fire. The colour drained from my face and my breath lodged in my throat. My chest throbbed with the pressure, as if I'd been held under water.

An unexpected knock at the door brought a rush of heat to sear my cheeks but I sat unmoving, unable to tear my eyes from the moving images in front of me. The sound of a key in the latch brought me to my senses and I sprang into action, fumbling with the mouse to click on the X. My fingers were so timorous that it took several attempts before the screen cleared, the doorbell growing ever more insistent.

Jogging to the hall, I felt grateful for my usual habit of locking the door whenever I'm home, if I have a child in placement. I had grown more security conscious after a parent had forced his way into my home a couple of years earlier. I had driven to a contact centre to collect his children after a contact session with their birth mother. The father had lain in wait in the contact centre car park and then followed me home. He was more desperate than angry but trying to convince him to leave the house had been a nerve-racking experience and one I wouldn't want to repeat.

My hands were shaking as I reached for my keys. My eyes strayed to the top of the stairs and a feather of anxiety brushed at my throat. I trawled my brain, trying to work out why a girl like Zadie would be drawn to looking up something so awful. It was a struggle to reconcile what I had seen on the screen with the introverted, withdrawn teenager having an anxiety attack in my bathroom. In my mind, she became even more of an enigma.

On the doorstep stood Jamie, his cheeks flushed, school tie askew over his shoulder. 'I forgot my locker key,' he said, groaning. 'Now I'm gonna be late.'

'Oh, Jamie,' I said, shaking my head. 'Don't worry. Grab your key and I'll give you a lift.'

'Ah, thanks, Mum,' he said with relief, all trace of adolescent bravado gone. He planted a rare kiss on my cheek and raced off to his room.

Up in the bathroom I handed Zadie a glass of water. She refused to meet my eyes but thanked me for the drink and took a few tentative sips. Perched on the edge of the bath, she looked so small and frail that I was tempted to draw her into a hug. I rested my hand on her shoulder but she instantly tensed, angling herself away from me. Overcome with a sudden feeling of *déjà vu*, I recalled the interactive dance played out between myself and Phoebe when she had first arrived – how she would draw me in with one hand and yet hold me away with the other. Sometimes I would catch the nine-year-old watching Emily, Jamie and me with a sad yearning, her past a barrier that held her in limbo, despite her longing to be part of a loving family. Phoebe kept her distance until the trust between us grew strong enough to overcome her fears, something that couldn't possibly happen overnight. I was beginning to suspect that with Zadie it was also going to be a case of playing the long game.

At some point we were going to have to have a frank discussion, but with the teenager still struggling to get her breath back and Jamie waiting impatiently in the hall, now was definitely not the right time.

Chapter 4

I drove towards Jamie's school on autopilot, trying to assemble my thoughts in some sort of rational order. Every time I tried to figure out what had possessed Zadie to search for pornography, naked bodies punctured my concentration. Sashaying to the forefront of my mind, they taunted my already churning stomach with grinding gyrations and twisted leers.

I considered the possibility that Zadie had stumbled onto the website by mistake. But whatever the reason, exposing a child to pornography was a form of abuse, and since it had happened under my roof and while Zadie was in my care, it followed that I was responsible. I let out a sigh, guiltily admonishing myself for not installing security locks before allowing Zadie to use the computer. I had tried parental controls before but quickly grown frustrated with them. The problem was that even tame sites seemed to be blocked by family-user settings, ones that Emily and Jamie found useful for homework, so I always ended up giving up on them.

My mind was so caught up in what had happened that I almost drove straight past Jamie's school. Fortunately we got there with a minute or two to spare. After dropping him at the gates I suggested to Zadie that we should take our walk then, rather than going out later in the day. The sky was already clouding over and I wasn't sure how long the dry weather would hold out. Zadie nodded in lacklustre agreement. She had seemed reluctant to leave the house, as if the walls were a protective shell she couldn't do without. As we headed towards the woods she seemed to withdraw even further into herself.

The traffic grew lighter with the school-run chaos over, and as I approached an almost empty crossroads an idea came to me. Swinging the car into a U-turn, I drove back through a small village and on to a fellow foster carer's house. Besides caring for three young boys, Jenny had recently taken in a rescue dog. Bobby, a Labrador, was still a puppy; just the sort of lively company I felt we needed. I knew that Jenny would probably be more than happy for us to give him some exercise.

As I'd thought, Jenny readily agreed. 'You're in luck, Bobby,' she called out, bending over to pat her knees. The excited puppy skidded along the wide hallway and collided into her legs, his tail wagging furiously. 'You do know they forecast rain, Rosie?' she said, clipping the lead onto the dog's collar.

'Hmmm, it does look overcast,' I said, leaning in conspiratorially and stroking Bobby's velvet ears. 'But we need a bit of a distraction ...'

Betrayed

'Ah, right.' Jenny nodded. 'Time for a catch-up, I think,' she said, leading Bobby to the car. 'When are you free?'

I cradled my chin with my forefinger. Zadie would obviously have to come with me, with her not being in school. I wanted to give the teenager a bit of time at home, a chance to get used to us before introducing her to lots of other strangers. 'How about the week after next? Monday?'

'Fine by me,' Jenny said, guiding Bobby onto the back seat. 'I'll ask Rachel and Liz along as well. Hi, Zadie. Lovely to meet you.'

Zadie lifted her chin in acknowledgement, her solemn face breaking into a rare smile when Bobby rested his heavy paws on her lap and nuzzled against her.

Jenny remained on her front step as I pulled away, waving silently in my rear-view mirror. I was looking forward to getting together with some of the other carers. Working from home can be an isolating experience, and when coupled with the need to maintain confidentiality it was often a relief to meet up with Jenny, Liz and Rachel. Apart from the company, each of us was able to share any concerns or challenges we were facing openly, instead of keeping them bottled up.

At the end of Jenny's road we pulled onto a wide, tree-lined street. We drove on, past a little park and then back through the picturesque village where rows of shops and restaurants were prettily co-ordinated with awnings in complementary shades and window boxes ablaze with jasmine and trailing lobelia. Soon we reached the main road that runs parallel to the river. The tide was high and a light wind was buffeting the blue-grey water into miniature, white-crested waves. As I crossed the steady flow of traffic, I noticed a colourful steam barge emerging from beneath an ornate bridge, the top deck dotted with passengers. 'Do you see that, Zadie?'

She glanced sideways. 'Oh, wow!' she said, the unexpected enthusiasm in her voice taking me by surprise. In the rear-view mirror I could see her smiling and craning her neck as Bobby strained to lick her face. In that moment she looked so carefree that I felt a spike in my throat, upset to think that someone so young could, within minutes of logging onto the internet, access images as disturbing as the ones I'd seen earlier that morning.

The memory brought an unpleasant roll to my stomach, my discomfort compounded by the fact that it had happened 'on my watch'. A fine mist lowered itself over the river and my windscreen clouded with condensation. Flicking the wipers on, my gaze drifted across the water where several ugly 1970s tower blocks stood. The featureless concrete buildings rose from their scenic backdrop to dominate the skyline, casting ominous shadows over the natural beauty surrounding them. Their incongruity struck me as fittingly apt; the corrupting influence of a fast-paced world on someone as fragile as Zadie seemed to be.

Three-year-old Charlie fell from a first-floor window of one of the blocks, into a large container of rubbish below. I would never forget how frightened he looked when he first arrived at my house, the cut on his head covered with a white bandage. I had recently heard how Charlie was getting on, living with his paternal grandmother; he was thriving and doing brilliantly at school. Pictures from the past often danced their way to the forefront of my mind, helping to boost my confidence at the beginning of a new placement. When things weren't perhaps progressing as well as I hoped, it helped to remember how resilient children can be. Charlie's rapid recovery was testament to that. Little did I realise back then that Zadie's problems would take far longer to mend than Charlie's cuts and bruises.

Despite the watery grey sky it was pleasantly warm, and as we pulled into a car park at the end of a narrow lane I felt my mood lighten. Zadie seemed to have relaxed. She was giggling and chattering softly to Bobby as I opened the rear door and beckoned them out. On reflection, there was no reason why I couldn't delay our internet safety chat until another day, by which time Zadie was likely to feel more comfortable in her new environment.

As we walked side by side down a gentle slope and through a canopy of trees, a rich, woody fragrance rose to greet us. A narrow path stretched ahead into the forest, as far as the eye could see, and when we were a safe distance from the road I let Bobby off his lead. He bounded off with his tail high in the air, every so often tripping over his large front paws in his eagerness to explore. We strolled without speaking, our eyes focused on Bobby as he darted between trees and sent squirrels scattering in all directions.

As we ventured deeper into the woods, the soft drone of traffic receded until it was barely audible. The loamy earth beneath our feet muffled the sound of our footsteps so that, apart from the occasional crack as we stepped on a twig, the scuffle of small pawed animals or the distant squawking of gulls, there was near silence. I began to chatter about other places we had visited in the past, hoping that Zadie might begin to reciprocate. She smiled politely and nodded in all the right places but, apart from the odd gasp when Bobby tumbled over, she remained more or less mute. Fortunately, just as I had hoped, the puppy's presence transformed the atmosphere so that our one-sided conversation felt companionable rather than strained.

Another hundred metres in, the path began to widen. Dappled light picked its way through the trellis of over-hanging leaves, the shadowed earth shrinking as we reached a glade. Fast-moving clouds swirled overhead and there was the odd rumble in the distance. Looking up at the hooded sky, I wasn't sure how long we would have before the rain set in. With the grassy area opening further, Zadie jogged ahead, trying to keep up with Bobby. She cut a soli-tary figure out there in the middle of the clearing and as I followed I hoped it wouldn't be too long before she was brave enough to reach out to me.

My drifting thoughts were interrupted by Bobby, bark-ing and leaping up at a fence. On the other side was a meadow strung with daisies. Further into the distance the fields sloped away to give a view of the village we had driven through and the lower foothills beyond. Zadie gathered her robe in her hands, lifting it above her ankles like a char-acter from a Jane Austen novel. Suddenly childlike, she ran towards Bobby and pointed to a stile beyond some bushes. 'Over here, Rosie,' she called out, her soft voice almost swallowed by the wind. Grasping Bobby around his midriff, she lifted herself to the top plank of the stile and slipped over in one smooth motion.

I climbed over with far less elegance, even though I was wearing jeans. Zadie waited nearby, her arm flickering at her side as if ready to catch me if I stumbled. I was surprised by her gentle consideration. 'You see over there, Zadie?' I said, slightly breathless, pointing to a large yellow sandstone building. 'Inside that hall are boxes of material from all over the country, from Cornwall all the way up to Scotland.' As we crossed the meadow I told Zadie about my mother's voluntary job at WEPH, Working to Eradicate Poverty and Hunger, a committee based at the local church. The group, mainly women, met regularly to fundraise; their latest project was to provide desks and equipment for a blind school in the Congo.

'What are they going to do with all the material?' she asked softly. I could tell that her interest was piqued. It was the first time she had voluntarily spoken since we left the house but, then, children in foster care are often fascinated by stories of hardship and tales of triumph over adversity. I think that hearing about other children in difficult situations gives them a yardstick to measure their own problems against, one of the reasons why all of the Jacqueline Wilson books in our house were so well thumbed.

Like adults who enjoy watching tragic or sad films, perhaps feeling relief that their lives could be worse, I think that children gain a sense of perspective and learn that they're not alone in their sadness and uncertainty. One of the therapeutic games I play with older children works on the same principle, where they have to imagine a situation worse than their own. It may sound like a grim activity but it often works a treat and it's surprising how many colourful and inventive scenarios they come up with.

I remembered playing the game with ten-year-old Taylor, who came to stay with her five-year-old brother. The siblings had endured years of witnessing domestic abuse between their mother and father and, using her personal experiences as a template for relating to others, Taylor would replicate the violence at school. She had a reputation for bullying and most of her classmates shied away from her. It wasn't unusual for hers to be the only book bag in the class without a colourful little envelope containing a party invitation inside, and she would often come home to me and break her heart over the rejection.

The sad truth was, the only way Taylor knew how to relate to anyone was by using physical force and harsh words. It wasn't surprising that parents steered their own children away, keeping their distance and encouraging them to have nothing to do with her. The awful, alternative universe situations she managed to dream up were truly terrible to hear, but we would always end the game with strategies for helping 'Alex who had lost his entire family and was sleeping rough inside a large rat-infested drain' or the teenager who was made to drink bleach by her drug-addled parents. Imagining what it must be like for others who experience hardship encouraged Taylor to see things from their point of view. It is a proven fact that when we empathise with others our brains release oxytocin, and slowly Taylor learned the simple lesson that showing kindness felt good. It didn't take long for her to stop hitting out and gradually her peers became less wary of her.

'They're going to make patchwork quilts. They have a small army of women working on them already, and since mentioning it on Facebook they have lots more people keen to sign up. I've started on one myself.' I twisted my mouth. 'Only I haven't got very far yet.'

I tapped my forehead. 'And that reminds me, Mum asked me to find out where they can sell the quilts that are already made. Another thing I haven't gotten around to.'

Zadie seemed so interested in the blind school that I wished I knew more about it. Making a mental note to find out more from Mum, I drifted onto other subjects, none of which caught her interest in the same way. She fell silent but I no longer felt like I was jabbering away to myself. Bobby loped ahead, every now and again performing an emergency stop to grab a stick or a stone between his teeth. Zadie delighted in his company, frolicking around with him in the long grass. Nettles stung my ankles as I waded after them and I was beginning to long for a cup of tea.

Eventually Zadie came to a halt by a cobbled stone wall. A large oak tree stood nearby, skirted by a wooden bench. When I caught up with her I asked, 'Shall we sit here for a bit?' Bobby's breath was raspy and his tongue was hanging out. 'It looks like I'm not the only one who could do with a rest.'

We sat down, Zadie planting herself a couple of feet away from me. She crossed her legs and rested her hands in her lap but then they tumbled over themselves in that nervous way of hers, continually smoothing invisible folds in her robe. I made a mental note to get some aqueous cream; her skin looked painfully sore. The wind was picking up and there was a sudden chill in the air. I wrapped my cardigan around myself and watched her movements surreptitiously.

She sat hunched over, her head trailing low. On closer inspection I noticed that her chapped fingers weren't just wringing themselves in a random way; they were strumming a particular beat. Not only that, but her lips were moving silently, as if she was counting or chanting something. Recalling the way she had rearranged her toast so fastidiously earlier that morning, I was beginning to suspect there was more to her twiddling than absent-minded nerves.

'Your hem is wet through, honey,' I said. 'Are you cold?'

Her fingers froze for a moment, then she rested them sedately on her knees. She shook her head.

I sat staring into the middle distance, trying to think of ways to get a conversation going that involved more of a response than a nod of the head. I told her about the time Emily and I went blackberry picking, her clothes getting so heavily plastered in squashed fruit that they turned her car seat blue. I talked about the day I took Jamie for a walk in the hills when he was just three or four. 'It started to rain and his wellies got stuck in the mud. I had to lift him out of them and carry him to the car. We never did get those little boots back.'

Nothing sparked a response that wasn't closed-mouth silence. Darker clouds gathered and the air around us was scented with the cloying dampness of impending rain. I listened to the stillness and decided to plunge right in with direct questions. It wasn't going to be an easy time for her in foster care unless she learnt that she could trust us. 'So, enough about us. Tell me about your family.'

She turned abruptly, a bit taken aback.

'There's not much to tell,' she said, twisting her lip.

'Well, do you have any other brothers and sisters, apart from Chit?'

She nodded. 'I have another older brother. Vijay.'

'And do Chit and Vijay both live at home?'

She nodded.

'So there are five of you?'

A shadow crossed her face. She shook her head again. 'Just my brothers, Papa and me.'

'Ah,' I said softly. 'I didn't know that.'

She lowered her head, the silent curtain of her headscarf shielding her expression. I could tell she was uncomfortable but then I remembered Peggy's earlier words: if we didn't find out something soon, Zadie could find herself having to return home. While I phrased the next question in my head, the silent pause worked its magic.

'I can't really remember much about her,' she said softly, risking a glance in my direction. There was a strained quality to her voice and for the first time her expression was transparent, the pain in her eyes diffusing across her whole face. Above, clouds shifted, closing in on us.

'Your mother?'

She nodded.

'When was the last time you saw her?'

She let out a breath so gentle it was almost masked by the strengthening breeze. Again her fingers tapped a secret rhythm on her knees. 'I think I was about five.' Bobby

47

began to whine. He trotted over and rested his head on Zadie's lap as if sensing her discomfort. Absent-mindedly massaging his chin, she said, 'I don't even remember what she looks like but I can feel her sometimes, as if she's still around.'

The heavy sadness in her voice brought a sudden lump to my throat. I nodded, hoping to communicate how much I wanted to understand, and all the while other thoughts whirled around my brain, like was her mother dead? Or had she walked out on her family? I was trying to think how to frame my questions delicately when the rain started. Grabbing my handbag, I brushed dried leaves from the back of my jeans and sprinted after Zadie who, slipping and sliding, ran ahead with her arms out, steadying herself. By the time we reached the fence the fine rain had fortified into a deluge. I stumbled over the stile but Zadie waited behind, calling out to Bobby. He ran around the field in wide circles, barking at the air and catching raindrops on his tongue.

When he finally reached us, yapping in excitement, we were both drenched. He jumped up to rest his muddy paws on Zadie's chest, lapping at her face with his tongue. She closed her eyes and threw her head one way and then the other, laughing loudly. 'Rosie, help!' she shrieked, her brown eyes full of life.

It was one of those moments that fixed itself in my mind so vividly that I can still picture every detail. I stood motionless for a few seconds with the rain lashing down on my back, captivated. Her teeth were very white, the front two crossing over one another slightly – not enough to worry about getting braces fitted but perfect for adding a touch of character to her smile. Her headscarf and robes became indistinguishable, clinging cold and heavy against her skin. Curves appeared where before they were hidden and it was clear from her silhouette that she wasn't as thin as I'd first thought. It was a relief to know that I wouldn't have to worry too much about her lack of appetite. Still giggling and with water pouring from her face, she closed her eyes and wrestled Bobby away.

'You jump in,' I shouted to Zadie over a rumble of thunder when we reached the car. 'I'll put Bobby on a blanket in the back.'

Ten minutes later we dropped a drenched, smelly pup back to Jenny. The foster carer gasped when she saw him but I knew she wouldn't mind. 'See you on Monday then, Rosie?'

'Yes, lovely.'

'I sent Liz and Rachel a text, so hopefully they'll be here too.'

On the way home I turned the radio on for some background noise. It seemed that a walk in the rain had broken the ice, as far as I was concerned at least. Zadie had told me something about herself, albeit reluctantly at first, but it was a start and it *was* only her first full day. Feeling much more at ease, I began singing along to the music. Zadie's expression in the rear-view mirror was a mixture of surprise and amusement.

* * *

'Would you like to use the bathroom first?' I asked as I stood in the hall shivering, water dripping down my nose.

Zadie nodded and slipped off her shoes, bending over to straighten them at a neat right angle to the wall. While she ran a bath I got a clean robe out of her rucksack and draped a fluffy towel over the radiator in the hall, so that it would be warm by the time she was ready to leave the water. Getting her things ready reminded me of when Emily and Jamie were small. Every Sunday afternoon we would go for a walk in the hills or by the river. More often than not, one of them would end up with their clothes soaked through or covered in mud. I relished the thought of getting them home, giving them a hot bath then wrapping them in their soft dressing gowns.

I think one of the reasons I enjoyed fostering so much was the opportunity it gave to lavish comfort on children who've sometimes not even experienced basic care. Often, when a child arrives in the foster home, they've never known the pleasure of tucking into a home-cooked meal or climbing, sleepy and safe, into a warm, clean bed. Being in a position to console someone in crisis is such a privilege, one I don't think I will ever tire of.

In the kitchen I made two mugs of hot chocolate and reached for the biscuit tin. Suffused by a feeling of optimism, I still had no sense of the traumas that lay ahead.

Chapter 5

Lunch was pasta with cheese sauce. Zadie had told me not to worry about special food for her as she was vegetarian and I had checked that it was something she liked, but she barely touched anything. She sat in silence, her eyes fixed on her plate as she twirled her fork in her right hand. Her left hand was out of sight under the table, no doubt tapping out nervous rhythms on her thigh.

Des, my supervising social worker, had called soon after we arrived home, to ask if he could pop in later to make one of his statutory visits. He was a gregarious character and always managed to bring out the louder side of my own personality, so I was looking forward to introducing him to Zadie. If anyone could bring Zadie out of her shell, it would be him.

The rest of the afternoon passed quietly, with Zadie up in her room reading *The Red Pony*. I was happy with her choice, confident that the classic was unlikely to cause offence to anyone. While she was occupied I sat in the conservatory to write up my daily diary. Recording our earlier conversation in the forest, I remembered how abruptly it had ended. It was a shame the rain had started just at the moment she spoke of her mother. I sat mulling over what she had said, itching to find out more.

When my records were up to date I invited Zadie to help me prepare a chicken pie for our evening meal, hoping that we might take up the conversation where we left off. Emily and Jamie were going to the golf driving range with their dad after school – although we had divorced years earlier, Gary remained dedicated to the children and saw them often – so we had a long afternoon to fill. She seemed content pottering around the kitchen and was adept at preparing food, even the meat, despite being a vegetarian. It was clear that she was well practised at preparing meals for a large family. Without any direction from me she tore the plastic from a pack of chicken and rinsed each fillet under the tap before deftly snipping slivers into some hot oil with a pair of kitchen scissors.

I began kneading the pastry and chattered on about the rest of our family; my mother and nieces and nephews, but, while Zadie seemed interested, she didn't join in or volunteer anything of her own. I remembered what Peggy had said about her father pressurising for Zadie to be returned to him and couldn't help feeling a sense of urgency, but I didn't want to force it so I avoided any more direct questions.

Emily and Jamie arrived home just after five o'clock. As soon as Zadie heard their steps on the gravel driveway she washed her hands and then left the kitchen. After a hurried greeting in the hall, she withdrew to the dining room, burying her head in her book.

Emily went straight up to her room and Jamie, following his usual after-school routine, raided the biscuit tin then switched on the Xbox. Leaning his head into the dining room, he invited Zadie to join him. She shook her head shyly, diving straight back into her book. A little pride swelled up in me; it was always so lovely to see my own children's efforts to welcome others in, even though their friendliness was often shunned in the early days. Jamie shrugged off her rejection and carried on with his game.

Des arrived just before dinner time, as was his usual habit. Jamie answered the door, greeting the social worker by thrusting an Xbox controller in his hands. Although half the time my son made an effort to show that he was now beyond all forms of play by shrugging nonchalantly and forcing a look of disinterest, computer games seemed to be an acceptable caveat.

'How about you let me take my shoes off first, eh, Jamie? He doesnae give me a chance,' Des muttered, removing his shoes using the heel of each foot and leaving them in the hall. 'Hi, Zadie,' he said casually when he passed the dining room, as if he'd met her dozens of times before. 'How do you put up wi' him, you lot?'

Jamie grunted, revelling in the banter. Zadie peered over the top of her book, a little intrigued. Des was such an affable character; he just had that way that some people have about them, of creating an immediate air of familiarity.

'Don't start another game yet, Jamie. Dinner's almost ready,' I said, leaning against the doorway. It was one of those moments when I wished I had thought to run a brush through my manic hair. I managed to tuck some of it behind each ear. 'Hi, Des. Would you like to join us?'

He looked at me sideways, his blue eyes shining with their usual glint of humour. 'What are you having?' There was no mistaking the caution in his voice and I couldn't disguise my smile. Des struck me as such a bold character. He was outgoing, charming and had travelled all over the world, yet he was such a baby about food. One sniff of something spicy and his lips would go pale. 'Not that I'm fussy,' he insisted, 'so you can stop looking at me like that, Rosie Lewis.'

'Chicken pie. We made it this afternoon, didn't we, Zadie?'

She raised her eyes, nodding silently.

'You didnae sneak anything hot in there, I hope?' he teased.

Zadie looked serious. She frowned, shaking her head.

'Don't worry, Zadie. Des thinks pepper is an exotic flavouring, don't you?'

The social worker snorted. Zadie pinched her lips in imitation of a smile but her features didn't soften accordingly.

'Yes, count me in then, if there's enough,' he said as I leaned my head into the hallway and called up to Emily. 'Dinner's ready, love.'

At the table, Des and Jamie argued playfully about the upcoming friendly football match between England and Scotland, Des going into a rant in imitation of a well-known sports commentator. Dark wavy hair that was usually swept back from his temple flew out at odd angles and soon Jamie was in fits of laughter. It was easy to picture Des in his earlier days, as a bit-part actor in dodgy American sitcoms. Tonight he surprised us by throwing into the conversation that he'd also been the lead guitarist in an unsuccessful rock band known as The Bad Natives. Lifting his leg, he wrapped one hand round his shin, strummed his thigh and threw his head back, launching into a rendition of 'Mustang Sally'.

Jamie whooped, drumming his palms on the table. Zadie raised her eyes, interested but a little taken aback by the banter. Every now and again she would cast a furtive glance around the table but whenever any of us looked her way she would stare into her plate and play lifelessly with her food. But she wasn't the only one. I could see that Emily was troubled too. I can read my daughter's expression from across a room, interpreting her mood from the angle of her head or slant in her shoulders, but that night I didn't need a mother's instinct to know she was upset. She was usually animated when Des came to visit but she prodded at the same speck of food with her fork, barely glancing in his direction.

'Are you all right, Ems?' I asked.

'Yes, fine,' she nodded. Des stopped teasing Jamie for a moment and turned to look at her. Emily smiled but quickly returned her attention to her plate, clearly stewing over something. It was unusual for anything to cloud Emily's brightly glowing aura. She was such a cheerful, buoyant soul that it was a surprise to see her gloomy. I wondered whether Zadie's brooding silence was affecting her, but then I dismissed the thought. Emily had grown used to children arriving in a much more distressed state than Zadie appeared to be in. I was wondering whether to say anything more when Jamie distracted my attention. 'Can I leave the table, Mum? I told Ben I'd meet him on *FIFA* at 7.'

As usual, his plate was clear. 'Go on then.'

We watched silently as Jamie sprang to his feet and disappeared from sight. Des can't be described as anything other than a people person; his ability to mingle was the trait I admired in him the most, yet without Jamie at the table he seemed to lose his momentum, as if the silence of the rest of us was contagious.

Our attention soon focused on Zadie. Holding her fork in her right hand, she separated the food on her plate into small mouthfuls; a couple of peas, a piece of her own mini-vegetarian pie and some mashed potato were dotted around the plate in small mounds. If a pea rolled away she manoeuvred it back to the required position with robotic movements. It was mesmerising.

A minute or two of silence passed before Des recovered. 'I've been thinking about reviving the old band actually,' he said, reaching for his glass of water. 'First there was the Spice Girls, then Take That. I think the world might be ready for a Bad Natives reunion. What do you think, Ems?'

That was it. Emily guffawed, much like her usual self. Zadie touched her forefinger to the tip of her nose and examined what was left of her pie. She tilted her head then set to work rearranging the layout, making minute adjustments. Des put his fork down and cocked his head, giving me a knowing look. I stretched my lips and gave a slight nod.

It wasn't unusual for fostered children to display symptoms of OCD, especially where food was concerned. But Zadie's compulsive behaviour went beyond that; the strumming, the counting under her breath, the tidying. And then it suddenly struck me: the chapped skin on her hands might have nothing to do with sleeping out in the cold for two nights, and all the time she spent in the bathroom may not have been just purifying herself for prayers.

'Had enough of social work then, Des?' I heard Emily ask Des.

'Funny you should say that,' he answered.

But their conversation faded into the background. I was quiet, absorbed by my own thoughts. I remembered Zadie washing her hands after doing the dishes. I had thought it was nerves but now it all fell into place – she was an obsessive hand washer.

Just after 8 p.m. Des stood at the front door manoeuvring his feet back into his shoes. With his uncanny ability to read me he looked down and touched me on the shoulder. 'Give it time.'

I sighed. 'She just seems so very far away.'

'She'll come out of herself,' he said, speaking with absolute conviction, 'once she feels comfortable.'

He always seemed to make me feel better. 'Thanks, Des. You would have been wasted as a rock star. You're in the perfect job, if you ask me.'

He gave me a look I couldn't quite decipher. 'Visiting you is more than just a job, Rosie. You do know that, don't you?'

I smiled, patting his arm.

'Anyway, looks like there might be changes afoot,' he said cryptically.

'Changes?'

Just then Jamie came into the hall and stood beside me, draping an arm around my shoulder.

'I'll tell you more on Saturday. You are going, aren't you?'

Des was referring to the foster carers' ball. Every year our fostering agency arranges a dinner dance for its foster carers. They often invite a motivational speaker along to give a talk and then to present long service and special recognition awards afterwards. It was an enjoyable occasion, although this year, feeling a bit guilty about leaving Zadie with a back-up carer so soon after her arrival, I wasn't as keen to go.

'Yes, I've booked my mum in to babysit.'

'Great. Maybe I'll persuade your mother to have a dance with me,' Des said, winking at Jamie.

'I wouldn't, Mum,' Jamie said. 'He might start singing.'

About an hour later, while Zadie was having a bath, I went into her room to look for any dirty clothes she may have left in there. Foster carers usually have to keep their wits about them, especially at the beginning of a placement when the child is assessing their new environment. Taken away from all that is precious to them and then catapulted into a relationship with unfamiliar adults, it's a natural response to react badly. I remembered the high drama of when 15-year-old Amy came to stay.

Betrayed

Amy spent her first week with us in a highly anxious state, withdrawing from cannabis as well as trying to deal with the commotion of coming into care. It's fair to say that our house took a bit of a battering during her period of readjustment. But there seemed to be none of that with Zadie, and her room was immaculate, with not a thing out of place.

If anyone had asked me to name three character traits of Zadie's after she had been with us for a couple of days, 'quiet' would most definitely have qualified. Above that would have been 'nervous', but I would have struggled with the rest of the list. There seemed to be no substance to her, nothing solid that I could put my finger on.

About to leave the room, I made a little triangle of her duvet by turning it back at the corner and grabbed her pyjamas from underneath the pillow. As I was smoothing them out on the radiator in the hall to warm them, I felt something knobbly beneath my palms. Frowning, I picked them up again, noticing for the first time how heavy they were. Turning them over in my hands, I felt several hard lumps in the material. Running them between my fingers, I found what felt like rough pebbles had been sewn into the hem of the top and the waistband of the bottoms.

'Zadie. What are these doing here?' I asked, surprised to find her standing behind me. She moved so lightly from room to room that all I had sensed was a wisp of air. I often have to remind the children I look after to keep covered up but Zadie had dressed back into her robe just to take the short walk along the hall to her bedroom. Her headscarf was off though, her damp, dark hair clinging to the robe and leaving a large damp patch at the back. It was surprising how different someone could look with the absence of one simple garment. She looked even prettier with her hair long and flowing.

'What?' she asked, though it was obvious she knew what I was talking about; she was staring straight at her pyjamas.

'Why are there pebbles in your PJs?'

She looked at me, chewing her lip. With the line of her elegant neck visible she seemed so much more vulnerable. 'I'd sleep on my tummy if they weren't there.'

I held them in front of me, staring. 'What's wrong with that?'

'I'm supposed to lie on my back.'

I shook my head as I passed them to her, still confused. 'Why?'

'Prophets sleep with their bellies facing upwards,' she explained, clutching them to her chest and lowering her chin into the soft material. 'I might be sent to hell if I sleep badly, so Chit sewed them in.'

I didn't know how to respond so I stood clutching her door handle for a moment before saying goodnight.

Downstairs, I picked up a book and slumped on the sofa. Holding it open, I ran my eyes over the first page then realised I had no idea what I'd just read. I tried again but gave up after the second paragraph, too preoccupied to take anything in.

And so, the night before the real problems began to emerge, I lay in bed feeling generally puzzled. I was a bit concerned about Emily. From the moment she was born she had been a textbook baby. She slept when I laid her down, like one of those dollies with the closing eyelids, smiling and cooing whenever she was awake; she skipped her way through the 'terrible twos', and even as a teenager she was rarely moody or difficult. I resolved to leave it a few days before pressing her any further. Emily tended to think things through for herself before blurting out what was worrying her.

Unlike Zadie. I knew that she would need lots of encouragement if she was to open up. My thoughts turned to our earlier conversation and I felt a flicker of unease. Funnily enough it wasn't the pebbled pyjamas that worried me. It seemed a bit of a draconian measure to me but it sounded like her family were doing what they could to keep her spiritually safe. All religions had their own special ways of negotiating their followers through an unpredictable world, I reasoned. I could see the logic.

When I was young, my father had a rigid routine of Bible study in place for when I got home from school. There was no relaxing in front of *Grange Hill* with milk and a biscuit for me. It was a case of working my way through the books of the Bible and memorising important texts to repeat to him when he got home from work. I had a feeling that Zadie's experiences were magnified tenfold on a scale of severity, but I could certainly relate to them.

What really unsettled me was the control her brother seemed to exert over her. Zadie said it was Chit who had taken it upon himself to correct her for sleeping on her back. It struck me as strange that a brother should involve himself in disciplining his sister so harshly, but then a little girl, Freya, tugged at my memory. Even though she wasn't quite five years old when she came to stay with me, she was well used to caring for her younger siblings. She knew how to prepare a bottle of formula milk for her baby brother and was so protective of her role as their carer that she became distressed when I tried to release her from it. I wanted her to learn to be a little girl again but she found it hard to relinquish what she saw as her responsibilities. Without his mother around, perhaps it was natural for Chit to take a more active role in caring for younger siblings, I reasoned.

And then there was Des. Usually so quick to comfort and calm, there was something in the way his eyes shadowed when he told me that changes were on the way that stirred up anxiety in me. I had a feeling that I wasn't going to like what he had to say.

Chapter 6

On Thursday morning I must have woken midway through a dream because when I opened my eyes I sensed the vestiges of something incomplete. I don't often recall dreams but this one was so vivid that it stayed with me as I went downstairs to make coffee. While the kettle boiled I leaned back against the worktop and closed my eyes. Flickers of black and white played across my eyelids as the dream came back to me, with Zadie and me back in the forest.

Dreary swirls of grey moved across a brooding sky, following us at a pace as we ventured further along a narrowing path. Driven deeper into the woods by a high wind and squally rain, I noticed that my feet were sinking into the sodden earth while Zadie's seemed to glide above it, like a character in a film that has been switched to fast forward. As I struggled to get free, a shadowy figure emerged from the labyrinth of trees surrounding us and hurried after Zadie.

Beginning to panic, I clawed my way out of my shoes and stumbled off in pursuit. Every so often I caught a glimpse of Zadie's billowing robes and the faceless stranger following her but, shapeless and fluid, it would float away in a wisp of black smoke whenever I drew near. Soon the undergrowth was too dense for me to follow and all I could do was watch helplessly as the shadowed outline rose up in front of Zadie and blocked her way.

Towering over her, the figure turned and whispered something in a low, mocking voice before reaching out its hand. With one touch Zadie shattered into a hundred tiny pieces, the fragments falling to the soil and rolling beneath tightly interwoven tree roots.

When the figure slipped away the undergrowth parted and I was freed. I ran to the spot where Zadie had been attacked and sank to my knees, scraping at the soil and calling her name. When my hands were too sore to continue I sank back and watched as droplets of blood sprang to colour my palms. Suddenly the dark clouds overhead scuttled away and a shaft of pale blue light pierced through a crack in the overhanging branches. A pathway opened up in front of me and at the end stood Zadie, beckoning. Somehow I knew that she was ready to give up her secrets.

My dream had ended there but in the kitchen I kept my eyes closed, convinced that if I had followed the path Zadie would have offered me the insight I craved. Nothing but ominous grey clouds danced against the backdrop of my eyelids and so, as I drank my coffee, a feeling of frustration lingered.

Betrayed

The house was so quiet that I realised Zadie must have gone back to bed after dawn prayers. It was something of a relief to be alone while I turned things over in my mind. Since her arrival, days earlier, I had found my tension increasing. In some ways, Zadie was the easiest placement I had ever had. Well behaved, courteous and helpful, there seemed to be no great challenges for me to overcome. I also got the sense that she was relieved to be in foster care, something I hadn't experienced before. Most of the children I have looked after crave their own home; they want to be with their parents, no matter what they've been through. They seem to spend their first few weeks in a suspended state, always waiting – waiting for news from the courts, counting down the sleeps until their next contact or passing the time until their forever parents came to claim them. With Zadie it was different. There was no resistance to being a looked-after child. Caring for her should have been a doddle.

And yet every time I looked at her I couldn't shake the nagging worry that she was in trouble and I should be doing something about it. I couldn't put my finger on why I felt that way; she was safe with us and we were taking good care of her. She wasn't eating much but she was hardly wasting away and I was sure her appetite would pick up once she felt more at home.

So why did I feel such a sense of urgency? Somewhere in my head was the sound of a clock, ticking rhythmically. I just couldn't figure out why, and my dream, rather than resolving anything, only made it worse.

Still bleary-eyed, I crept upstairs and checked myself in the bathroom mirror. My skin was a pasty tone and I noticed that my expression was pinched with anxiety. Bunching a handful of blonde curls on top of my head, I fixed the bundle into place with a large grip, hoping to reduce the hassled look that often besieges foster carers. We were to meet Zadie's brother in a few hours and I wanted to give the impression that I was a decent, responsible woman, especially since the family had reservations about the placement.

Splashing some water on my face and patting my skin vigorously with a towel to get the blood flowing, I took another hopeful look. A tired, middle-aged woman with eye bags and curly blonde hair stared back at me, but my ever-present optimistic air remained, and, though I tend towards self-deprecation, a definite kindness. When combined with a reassuring smile, I hoped that Chit would see that his sister was safe in my care.

In my bedroom, I ran my hands through the clothes in my wardrobe, opting for a smart dark-blue shift dress and tailored cardigan rather than my default jumper and jeans. An hour later the residual anxiety from my dream was displaced by the bustle of breakfast time. Jamie sat at the table pouring a generous portion of Cheerios into his bowl and Emily, still in her dressing gown, was quietly making herself a cup of tea, a faraway look in her eyes.

'How was your night, honey?' I asked.

'Fine,' she said, forcing a smile. She looked tired, no trace of her usual exuberant good humour. 'Yours?'

'Not bad,' I said. 'Everything OK?'

'Yes, why do you ask?' she asked, returning the milk to the fridge.

'You seemed preoccupied yesterday.'

Emily dropped a teaspoon into the sink. 'Don't start, Mum, please,' she sighed.

'I'm not starting. I just want to know –'

'Whether I'm all right,' she interrupted, closing a cupboard door with her hip. 'And yes, I am, so you can stop going on about it.'

'Emily,' I said, gently chiding. It was only the second time I'd asked her.

She softened. 'Really, Mum. I'm fine,' she assured me. 'I'm just tired, and we're getting stacks of homework at the moment. But there's nothing wrong.' She pecked me on the cheek. 'It's all good,' she said, grabbing a bowl from the draining board and turning to leave.

I gave an internal sigh. It had been so easy when Emily and Jamie were small. If something was worrying them it would usually come tumbling out as I gave them a bath, or when they were snuggled on my lap ready for a bedtime story. There were times when I missed those intimate moments that come so few and far between once children reach adolescence.

'How about we have some time together this evening?' I suggested, following Emily through the living room.

'Sure, OK.'

In the dining room Zadie was fully dressed in a beige-coloured robe, matching headscarf and the same baggy cardigan that she had worn every day since she arrived. She stood at the table, pulling at the front of her threadbare robe as if it was damp and sticking to her skin. Resolving to take her shopping to get some new clothes, I reached for a plate from the centre of the table and helped myself to the toast I had prepared earlier. I sat next to Jamie, and Zadie, finally finding the courage, sat opposite, though she ate very little.

After Emily and Jamie had left for school I sat beside Zadie on the sofa and asked what she had planned for the morning. We weren't due to meet her brother until two o'clock so I suggested that we go shopping and buy her some new clothes. 'We'll be back in time for prayers before we have to leave for contact.'

'I'd rather stay home, if that's …' she said quietly. She rarely seemed to finish a whole sentence. It was as if the sound of her own voice was so embarrassing to herself that she couldn't bear to continue.

'OK?' I offered. When she nodded I agreed, though I didn't like the thought of her drifting aimlessly through the morning and I had some chores to catch up on. 'So, what would you like to do?' I asked, knowing what she was going to say before I had even finished the sentence.

'May I use the computer?' she asked softly.

'Erm …,' I hesitated, knowing the grim task of confronting her about what she had been looking up couldn't be delayed any longer. 'You can,' I said slowly, 'but first we need a chat.'

Her face flushed crimson.

I felt immediately sorry for her. She knew exactly what I was going to say. 'The internet is great,' I said, tempering my serious tone with a touch of gentleness. She still looked mortified, though, so much so that it was actually uncomfortable to watch. 'But there are some horrible sites on there that I wouldn't want children to look at.' She kept her gaze averted so I went on to explain to the side of her head-scarf that, as a foster carer, I would be struck off if offensive material was found in my home, whether I was aware of it or not. Zadie nodded the whole time, but continued to study the wall beside her. I patted my knees, thinking here goes, then took a breath and said, 'I was a bit concerned about what you were looking up when you last went online, honey.'

Zadie covered her face with her hands and made a small noise somewhere between a groan and a sigh, then let her hands drop to cover her mouth. 'I'm sorry, I didn't mean to,' she said, her voice muffled. 'It just popped up and I kept clicking on the cross but …' Her voice was wobbling. She sounded close to tears.

'But you must have entered some strange keywords for *that* to come up, surely?'

She shook her head emphatically, her fingers knotting over themselves ten to the dozen. 'Someone emailed me the link,' she admitted eventually. 'I shouldn't have clicked on it. I'm sorry, Rosie.'

'Who would email something like that to you? One of your friends?'

'I don't have any friends,' she said quietly. 'It was spam.'

She spoke without self-pity but what she said tugged at my heart, throwing me off-kilter so that I accepted her explanation even though I didn't believe it. I realise now that I probably shouldn't have, but being a foster carer is much like being a mother; many mistakes are made along the way.

I hardly saw anything of Zadie for the next couple of hours. When she wasn't reading in her room she sat at the computer. I leaned my head into the dining area every now and again, partly to make sure she was OK but also to let her know that I was keeping an eye on her. Blue light from the screen flickered across her serious face as she stared in utter concentration.

About 11 a.m., just as I was putting a wash on, I heard the printer juddering into action. A few minutes later Zadie came into the kitchen and shyly offered me a wad of paper.

'What's this?' I said, taking it from her. On the top page there was a chart. The left-hand column, highlighted in blue, listed the names of markets in the local area. The next one, in yellow, showed the cost of hiring a stall and the days available. Across the top, underlined, was the title 'WEPH – Project Congo'. I was so moved that for a moment I couldn't speak. Leafing through the pages, I saw that she had researched the telephone numbers needed for booking a sales tent and had even included directions for each location.

I remembered blathering on about the quilt making to Zadie on the day we went for a walk. She had shown a glimmer of interest at the time but I had no idea she had taken so much in.

'Zadie, how lovely of you!' I exclaimed, wanting to reach out and catch hold of her hand, though from her stiff demeanour I sensed she wouldn't want me to. 'Thank you so much.'

I could hardly believe it. It was the first time I noticed another dimension to Zadie, layers of warmth behind the unbreakable wall, but I was about to get an even bigger surprise. Shifting the weight from one foot to another and fumbling beneath her long sleeve, she produced a ten-pound note and handed it to me.

I frowned. 'What's this for?'

'To put towards the collection for the school desks,' she said, turning on her heel and scampering off before I had time to react. I stared at the money, my heart opening with a sudden rush of affection. I had given her some pocket money a few days after her arrival, her part of the weekly allowance that foster carers are paid by the local authority. Not wanting to discourage her generosity, I slipped the note into a side pocket in my bag with the intention of adding it to the savings account I was going to open for her.

I finished loading the whites into the washing machine, stunned and deeply touched.

Peggy had arranged for us to meet at the Lavender Fields, a location midway between the Hassan family home and our house. Zadie and I arrived a few minutes early and since there was no sign of her brother we waited in the gift shop. Unable to resist, I began working my way through the entire selection of lotions and aromatherapy essential oils arranged along the shelves of an ornate white dresser, sniffing at each tester pot then asking Zadie if she would like to try. She recoiled as if she'd been shot, her face quickly turning green.

It was a few minutes after two o'clock when Chit Hassan arrived. Just as Zadie was pointing out a lilac candle that was so highly decorated it looked more like a cake, I spotted his dark head crossing the car park. I nudged her. 'I think your brother is here.'

Pausing in the doorway, Chit's eyes swept the aisles of glossy coffee-table books and embroidered lacy cushions, eventually settling on his sister. Zadie immediately froze, morphing once again into a figure carved from granite. Chit was a good-looking young man with a square chin and cheeks so lean they gave the impression he was sucking them in. His hair was the same rich dark brown as his sister's, though his was tinged with a reddish gold and his expression was alert, assessing. After a brief smile in his sister's direction his eyes met mine.

I smiled, mouthing hello as we made our way towards him. Dipping his head in acknowledgement, his stare did not waver as I closed the gap between us and held out my hand. His gaze dropped, registered my proffered hand then flicked to his sister, the expression on his face serene. Thrown off-kilter by the rejection, my smile evaporated and my redundant hand flitted to my hair to tuck imaginary loose curls behind my ear.

'Lovely to meet you, Chit. I'm Rosie. Did you have far to come?' I asked, aware that I was talking quickly, something I did when trying to recover my equilibrium. It was a futile question; I knew exactly where the family lived. 'I mean, did you find it OK?'

'Yes, thank you,' he said politely, without taking his intense eyes off his sister. Up close I could see that they resembled Zadie's, as striking, though not quite so thickly lashed. She was facing him but seemed to be staring at a point somewhere between his chin and his chest. I glanced uncertainly from brother to sister, oddly embarrassed by whatever it was passing between them.

'I thought you two might like to go for a walk,' I offered, realising suddenly that Chit's refusal to shake my hand probably had something to do with his culture, rather than a personal rebuttal of me. I remembered reading that non-essential touching between genders is forbidden in Islam and that the avoidance of physical contact is seen as a sign of humility. Chit would probably consider it disrespectful to touch me. 'I'm sure you have lots to catch up on,' I said, feeling a little foolish. My mind flicked to earlier that day, as I stood in front of my wardrobe worrying about which outfit I should wear to make a good impression, and yet within 30 seconds of meeting Zadie's brother I'd already made my first gaffe.

'Yes, thank you,' Chit said crisply, dipping his head respectfully then gesturing towards the door that led to the fields. Zadie tugged at her robe and looked at me, swirling the dark material around her fingers. I got the impression she was seeking some sort of approval so I smiled reassuringly. I had thought that Zadie might be relieved to see a familiar face, but with her hunched shoulders and trembling hands she seemed more cowed than anything else.

Turning away from me, Chit held out his hand towards Zadie's back, guiding her out with a proprietorial air, though I noticed he was careful not to make contact with her. I followed them, watching with a disquieted interest.

Outside, fields of lavender stretched for miles, broken only by the odd farmhouse, the purple-blue blanket following the contours of hills and rolling out of sight far into the distance. The wild, luminous beauty of the view and the sweet, soft fragrance were breathtaking, discordant with the tension between the three of us. On almost any other occasion I would have delighted in the comfortingly natural surroundings; it was a pleasantly mild day and the sun was doing its best to break through the stubborn hazy cloud, but the warmth on my face did nothing to quell my discomfort as I watched Zadie and her brother weave their way through the waist-high rows of woody shrubs.

Supervising contact is rarely a pleasant experience. Relatives usually detest being watched and it can be uncomfortable coping with the vibes of resentment and occasional open hostility. But as I trailed a few metres behind Zadie and her brother, navigating through the narrow furrows between rows of foliage, I realised that I felt more conspicuous than ever before.

There was symmetry in the siblings' stride, their arms hanging stiffly at their sides, though Chit, at almost 18, was much taller than Zadie. They were moving so slowly that I had to keep at a snail's pace so as not to get too close to them. Chit seemed to be doing most of the talking, his head bobbing animatedly as he twisted to look at Zadie. He put me in mind of a parent, checking to make sure that their child was paying attention. Every now and then he stopped, gesticulating with his arms as he spoke as if to underline his words. Zadie turned her head towards him once or twice, but mainly she stared at her feet. When they reached the end of the first row they turned right and kept on going, skipping several lines of plants before returning the way they came, probably trying to keep their distance from me.

Straggly stems from the plants' woody centres cascaded over the path, their softly jagged flowers brushing against my legs and almost tripping me up. Deciding it would be daft to stalk them for the entire hour, I searched for somewhere to rest and found a bench nearby, abandoned against the wall of a derelict barn. Making myself as comfortable as I could on a seat with several slats missing, I pulled a book from my handbag and started reading. Every now and again I glanced over the top of the page to check on the pair, who remained within eyesight. Snatches of their conversation floated to me on the scented breeze but I couldn't pick out individual words and wasn't even sure whether they were talking in English, although Chit's authoritarian tone was unmistakable. I had been reading for quite a while when I noticed that they had stopped halfway down one of the rows, roughly 30 feet away from me. Chit was leaning over Zadie with his hands resting on his hips, again giving the impression that he was an angry parent, dressing down a rebellious child.

Foster carers often have to make a judgement call on the spur of the moment, if relatives seem to be overstepping the mark. I usually try to keep an equal measure of trust and wariness and wanted to give Zadie and her brother space to make the most of the short time they had together, but an unnerving feeling in my stomach was bugging me to intervene. Just as I was reaching for my handbag they set off again at a gentle pace and I thought maybe it had been just an animated conversation after all. I checked my watch, telling myself I was being silly – all I had heard were the rising tones of a probably innocuous conversation that I knew nothing about.

But anyway, it was almost three o'clock. Contact had been scheduled for one hour so their time was almost up. Relieved, I made my way over to the pair. Closing the gap between us to a few feet, I called out to them. 'Zadie, Chit. I'm afraid it's time to head back.'

Chit turned sharply, fixing a serene half-smile on his face, but there was something frozen in his eyes, as if he was flicking back in his head, trying to figure out what he had been saying and whether he might have been over-heard. Zadie said a sombre 'OK', and they turned in unison, heading towards the gift shop and way out.

'Well, it was nice to meet you, Chit,' I said when we reached the car park.

He smiled and made a noise in his throat that I, giving him the benefit of the doubt, took to mean 'likewise'.

'OK, well, we'll see you soon I expect,' I said cheerily.

'I doubt it. Zadie will be home soon.' He bobbed his head in the same habitual way as his sister, although with Zadie it was usually accompanied by an endearingly shy smile. Chit wasn't in the least bit rude but there was an element of arrogance to his manner and a barb in his tone.

Chit waited in the car park, watching as we pulled away. Zadie sat in the back of the car, silent and withdrawn. I thought about what her brother had said about her return-ing home. There was no sign that going back to her family was something she wanted. Strolling beside him, she had seemed fragile and lost. But unless she could find the courage to tell me why, she might soon have no choice but to leave her foster placement. I worried about it all the way home; her unsettled sadness, her reluctance to trust. How could possibly it work itself out? I wondered, and just where was it all going to end?

Looking back, there were already clues to what the future held. If only I had been more alert. Instead of fretting over the small things, like rejected handshakes and clipped tones, I should have been looking for something far more sinister.

That night the sound of howling reached my ears before I was fully awake. Thrashing around in the dark for my dressing gown, I had awful visions of one of the children injured. Running full pelt along the hall, I followed the wolf-like noise to Zadie's bedroom and hesitated for just a second on the landing to reassure Emily and Jamie, who wondered what on earth was going on. I took a breath before throwing the door open and flicking on the light.

Zadie was sitting up in bed, her eyes open but cloudy and far away. I knelt beside her bed, my legs still shaking from the shock of hearing her screams. I stroked the hair back from her face and put a palm to her forehead, flipping it over to feel with the back of my hand. I made soothing noises to try and calm her; she was sweaty and dazed. I assumed she was having some sort of lucid dream so I tried not to wake her, fearing she might become even more disorientated. But she must have sensed my presence because she stopped screaming, though there was still a rigid cast to her shoulders. She looked stiff with fright.

After a few minutes her breathing began to settle and she sank back onto the pillow. Rolling onto her side, her lips began moving as if she was trying to speak. It seemed as if she was repeating the same thing over and over again but I couldn't distinguish her words. Gradually her lips stilled and her eyelids stopped fluttering. I was about to turn off the light when she began thrashing her legs and, moaning softly, she rolled over to her other side. Her duvet slipped off her shoulders and half-dangled on the floor. I reached down to pick it up.

And that's when I noticed the blood. I froze, my eyes flicking from her stomach to her face. Red streaks followed the line of buttons on her pale-blue pyjamas, running from her chest to her navel. My breathing faltered as memories of nine-year-old Phoebe surged into my mind. Tortured by an abusive past and terrified to tell anyone about it, the nine-year-old had cut herself in the same bed that Zadie now slept in. My stomach twisted uncomfortably as I scanned her from top to toe, trying to find the source of the injury.

There were no obvious cut to her wrists or neck, I registered with relief. The bloodstains were light, as if from scratches rather than deep cuts. She was such a private person that it seemed disrespectful to check her while she was asleep so, reassuring myself that she wasn't going to bleed to death, I draped the duvet back over her side and tucked it around her chin. She twitched, her breathing still unsteady. Tiptoeing around the room, I checked her drawers and bag for sharp objects.

Satisfied there was nothing that could cause serious damage, I straightened and switched off the light. Standing at the door, I listened to her uneven, troubled breathing for a few moments, filled with a longing to understand her secrets.

Five minutes later I lay in bed, awake, restless and still trembling. The only reason I hadn't gone into nursing when I had left school was because I didn't have the stomach to cope with the sight of blood. Mucky nappies and upset tummies were a breeze, but the sight of blood had the power to make my bones go soft so that it was an effort to hold myself upright. Tugging the duvet around my ears, I rolled one way and then the other, poked my feet out then trawled one of them back in. Not warm but unable to bear the weight of the bedclothes on my restless limbs, I went downstairs for a glass of water. Still edgy and unsettled, I tried a glass of milk then prowled the bedroom a couple of times in a pair of fluffy socks. Wrapping my dressing gown around myself, I stood at the window and stared at the night sky flecked with stars, stirring memories of the hours I had spent pacing the same piece of carpet with Sarah in my arms, a baby who had been born addicted to heroin.

Since Sarah had moved on to adoptive parents I had tried not to let my mind stray to nostalgic thoughts of her. Having nursed her for the first six weeks of her life, I felt a strange sense of incompletion whenever I remembered her soft vulnerability, as if I'd started some vital research and had recklessly abandoned the task at some critical point.

My nerves jangling, I went downstairs and switched the computer on. I remembered reading, during my hurried research about Islam, that some Muslims practise self-flagellation. Clutching at straws, I entered 'self-harm' and

'Islam' into Google. I found myself holding my breath as the screen flickered, half-knowing that I was searching for other explanations because I was reluctant to believe that Zadie was hurting enough to want to harm herself. But deep down I think I was also afraid to acknowledge that I was missing something vital and, more painfully, that Zadie didn't trust me enough to tell me what it was.

As is often the case, there was to be a huge range of conflicting information online. It seemed that some Shi'a Muslims beat their bodies with knives and chains to show their devotion to their religion, but then I knew that some Christians inflicted pain on themselves in atonement of their sins.

It seemed that every culture, whether Muslim or not, had its own guidelines on the subject of self-harm and its own set of traditions. I switched the computer off and strummed the desk with my fingertips. There was only one way of knowing what drove Zadie to injure herself and that was to ask her. I climbed the stairs, dizzy with tiredness but still plagued with the same restless feeling, as if the blood in my veins had been drained, replaced by an army of adrenalin-crazed ants.

Chapter 7

Friday was a teacher-training – or inset – day so there was no need to set my alarm but I woke early to the sound of Zadie washing for morning prayers. It was just before 5 a.m. and it felt like I'd only slept for half an hour. My eyes ached from socket to brow but, plagued by that horrible sweeping sensation I get in my stomach when I'm nervous, I knew I wouldn't be able to get back to sleep.

I went downstairs, splashed water on my face and made some coffee instead, still feeling a little ragged. I knew that if I sat down my stomach would take over where my feet left off, so, sipping at the piping hot drink, I pottered around the kitchen, putting cups away with my free hand.

I wondered whether I was feeling frayed because of the shock of being woken by the sound of Zadie's screams. But it wasn't just that; after years of fostering I was used to unsettled nights. It was the thought of those pebbles in Zadie's pyjamas that kept niggling at me, more than I thought they should. Something about them was wrong, though I hadn't the faintest idea what. And then there was my wretched dream. Every time I closed my eyes I pictured Zadie in the woods, trying to outrun the shadowy, menacing figure that was chasing her and taunting me.

However much I tried to push it from my thoughts, I couldn't escape the feeling that I was supposed to do something about it.

My anxiety about Emily's low mood still hovered as well. There had been no change in her and I wondered again whether the introduction of another teenager in the house might have something to do with it.

By 9 a.m. there was still no sign of her or Jamie but Zadie was up, nibbling at some muesli. Sitting opposite her at the table, I thought I saw her wince in pain once or twice but she disguised it so well that moments later I wondered whether I had imagined it. Finishing the last of my toast, I took a sip of coffee and then cleared my throat. 'Your hands look very sore, sweetie. Have you been using that cream I gave you?'

Immediately shamed, she dropped her spoon and buried her hands beneath the table. 'Sorry,' she whispered, reddening.

'No need to apologise. It's just that they must be painful and we don't want them to get infected.' I paused and then said gently, 'I think perhaps you're washing your hands too much.'

She looked up at me and swallowed. There was a look of mortification on her face, as if I'd just accused her of stealing. I felt a moment's encouragement – she was becoming less able to hide her emotions from me, which was a sign of progress.

'It can become a bit of a habit,' I continued, trying to keep my tone light and gentle. 'Some people, when they're feeling anxious, get stuck in a cycle of doing repetitive things like rearranging tins in a cupboard or walking around the block several times before allowing themselves to go home. But I know a little trick that can help whenever you feel that way. Would you like me to show you?'

Her cheeks were still red but there was a flicker of interest in her eyes, a slight hopefulness.

I trotted off to the kitchen, grabbed something from one of the drawers and then sat back down beside her. 'These are for you,' I said, handing her a pot of elastic bands.

Her brow furrowed as she took it but there was a smile of intrigue playing on her lips.

'Right, so, what you do is put a few on your wrist.'

'Like this,' she asked shyly, pulling several coloured bands over her sore hands.

'That's right. Now, whenever you're tempted to wash your hands when they're already clean, pull one of the bands out and ping it against your skin.'

She cocked her head, frowning, as if she wasn't sure I was serious, though she was smiling as well.

'It works like a charm, honestly. I use it when I have to talk in front of a group of people. Public speaking terrifies me but whenever I get scared I ping myself and it relaxes me.

She laughed out loud then. 'Really?'

I smiled. 'Absolutely. Try it.'

'OK,' she said quietly and picked up her spoon again.

After a few moments I spoke again. 'You called out in your sleep last night, honey. Do you remember?'

Zadie shot me a look of surprise. 'Did I?' She rested her spoon gently on the rim of her bowl and ran her teeth over her lips, watching me cautiously. 'What did I say?'

'I couldn't make it out but you were pretty upset.'

Her shoulders sagged as if she was relieved. She picked her spoon back up, though she didn't lift it to her mouth.

'Do you often have nightmares?'

'No,' she said a little too quickly, and then, 'I don't think so.'

I paused, watching her. She didn't look up but held herself very still. 'You know you can talk to me if there's something worrying you, don't you?'

She made a noise of assent in her throat, still staring at her unfinished muesli.

'Only, you seemed to have hurt yourself as well.' I stopped for a moment, letting the words sink in. Her eyes were downcast but they darted from side to side, as if searching for a means of escape. Quivering, she let go of her spoon and it clattered against the bowl, making her jump. Her hands fell to her lap. After a moment I continued, 'There was blood on your pyjamas.'

Her hands flew to cover her cheeks. 'I'm sorry,' she said, her voice trembling.

'No, sweetie. There's absolutely no need to apologise. That's not what this is about.' I leaned over the table and, crossing the invisible boundary between us, I gently prised her hands from her face and held them in my own. I could feel her trembling. 'If you're hurting, Zadie, I want to help you.'

Her face crumpled in anguish and her eyes filled with tears. She held my gaze for a few beats, the longest she had ever managed. The skin around her mouth puckered as if she was trying to form a reply, but no sound came out. It wasn't the first time a child had struggled to confide in me. I think that giving life to words can somehow make fears or memories seem too real.

'I ... I ...' she faltered, staring at me intensely, but then a shadow crossed her face and she gently pulled her hands away, as if she suddenly thought better of what she was about to do. 'Please may I go ...?' She pointed straight to the ceiling, gesturing to her room.

I forced a smile. 'Of course you can.'

She fled the room and ran upstairs, though she was so light-footed that she barely made a sound. Staring at her unfinished muesli, I sighed, wondering whether it had been a mistake to confront her over breakfast, particularly as she had been making a rare effort to eat. But in some ways I felt reassured by her distress. At least we were making some progress in getting to know each other.

After clearing away the breakfast things, I decided to take advantage of the time alone by calling Peggy. I picked up the telephone and dialled her number. She needed to be told about last night.

Around 11 a.m. I managed to persuade three reluctant children to come into town to buy some new clothes. Emily, despite her age, still had no interest in fashion but her ever depleting wardrobe was in desperate need of replenishment. Zadie, I was beginning to suspect, was suffering from mild agoraphobia, and Jamie would rather visit the dentist than trawl around the shops. My suggestion was met with a chorus of sighs and it took the promise of a hot chocolate and a doughnut with all the trimmings to get them all moving.

Leaving the car in the multi-storey car park on the outskirts of town, we walked along the riverside and then through a network of grass-lined streets of Victorian terraces, towards the main shopping centre. Jamie walked beside me chatting animatedly and the two girls followed behind, both reserved and silent. I was willing one of them to strike up a conversation but I knew Zadie was far too shy to make the first move and Emily was still unusually subdued.

Despite nearing the end of May it was a damp, cold day. The grey pavements mirrored the leaden sky and so it was a relief when we reached the brightly lit department store with its colourful displays of beach and bridal wear. Standing one behind the other, we rode the escalator up to the clothing department. When we reached the third floor Emily surged ahead and within five minutes she was zigzagging her way back to us through the dense aisles, several items of casual clothing draped over her bent arm.

'Aren't you going to try them on?' I asked. Desperate to end her shopping torture, Emily always chose blindly, barely glancing to check whether she even had hold of the right size.

'They'll be fine,' she said with a wave of her free arm. 'Are you ready to go?'

Betrayed

I scanned the aisles one more time, trying to see if there was anything suitable for Zadie. 'Seen anything yet, Zadie?'

She shook her head. 'I've got these,' she said, giving her robe a tug. 'I don't need anything else.'

In some ways it was nice that she was so easily pleased but I had been through her clothes and she only had four robes, a few headscarves and two ropey cardigans. I had pointed out a rack of modest, ankle-length skirts that I thought she might go for but her eyes widened in horror at the very thought of wearing them.

'Hmm, we need to get some more robes then,' I said, tapping my chin. A young sales assistant dressed in a smart black trouser suit gave us a quizzical look as she slipped empty hangers on the end of a rack. Moments later she arrived at our sides in a fragrant cloud of strong perfume. 'Can I help?' she asked.

'Hmmm, possibly. Do you sell robes?'

'There's a shop on the other side of town that sells stuff like that,' she said, her eyes running quizzically over Zadie. 'Near the station.' The girl went on to point out some long flowing skirts and dark linen trousers. She was making an effort to be helpful and I was grateful but she seemed oblivious to Zadie's discomfort. The teenager's face was as benign as ever but I was getting better at reading her and I could see she was withering under all the attention. Sinking her hands deep into the pockets of her cardigan, she straightened her arms and raised it like a tent around herself. I got the feeling she would have liked to pull it right over her head.

As we rode the escalator to the ground floor, I was more convinced than ever that Zadie wouldn't have run away over some minor, teenage disagreement. She seemed so gentle and mild mannered. When I had called Peggy earlier that morning to tell her about the blood on Zadie's pyjamas, the social worker had said that time was running out. Since Zadie had been taken into police protection, social services were technically only allowed to keep her for 72 hours. Zadie's father was seeking legal advice, although he had reluctantly agreed to a Section 20, meaning that Zadie would stay with us voluntarily. Peggy told me that a decision would soon have to be made about reuniting her with her family. Fearing that Zadie would clam up even more if she knew that, I had kept the conversation to myself, but as the morning went on the clock in my head ticked that little bit louder.

It began to drizzle soon after we left the department store. Hurriedly, we made our way across the town square and then through the network of narrow cobbled streets that led to the station. As we left the shelter of the tightly knit lanes and turned into the main road, sharp gusts of wind drove the rain horizontally so that our coats were soon wet through. Drivers switched their headlights on, raindrops shimmering in their cones of light.

Shouts from behind muffled the whooshing sounds of tyres on wet tarmac. We turned to see a crocodile of delighted children behind us, flanked by some rather harassed looking adults. Smiling, we stood to one side on the kerb to let them pass by, listening to their excited gasps as a bus sped by. Its wheel skimmed the kerb, whipping grey water into an arch above our heads. Emily caught the worst of it. She gasped, her arms flailing at her sides. Jamie shrieked with laughter at the sight of his sister, water dripping from her sodden hair and down her face.

Next to the station I noticed a café. 'In there,' I shouted, pointing at the sign. The rain was pouring so heavily that we could hardly see. Emily squinted, then grabbed the carrier bag with her new clothes in and ran ahead.

Up close I could see that the outside of Jim's Café was shabby. Dirt clung to the corners of the windows where, in picture postcards, snow would gather, but with Emily soaked through and in the absence of one of the many quaint little tea shops that lined the river, it was a case of any port in a storm.

Inside was dim, partly down to the grimy plastic covering the strip lights. I wasn't sure if the Food Standards Agency ever issued negative scores but, if they did, Jim's Café would probably be right down there among the worst the town had to offer. It was a relief to be out of the rain, though, if nothing else, and Emily was already using the facilities to get changed, so I decided to order some drinks.

Leaving Jamie and Zadie to find a table, I went up to the counter. Standing third from the front in a queue, I turned and noticed a group of teenage girls sitting at a table in the corner, pointing and laughing at passers-by through the almost opaque windows. There was a hard edge to their banter that seemed more than high spirits and so I was relieved to see that Jamie had settled himself several metres away from them. Zadie hovered between tables, probably too shy to sit at the table with Jamie alone.

My heart sank when I saw that one of the teenagers, an overweight girl with long hair on one side and shaved around her ear on the other, had turned her attention to Zadie. Feeling a prickle of heat creeping up my spine, I found myself clenching my hands and willing Zadie to move away. She seemed terribly vulnerable standing there, and Jamie, leafing through a grubby plastic menu, was completely oblivious. Zadie's shoulders sagged a little under the scrutiny but she was doing her best to ignore it. Her expression, as usual, was impassive.

The elderly lady in front of me dropped some change and I stepped back, kneeling to help her pick it up. Angling my head, I took another glance across the café, noticing that the plump girl was nudging her friends, tilting her head in Zadie's direction. Their chins simultaneously dropped over the top of their frothy milkshakes. Still gathering coins, I heard loud scrapes as the group angled their chairs to get a better view. By the time I straightened there were smirks all around as the girls goaded Zadie with their eyes.

'Thanks so much, dear,' the elderly woman said. 'I'm all fingers and thumbs this morning. Everything's so damp I can't get a grip on anything. Awful out there, isn't it?'

'Yes, terrible,' I answered, glancing back over my shoulder and straining to hear what the girls were saying.

'Where did you get your dress from? We love it,' the girl sitting next to the overweight one said in mock praise. A smirk twitched on her upper lip.

Zadie froze. Her serene expression evaded her and an agonised one took its place. Feeling a pang of pity, I flapped my hand through the air, trying to get her to move away from them. She didn't notice: she was busy pinging a band against her wrist. My heart tugged unbearably and a flush of anger burnt my cheeks. My feet were tingling with the urge to charge over and give them a piece of my mind but I wavered, wondering whether my interference would increase Zadie's embarrassment and make more of a scene.

'Would you mind helping me, dear?' the old lady asked, pressing her soggy purse into my hands. It seemed that her glasses were buried deep in her handbag and she couldn't find the correct change to give the assistant who, bored and unhelpful, was staring into the middle distance, avidly chewing on some gum. With her greasy hair and sludgy eye make-up, she looked at home in her surroundings.

'Of course,' I said, hurriedly counting out the right money so that I could keep an eye on whatever was unfolding across the room. Handing the coins to the assistant, I turned to watch the group.

'Is it a Victoria Beckham design?' the girl who had been silent asked in an exaggeratedly sweet tone.

Jamie raised his head, half-studying the menu, half-watching the girls. He frowned in puzzlement.

'I think you can buy them from the council recycling department,' a girl with blonde hair trilled. Her false eyelashes were so long that one of her eyelids hung lower than the other with the weight. Her voice was deep and raspy, her tone sickly sweet.

Zadie scratched her arm through her sleeve, her slender fingers digging at her skin. She looked so cowed, standing with her fingers knotted up in her robe. Having reached the point where I felt I needed to intervene, I turned to abandon my place at the front of the queue and was about to walk over when Jamie stood up and went to Zadie's side.

'Do you want to come and sit over here, Zadie?' he asked gently, shooting a quick glance towards the group.

I took my place back at the counter, relieved to see Emily coming out of the toilets just as Jamie and Zadie began navigating their way through the maze of tables. Buoyed by their attempt to retreat and no doubt disappointed to be losing such easy prey, the overweight girl stood up and blocked their path. 'Aren't you gonna tell us where we can get one then?' she asked, slipping her thumbs into the pockets of her jeans and resting her fingers casually on bulging hips.

My heart began to pound. Emily, narrowing her eyes, quickened her step.

'What can I get you?' the girl behind the counter asked between slurpy, open-mouthed chews.

'One tea,' I said, twisting my head to keep the group in view, 'and three hot chocolates, please.'

'I think she must have forgotten to take the towel off 'er head after 'er bath, don't you?' the one with the raspy, smoker's voice asked, her tone now openly cold.

Jamie was several metres away from where I was standing but his voice carried over, loud and firm. 'Leave her alone,' he said, his courage galvanised by his approaching sister. It was more of a command than a shout but the café fell silent. Some customers averted their eyes but most turned to stare at him.

Paying for the drinks as quickly as I could, I turned and saw, with a surge of grateful relief, that Emily had positioned herself at Zadie's other side. It was as if both she and Jamie were closing in protectively, cushioning Zadie.

'Move out of our way, please,' Emily said. 'Go and find someone else to annoy.' I was amazed at the authority in her voice. I knew that both Emily and Jamie possessed a strong sense of justice but my daughter also tended towards shyness and hated being the centre of attention. Her cheeks were flushed but she stood her ground, giving the teenagers an unflinching, steely glare.

The plump girl swallowed then glanced at the others, as if sizing up their support before deciding whether to have another dig. Her friends shifted uneasily in their seats and angled themselves away from her, feigning boredom. Shooting Emily a look with her lip curled in a sneer, the plump girl grabbed her coat and shuffled towards the door. The girl with the raspy voice shouted 'Arseholes' in a parting shot before following her friends out and slamming the door with a flourish. Emily rolled her eyes and put her arm around Zadie's shoulders, gently guiding her to a table. Zadie glanced sideways, a tenderly grateful look on her face.

As we sat with our drinks, I tried to make light of the episode, writing it off by telling Zadie that the girls were probably having a bad day and being indiscriminately rude to everyone. Our town had its share of problems, much like any other, but on the whole there seemed to be harmony between different cultures and the younger generation were even more tolerant. I didn't want to believe it was the colour of Zadie's skin that had provoked the girls into confrontation. I convinced myself that it was the way she was dressed. Ignorance was easier to swallow than outright malice and the foster carer in me couldn't help but pity the girls, wondering what experiences might have led to having such a short supply of kindness.

By the time we left the café the rain had abated but it didn't take much persuasion from Jamie to convince me to abandon the idea of more shopping. Watching Zadie cowering under the critical gaze of those girls had left me fuming, although the feeling was tempered by admiration for Emily and Jamie. It was one thing to be offended by injustice but to stand up against it took courage and as we walked together through the watery streets I felt very proud of them.

Back at the car I swallowed down another rush of anger. I had wanted Zadie to realise that the world around her was a warmer, friendlier place than she imagined it to be, so that she might feel able to reach out and trust us. The scene back at the café was over in less than a minute or two but I suspected that its impact might reverberate far longer than that.

So I was surprised to find, when we arrived home, that the incident seemed to have had the opposite effect. As soon as we got in Emily dropped her bags in the hall and asked Zadie if she wanted a drink. Zadie, rather than shaking her head and finding a corner to hide in, answered 'Yes please' in a voice that was audible enough for me to hear over the click as I closed the front door. Jamie, suspecting his luck might be in, switched the TV on and invited Zadie to play one of his Xbox games. When she agreed he gave a whoop. As I straightened Emily and Jamie's abandoned shoes, lining them up with Zadie's neatly positioned ones, I was tempted to give a little cheer of my own, feeling as if we were all a bit closer than when we left the house just a few hours earlier.

That evening, for the first time since her arrival, instead of taking herself off to her room after dinner, Zadie sat up and watched television with us. I think that by leaping to her defence, Emily and Jamie had fixed themselves as fellow comrades in her mind, showing that there was a place for her in the matrix of our family.

Chapter 8

So when I headed off to the foster carers' ball on Saturday evening, it was with a guarded sense of optimism. We had spent most of the day indoors, and thanks to the weirdly fortuitous encounter in the tea shop the atmosphere was perceptibly lighter. My efforts to include Zadie in our conversations were no longer strained and there had certainly been more interaction between her, Emily and Jamie. It was as if their show of solidarity had opened up a channel of trust.

After preparing their dinner I had left them to eat together while I got myself ready, and when I stepped out of the shower I could hardly believe the banter that was drifting up the stairs. Changing into the only decent dress that I own, I could hear Emily and Jamie doing most of the talking but Zadie was chipping in occasionally, mostly with quiet giggles. Peering into the living room, I saw that a half-naked, orange girl gyrating across the television was the source of their amusement – they were watching *Big Fat Gypsy Weddings*.

'Oh no,' I said, reaching for the remote control. 'I don't think this is the best idea. Choose a film to put on instead.'

'What? Why?' Jamie asked with a frown. Half-expecting him to blurt out that we often sit and watch the programme together, I gave him a quick warning glance. There was a pause then Emily leapt in with a helpful, 'Oh, yes, OK, let's download something.' Jamie seemed to take note, pulling a face but slumping back in his chair without another word. Impressed that he was finally learning the art of diplomacy I pulled some washing from the radiator and walked through to the kitchen, folding it as I went.

Jamie hurled the grenade once I had disappeared from his line of sight. 'She thinks you'll find it offensive because you're a Muslim,' he commented casually. I sighed and ran a hand over my brow.

When I had asked my mother to babysit a few days earlier I had warned her to expect a wooden atmosphere, and so when she arrived, just after six, she raised her eyebrows, as surprised as I was by the genuine camaraderie between the three of them. Closing the door to the sound of laughter that evening was immensely uplifting.

The ball was to be held at a hotel about five miles from my house and as I pulled into the car park I met Jenny and her husband, Aiden. It was a chilly evening and, with me nestled between them, the three of us walked towards the hotel, our arms interlinked. Tiny lights glittered around the stone-arched entrance to the hotel and as we pulled open the heavy oak door, warmth spilled onto our heads from an overhead heater. In the foyer, a young woman wearing a fitted black dress and white apron with frilled edges smiled and came over, her arms outstretched ready to take our coats.

'We're here for the Bright Heights do,' Aiden told the waitress. He was a handsome, well-built man with salt-and-pepper, short hair and kind blue eyes.

'Ah, yes. The Glamorgan Suite. This way please, sir.'

Waiters passed us with trays of food that looked too pretty to eat and, feeling oddly out of place, my stomach did a slow somersault. I was pleased to see another friendly face waiting at the large double doors leading to the Glamorgan Suite. Des was standing next to a small round table decked with dozens of champagne flutes arranged in neat lines. When he saw us he smiled broadly and handed each of us a glass, his eyes lingering on me for a moment or two.

'Doesn't she look lovely?' Jenny asked, embarrassing me.

'Aye, she does,' Des said. He leaned in and planted a brief kiss on the top of my head, adding, 'Shame she does-nae make the effort more often.'

It was just the sort of comment I felt comfortable with and I laughed loudly. 'Someone's starting early with the charm offensive tonight,' I said, with a playful nudge of my elbow.

The Glamorgan Suite was a large room about the size of our local mother and toddler hall, although the wooden floor was quite different: highly polished and unscratched, without a splodge of dried paint or clump of Play-Doh in sight. Tall windows stretched the length of one side, over-looking a rectangular courtyard. At the far end of the room was a raised dance floor where band members were in the process of setting up their equipment. There were already about 40 foster carers milling around the space and a few supervising social workers that I recognised from the agency. Huddled together in several overlapping circles, I imagined their conversations drifting from the children in their care then brushing lightly over other subjects before returning quickly to fostering. It was a subject that united but also interested us and, whenever we got together, we always ended up on the same topic. I made my way across the room, stopping every so often to hug people I knew and occasionally feeling a pat on the back from an unseen hand.

The meal was lovely – chicken fricassee and sauté potatoes with a side dish of vegetables – and it was a treat to eat something I hadn't cooked myself. There was no one around me that I knew well and so I sat quietly at first, surveying small knots of people as they interacted around their individual tables. As I listened to their friendly banter I had a sudden memory of the incident in the café, where the girls had picked on Zadie because of the way she was dressed. Just let anyone try that again, I thought to myself. If there was so much as a hint of anyone stepping over the line in the future, heaven help them, because this time they wouldn't get away with it so lightly.

Irritated by the memory, I shook my head and frowned, trying to concentrate on the conversation around me. It was light and friendly and I soon found myself drawn in. Next to me was a couple from a nearby town who had been fostering for 20 years and had recently adopted a sibling group of two after attending an adoption party, where would-be adopters mingled with looked-after children hoping to find a forever family. Both local magistrates, they struck me as stern at first and I found myself wondering how a child, perhaps with little previous experience of discipline, would take to living with them, but I quickly discovered that they shared a dry gentle wit and our chatter was interspersed with regular outbreaks of laughter.

Across the table from me sat an ex-dancer and her female partner. The pair had just passed panel and were waiting for their first placement. They were eager to hear about the children the rest of us had cared for and we were only too happy to regale them with our experiences. We all spoke so fondly that I could almost feel the couple's longing for the phone to ring with that much-anticipated first placement so they could get started on the path of caring for other people's children, a feeling most foster carers remember well. We finished dessert, opened more wine, although I only sipped at mine, and the evening lengthened quickly so that soon it was time for the band to play. The waiters started bringing out coffee in tall silver cafetières and tables emptied as people stood to stretch their legs and mingle.

'Rosie?' Des came over, a glass of red wine in his hand. 'How's it going?'

'Good,' I said, smiling. 'Well, better. I think Zadie's beginning to loosen up. Emily and Jamie are getting used to her too.'

'Great.' He bumped my arm gently with his own. 'What did I tell you?'

'Hmmm. There's still some teenage parallel play going on,' I said, smiling, 'but we're getting there.'

Betrayed

Des eyed me as he took a sip of wine. 'S-o … What's the problem?'

'What makes you think there's a problem?' I asked.

He held my gaze.

I stared at him, narrowing my eyes.

'What can I say? It's my party trick.'

'It's disconcerting, is what it is,' I said with a smirk.

'GCHQ has identified me as a person of interest for my people-reading skills,' he said, laughing. 'Seriously, though, I can tell there's something on your mind.'

'I have no idea, Des,' I said. 'There's something,' I said, shrugging, 'but I don't know what it is.'

He patted my shoulder, told me he'd visit in the next few days for a 'proper chat' then drifted into another conversation with one of his colleagues. Liz, an ex-head teacher and a friend of mine, came over and gave me a hug. It was so unusual to see her wearing make-up that I almost did a double take. Liz was one of the foster carers I met up with outside of the usual courses and support groups and, while Jenny and Rachel often dressed well, Liz and I tended to wear clothes we didn't mind crawling around in. She told me about her newest placement, Kingsley, a two-year-old boy. 'He's so cute! Swears like a docker, though. You'll meet him on Monday.' Her voice had softened with affection. 'Still OK to meet up?'

I nodded. 'And you'll meet Zadie then too. She's not at school so I'll be bringing her along.'

'How's it going?'

I tilted my head to one side, pursing my lips. 'I was just saying to Des, she's beginning to settle but my mind keeps snagging on something. I get the sense something isn't quite right, but maybe it's just me. I get a bit uneasy when life seems to be going too well.'

Liz laughed. 'Yes, I know that feeling. Oh, well, if anyone can get to the bottom of it, it'll be you, honey.'

I smiled gratefully. 'Let's hope so. Although I could do with some of Des's intuition to figure this one out.'

'Yes, it's such a shame, isn't it?' Liz said, reaching out to take a chocolate mint from a nearby table. 'I wonder who we'll get next.'

'Next? But you've only just accepted a new placement.'

'No,' she said, waving the silver wrapper through the air and popping the sweet in her mouth. 'I meant, who will supervise us when Des leaves?'

I frowned, a little taken aback. 'Leaves? What do you mean?'

'Did he not say?' She paused, sensing my unease. 'He's moving …' she was nodding slowly as she spoke, as if it was information that had slipped my mind, 'to the US.'

Stung by the news, I turned my face away for a few seconds.

'I wonder why he didn't tell you. Sorry, I thought the two of you were friends.' She touched my arm. 'Are you all right, Rosie? You look pale.'

'Yes, course I am,' I said after a few beats, trying not to reveal the flips going on inside my stomach. 'He's probably not gotten around to it yet, that's all.'

Someone I didn't recognise slipped his arm around Liz's shoulder and she turned reluctantly towards him, her concerned eyes lingering on me for a moment or two. I was relieved to be left alone. My eyes scanned the room and I caught sight of Des's back. He was standing in a large circle, moving his arms as he spoke with his usual effortlessness. I drifted into the shadows near the window, listening to his voice as it pitched high and loud at the tail-end of one of his anecdotes, the group around him dissolving into laughter.

I marvelled at the intangible gift people like Des seemed to possess, the ability to reveal themselves so easily to a crowd, and yet someone like Zadie was compelled to hide away. She seemed to be gaining confidence in our company but it was still rare for her to speak above a whisper, even when it was just the two of us together. I wished I could whisk away a fragment of whatever it was Des carried within and share it with Zadie. She was beautiful and intelligent but so unaware of her value, so lost and sad.

Overhead, the chandeliered lights dimmed to a soft glow and candles shimmered to life on tables where napkins lay scattered beneath overturned place mats.

'Everything OK, Rosie?' Des asked softly.

I hadn't noticed him approach and I whirled around, startled. 'When were you going to tell me?' The question was out of my mouth before my mind had stopped spinning. I had rounded on him, surprising myself by the accusatory tone in my voice.

He studied his hands. When he looked up there was a half-cocked smile on his face. 'I'm sorry. I was going to mention it on my last visit. There just didnae seem to be the right moment. You were busy with Zadie and …'

I felt a little pinch in my chest. 'So it's true then? You're leaving?' I asked, finding it difficult to look at him. Turning away, I straightened the used cutlery on the table beside me and, through force of habit, swept a few crumbs from the tablecloth into my waiting cupped hand. Realising what I'd done I tutted at myself and closed my eyes, releasing the crumbs in a neat pile, back on the table.

When I turned back to Des he was watching me with amused wonder. After a moment he frowned, a question in his eyes. 'Well, yes, I am. An opportunity has come up on the other side of the pond. Not that they understand a word I say over there.' He smiled wryly, his amusement dissolving quickly when he caught my expression.

'When?' I asked, trying to keep the quiver out of my voice while telling myself that whatever Des planned to do with his life was no business of mine.

'As soon as they can replace me. The department is looking for a social worker to go to Boston to research a new behavioural scheme for teenagers that's working well there. You's know I like to travel, and besides,' he levelled his gaze and held his hands open, palms upwards, 'I have nothing to stay for, Rosie,' he said simply.

'But I thought ...?' I didn't finish my sentence because I couldn't remember her name, but Des had moved in with his partner some months earlier.

He shook his head. 'She left.'

'Why?'

Again he looked at me questioningly, his eyebrows tilting up a trace. Perhaps he was wondering why I considered his love life to be any concern of mine. 'I wasnae around much, I suppose,' he said, answering anyway. He scratched his chin, sighed and looked at me. 'My heart wasnae in it, if I'm really honest.'

I was working on a reply when a noise from across the room drew our attention. It was the manager of our fostering agency, tapping on a microphone.

'Ladies and gentlemen, can I have your attention please?' Lesley Evans, a short woman in her mid-forties with dark hair cut into an angled bob, stood on the stage where the band members had temporarily retired their instruments and were having a drink at the bar. It was time for the presentations.

Lesley opened with a speech, welcoming newly appointed foster carers and updating us on administrative staff changes. My mind began to wander and I thought again about Zadie and her immutable sadness. I'm not sure if it was the effect of the few sips of champagne or the heat in the room but somehow my thoughts began to float, freewheeling back through the last couple of weeks with me making no conscious effort to concentrate.

The realisation hit me almost physically, although I knew that my subconscious had been preparing to unleash itself for days. My mind had been grappling with something since my dream and I had finally joined the dots – if, according to Islam, the sexes were supposed to be segregated, how did her brother know what position Zadie slept in? For a few moments I was in such a daze that I barely registered which carers were going up to collect their long-service awards from Lesley, or had she already moved on to commendations? I only realised that my own name had been read out when I felt the heat of everyone's attention focused on me. Blushing, I felt Des's hand in the small of my back, gently propelling me forward.

With a few nerves fluttering in my stomach I made my way to the stage, the sea of faces in front of me merging into one as I tried to push Zadie from my mind and focus on what the manager was saying. Lesley gave me a warm smile when I reached her, giving my hand a vigorous shake and setting a large bouquet of flowers in my arms. 'All of us here at Bright Heights are proud of the wonderful work you did with your last placement, Rosie. May there be many more successes to come.'

The sound of applause wrenched all other thoughts from my mind and I realised that I had been chosen to receive that year's special recognition award for my work with Phoebe. I was overwhelmed and chuffed as anything, but then very quickly ashamed. I thanked Lesley and hurried from the stage, suddenly conscious of the click of my heels on the hardwood floor. It was lovely that the agency had thought of me but I felt like such a fraud, accepting their praise. If truth be told, I had muddled my way blindly through the placement. Thankfully only Des knew how close I had been to giving up on Phoebe and I thought of my fostering friends, knowing that any one of them would have achieved the same result as me, perhaps sooner than I had managed to.

Liz gave me a hug when I reached her. With her previous experience of teaching, she may have picked up that Phoebe's strange gait and frantic, whirling arm movements were stress related rather than symptoms of autism. And then there was Jenny, so full of wisdom and able to strike up an almost instant rapport with children of any age. For a fleeting moment I wondered whether Zadie would have been better off with one of them. Being allocated a foster carer was a bit of a lottery and children had to take what they were given. The wheel had spun and Zadie happened to have landed with me. With my self-esteem dislodged, I felt a wave of pity for her.

I left soon after the motivational speeches and as I drove home I worried how I would cope on my own, without Des around. Though I rarely called on him for help, knowing that he was unreservedly on my side gave me a confidence boost whenever things got a little bumpy.

Gripped by the uncomfortable feeling that events were slowly unravelling, my thoughts turned back to Zadie. Apart from my impression that something with her brother wasn't quite right, I still knew very little about her. But I had a feeling deep down in the pit of my stomach that it wouldn't be too long until I found out more.

Chapter 9

Lying in bed that night, I couldn't stop myself going over and over Chit's knowledge of Zadie's sleeping habits, but with the arrival of daylight my unease seemed a little bit petty. Picturing Chit as he guided his sister out to the lavender fields, with a chivalrous arm careful not to make contact with her clothing, I dismissed my anxiety as paranoia. It was a respectful, gentle gesture and he had been perfectly polite.

Stowing the milk back in the fridge at about 6.30 a.m., I came to the conclusion that I had been over-dramatising the situation because I was anxious about Des leaving and hurt that he hadn't thought enough of me to tell me the news himself. But whatever way I looked at it, the clock was ticking. Zadie was in voluntary care and could be taken by her father at any moment. Strictly speaking, families are supposed to give the local authority 28 days' notice if they wish to withdraw their agreement to voluntary foster care, but it rarely happened that way. I needed to get Zadie talking, and soon.

Betrayed

I sat at the dining table sipping my coffee and watched Zadie through the patio doors as she bounced on the trampoline. It was something she had taken to doing in the last few days and was spending increasingly more time on it. I presumed the exercise was her way of relieving some stress; she certainly threw all of her energy into it, but there was something oddly manic in the way she launched herself into flips and dives, especially so early in the morning. She was such a placid, gentle-natured girl and yet she was throwing herself around with as much vigour as Jamie and his friends, whenever they got together on it. Knowing that anorexics often exercised obsessively, I began to wonder whether Zadie was suffering from an eating disorder. It was another mystery to add to the rapidly growing list.

After nigh on an hour of intense exercise she came in, her face rosy pink with exertion. It being Sunday, we had nowhere in particular to go and so, while Emily and Jamie caught up on their homework, Zadie sat in the dining room using the computer. I tried to limit the amount of time the children spent on screens so about an hour after she had logged on I invited her to join me in the garden.

She immediately tensed, twirling her fingers in the front of her black robe. 'Don't look so suspicious,' I said, laughing as I opened the back door. 'I thought that while Emily and Jamie are busy we might play a game of cards or maybe have a chat.'

Horrified at the prospect of talking, she quickly opted to play a game. 'But I don't know how to play cards,' she said, biting her lip.

It was the reply I'd been counting on. 'We'll do something else then,' I said as we walked towards our swing at the end of the garden. Glancing sideways, I could see that her robe was once again at the sharp, receiving end of her anxiety. After giving it the customary tug, she twisted the linen across her stomach so tightly that when she let go a silvery web of tight creases was left behind.

I sat at one end of the swing and patted the seat next to me, remembering how Phoebe, just a few years younger than Zadie, had found it much easier to talk to me when we were in the garden. It was while we sat together on the swing that I began to get a sense of how traumatic Phoebe's past had been. Some children, I have noticed, find face-to-face chats confrontational and are far likelier to open up if sitting side-by-side or when riding in the back of a car, and with Phoebe it had certainly been that way.

Zadie sat a couple of feet from me and stared into her lap, her fingers flicking at the bands on her wrist. I was pleased to see that her hands were looking less raw – the bands were clearly doing their job. I started telling Zadie about Phoebe, although I didn't use her real name and glossed over most of the details. 'And there was a memory game she used to love. Shall we give it a try?'

She looked across at me and nodded, a glimmer of interest in her dark eyes.

'OK, so you go first. Tell me about your earliest memory ...'

She bit her lip. I don't think it was the sort of memory game she was expecting but she put her finger to her lips and frowned in concentration. It was a game I had played before with other children I had cared for and I found it useful in helping to reveal feelings that they might not have been able to express through conversation alone.

I came up with the idea after reading somewhere that a person's earliest memory usually captures the nature of their entire childhood.

'I have quite a few memories from when I was about four or five, but I'm not sure which one …'

'Is the earliest?' I asked. She nodded. 'R-ight,' I said slowly. It actually didn't matter which one was the earliest. It was the memory that Zadie selected that would be important. 'Then just choose the one that you think might be the earliest and tell me about it.'

There was a pregnant pause. 'It's not a very nice one,' she said eventually, sounding apologetic.

I smiled. 'It doesn't have to be a nice one, just an early one.'

'Well, I remember there was one day when I was playing in the garden and everyone else was in the house. I was skipping or spinning around and then I fell over and hurt my knee. I was crying and I tried to get back in the house but someone had locked the door. And that's all I can remember.'

I was silent for a moment, absorbing what Zadie had said. Children that have known an attentive, loving carer are likely to view the world as a friendly place and tend to be optimistic in nature. If a child has experienced insecure, unreliable attachments it is probable that they will hold a pessimistic view of the world beyond their family. So a child who has been abused or mistreated is likely to choose a sad memory from all the ones available to them – and Zadie had chosen a sad memory.

She turned to me. 'So what happens now?'

I could have continued along the same vein, allowing her to ask me the same question and then moving on to early memories of seaside trips or holidays, the sort of game that works well with younger children, but for some reason I didn't. I don't know why. 'Now you tell me how you felt, alone in the garden.'

She narrowed her eyes. 'This isn't really a game at all, is it?'

I gave her a crooked smile. 'Well, not really a game as such. More of a conversation opener.'

'Some conversation,' she said with a grimace. 'I'm doing all the talking.'

Her reply gave me another glimpse of the authentic, three-dimensional Zadie hiding beneath the loose-fitting clothes and anonymous head scarf and I grinned. 'OK,' I said, holding my hands up in mock surrender. 'But you're not the easiest girl to get to know.'

She quickly grew serious. 'I'm sorry.'

I patted her knee. 'No need to be sorry. But, the thing is,' I said, angling myself around to face her, 'if you don't give me some idea about what the problem is at home I'm afraid there's no way we can keep you here for much longer.' I paused for a moment. 'It doesn't have to be me. If you'd rather talk to someone else I can arrange –'

'No,' she interrupted, looking straight at me. Her expression was earnest. 'I want it to be you.'

I smiled and grabbed her hand, giving it a squeeze. 'The world won't end if you stand up for yourself,' I said softly.

'You might think it will, but trust me, it really doesn't.' Her eyes misted over, then she dropped her gaze to her lap. We sat in silence for several minutes, the swing gently rocking.

'I'd feel guilty talking about my family,' she said suddenly, adding with a whisper, 'I don't want to be disloyal.'

Sensing that Zadie might be close to opening up, my heart quickened and I took a little breath to steady myself. 'Yes, you're right. You probably would feel a little guilty. I understand that, honey, really I do. But you can't spend your whole life tiptoeing around in case you upset somebody. If you do, what sort of life will you have?' I paused. 'The thing is, Zadie, I think you're frightened of something. Is loyalty so important that you'd put yourself at risk to honour it?'

She frowned but stayed silent.

'Being loyal is admirable, but some things trump it, Zadie, and safety is one of them.'

She thought about that for a moment then gave a decisive nod. 'I want to be safe,' she said, her voice hoarse.

'Good,' I said, reaching for her hand again. 'You're safe here. And you can trust me. I'll support you, whatever you tell me.'

She let out a noise, somewhere between a sigh and a squeak. 'But maybe I'm not seeing things straight. I wanted so much to make my family proud –' she broke off, her voice cracking. After a moment she said, 'What if it's me that's wrong?'

I thought about all the children I had cared for and the power their parents wielded over them, even in their absence, remembering the sometimes maddening depth of loyalty they showed their mostly undeserving parents, no matter what had been done to them. It was easy to understand how Zadie would find it near impossible to escape the tunnel vision of her own family and gain a true sense of the world, especially when the counterbalancing effect of school had been taken away from her.

'I think you have to trust your instincts, honey. If you feel something is wrong you have to stand up against it, no matter how many people shout you down.'

'But it's not just my family I'll bring shame on if I talk. It's my whole community. They can't all be wrong.' Her voice wobbled. 'It must be me. I have bad blood.'

'Zadie,' I said firmly, grasping her hand even tighter. 'There's no such thing as bad blood. Children tend to believe what their parents tell them. If a parent insists that the world is made of custard and controlled by giant jelly babies, then that will become their child's frame of reference.'

She laughed quietly.

'Seriously, though, it's very difficult to disbelieve something we've heard from infancy, especially when it's reinforced by a whole community. But you need to realise that feelings are not wrong if they're truly your own. You're getting older now. It's natural to start questioning things.'

I paused for a moment, hoping that what I had said would sink in. When she didn't say anything I added, 'I understand your feelings towards your family, perhaps more than you realise. Take me, for example. For years I felt guilty about not being the good church girl my father wanted me to be.'

She turned sharply and stared at me. 'Really?'

Betrayed

I nodded, sensing that if I wanted Zadie to open up I would have to give a little bit of myself first. And to my surprise, I was beginning to suspect that in some ways she might be a kindred spirit. 'My father is a very religious man. He wanted me to leave school at 16 so I could devote my time to doing outreach work for the church. I did, even though I had dreams of going to university. For years I tried to do what was expected of me, but to be honest it didn't do any good. I've never felt as if I could ever measure up to his high standards, especially since I got divorced. I've always felt compelled to make up for being such a disappointment.' I held up my hands, then dropped them softly to my lap. 'I really don't know why.'

Zadie was watching me avidly, staring at my lips as if she wanted to hear more.

'It's not his fault, to be fair. My upbringing was staunchly religious but nurturing. I've never felt unloved.'

'And you're close to your mum, aren't you?' she asked.

'Yes, we're close. But I even feel like I've let her down.'

Zadie frowned. 'That doesn't make any sense.'

I shrugged and gave her a wry smile. 'Emotions often don't.'

'Your mum told me last night that you have a heart of gold. That you would do anything for anyone.'

'She said that?' My mother is a bit thrifty with compliments and so I was a bit taken aback. 'Really?'

'Yes,' she said. And then she giggled. 'Although she also said you can be a bit naïve.'

I laughed. 'That sounds more like it. What made her say that?'

Zadie blushed. 'I was telling her how kind you've been.'

I smiled and rubbed her knee. She looked shyly away. I noticed that she was finishing her sentences. It was the first time she had managed to since we first met. I let a few moments pass and then I said, 'So tell me about the way things were at home, before you ran away.'

It's funny how giving a little of yourself can sometimes change the course of a relationship. Perhaps seeing that every family has its own secrets made Zadie feel more able to reveal her own, or maybe she recognised that my feelings of guilt chimed with hers, but I sensed that something basic had changed between us. The polite veneer of formality had been brushed aside and we started to talk openly.

It seemed that she remembered very little about her mum but had spent years longing for her.

'So what happened to her?' I asked gently.

'I don't know. All I can remember is the way I felt on the day I realised she'd gone. I've tried asking Papa about her but he gets angry and refuses to discuss it. My brothers never talk about her either. It's like she never existed.'

Zadie went on to tell me how unhappy she was when she was told she wasn't allowed to go back to the school she loved. From early childhood she had nursed dreams of becoming a vet and worked hard at her studies. She had been doing well but her father felt that she was neglecting her prayers. 'Muslims who neglect their prayers can expect excruciating torment in the next world. Papa was worried that school was distracting me from my duties.'

She went on to say that her father regularly complained to the school about their lack of provision for Muslim students. Apparently the dinner ladies neglected to use different utensils for serving halal meals and the PE teachers had allowed Zadie to swim in a mixed session, even though they were aware that her family would consider it indecent.

And then she told me that her father questioned her daily when she got in from school, asking where she had changed for PE and whether there was any chance someone had caught an indecent glimpse of her. I was shocked. It seemed to me that the men in her family were behaving more like jealous lovers than blood relatives but I didn't want to come across as judgemental so I fell silent and let a few moments pass.

'So when did you leave?' I asked. In my head I was trying to work out what stage Zadie was at, academically, wondering whether I could enlist the help of Liz, my ex-head teacher fostering friend, to set some work for her. 'At the end of year 7?'

'No,' she shook her head. 'In the middle of year 8. My father drove past the school one day and saw me wearing school uniform. I wasn't allowed back after that.'

I looked at her, frowning. 'Wearing school uniform instead of your burqa?'

She stared blankly at me for a fraction of a second before it dawned on her that this was news to me. Her face clouded with realisation and she reddened, her eyes darting away.

'So you preferred not to wear your robe to school?'

She shrugged sheepishly, keeping her eyes averted. 'I just wanted to be like everyone else,' she whispered, reaching a hand beneath her headscarf to scratch behind her ear.

'Of course, I can understand that. So where did you get the uniform from?'

'The school had a lost property sale at the end of year 7. I used to wear my robe over the top and then take it off when I got to school.'

I felt a niggle in my stomach at her words, although there was certainly nothing unusual about a child wanting to fit in. I could understand that. Before I had a chance to analyse the feeling Zadie interrupted my thoughts, asking, 'So why did you ask about my earliest memory?'

'Because a child's early experiences shape their view of the world,' I said softly. 'And I want desperately to understand what's happened in your family. And how it brought you here.'

She nodded solemnly, picking at her bands again. She let them go with such force that I winced. 'But I had other memories. You told me to pick any of the ones I had in my head.'

'Yes, because from those that you grasp hold of, you were likely to choose one that encapsulated the mood of your early years,' I said, pausing again. She didn't reply so I added, 'It doesn't always work out but …'

I stopped in mid-sentence as Zadie took a loud intake of breath. I thought she was going to cough but instead she turned to me. 'It did work, Rosie,' she whispered. And then unexpectedly, she began to cry. Huge gulping sobs that made her physically tremble.

Reaching out, I pulled her towards me and encircled her with my arms. Resting her head just below my neck, she cried for several minutes. I could feel her shaking as the sadness pulsed through her, although she made almost no sound. When her sobs subsided she thanked me, then apologised profusely.

I gripped her by her upper arms. 'Zadie, please. Stop it. You've got absolutely nothing to be sorry for, do you hear me?'

'Yes, thank you,' she said, her expression agonised. 'Can I go now?'

'Of course you can, sweetie,' I said, trying to keep the puzzled frustration out of my tone. I was so pleased to be able to offer her some comfort, but I still had absolutely no idea why she was so upset.

Chapter 10

The next day was Monday and as arranged we went to Jenny's house for coffee. Liz and Rachel arrived at the large detached house a few moments after me, looking slightly frayed around the edges after tackling the morning school-run traffic. We hugged at the gate and then I introduced Zadie who rocked nervously on her heels, eyeing Liz as if she were the foreman of a jury, ready to drag her off to the gallows.

'Hi, Zadie,' Liz said, releasing her grip on the young toddler in her arms. The stocky black boy slid down her body, barrelling off across Jenny's front garden as soon as his feet touched the ground. Rachel reached around me and patted Zadie's shoulder.

As we walked up the path together, two-year-old Kingsley careened along the neat rows of spring flowers and then began zigzagging through them. 'Don't do that, Kings,' Liz called out, holding out her hand and wiggling her fingers. 'Come over here and say hello to Rachel and Rosie.'

Betrayed

'Nah, don't wanna, silly cow,' he chirruped, stamping on the dewy petals of some pale-yellow flowers.

'Oooh,' I said in my most enticing tone, 'shall we see what toys Jenny has for you, Kingsley?'

He stopped in his tracks and looked at me, considering. A moment later he dismissed the idea. 'Go 'way, silly bitch,' he said in a loud voice, having decided it was more fun to squat in the middle of some pink hydrangeas. The spiral curls of his afro hair were just visible over the top of the bush.

Standing behind Rachel, I could see her shoulders quaking with suppressed laughter. I breathed out my own chuckle into the collar of my jacket while Liz marched across and grabbed Kingsley around his middle. 'Oh the joys,' she said, puffing as she tried to keep hold of his wriggling form and avoid his kicks at the same time. The bottoms of his trousers were damp with dew. 'Remind me why I resigned from my perfectly good, well-paid job,' she said with a wry smile.

'Oh, you love it really,' I said with a laugh, ringing the doorbell then turning back to Kingsley. There was something about mischievous little boys that was beyond adorable and I couldn't resist giving him a playful poke in his tummy. His face creased into an angelic smile before attempting to deliver a swift kick to my stomach.

'Sorry about the mess,' Jenny said by way of a greeting as she manoeuvred an excited puppy back with her foot, 'but it's all I can do to get the boys dressed and off to school on time.'

'Course it is,' 'Tell me about it' and 'I know exactly what you mean,' we all chimed as we kicked off our shoes, quickly on our knees and helping to clear away the detritus of the early morning rush in the wide hallway. I was surprised to find the floor scattered with tiny crumbs and, in one place, something sticky that attached itself to my sock. Lego pieces, football cards and comic books littered the floor, a trail that continued through to the living room. Zadie, bless her, joined in and helped to sweep all the small bits into a cupped hand without being prompted. Billy, a four-year-old boy who had lived with Jenny for just over a year, hovered at Jenny's side and stared at Zadie with a puzzled interest, seemingly intrigued by the existence of a headscarf where hair would normally be.

Jenny's place was usually immaculate but she had recently accepted a new sibling placement and there was nothing like it for reducing even the most organised household into chaos. Besides all the extra toys, games and clothes to find space for, an individual daily diary had to be written for each child and then there were the education plan meetings, reviews and social worker visits on top of the usual washing, ironing and trying to find enough time left over to play with them.

After tidying, Zadie volunteered to take Kingsley and Billy into the garden, perhaps seeking solace away from the unfamiliar faces. I stood at the window and watched them for a moment, my thoughts drifting to my earlier phone conversation with my mother. According to Mum, Zadie had said that she had no idea where her mother was or even if she was still alive. When Mum tried to probe further, Zadie apparently clammed up and she was left with the feeling that the teenager was holding something back.

Betrayed

I was afraid that we had barely scratched the surface of Zadie's problems. Her family were strict and overprotective, I knew that much, but I still had no idea what led her to run away, or why she was too frightened to go back. A light wind tugged at Zadie's headscarf and as she reached up to flatten it I remembered what she had said about wearing a uniform to school. It struck me as odd that she went to the trouble of buying the clothes herself and kept them hidden from her family, and yet now, when she was in a place of safety, her robe was all she wanted to wear. I wondered whether it was her way of hiding away from us; the anonymity of the robe a sort of armour against strangers.

Rachel, Liz and I each found a spot on the comfortable sofa or matching armchairs and Jenny, after taking drinks out for the children and a blanket for them to sit on, brought us some tea. I took one of the steaming mugs, then curled up, relaxing into the sofa. Tucking my feet between the cushioned end and my hips, I let out a gasp, the unforgiving arm of a Transformers toy catching the delicate area between my toes.

As usual, the conversation drifted to fostering and we began comparing notes. Besides Kingsley, Liz was fostering a teenage boy who had been with her for almost three months. 'Feels like *so* much longer, though,' she said, collapsing at her middle so that her shoulders sagged in a mime of exhaustion. 'Bless him, he's amazingly sweet. It's just the tunnelling that gets me down.'

'Tunnelling?' Jenny asked, incredulous.

Liz first noticed something awry a few days into Ryan's stay when little mounds of dust began to appear in random places. She had no idea where they came from and no one in the house would admit to knowing anything about them. Liz became convinced that they must have been invaded by an army of mice or some sort of insect.

She decided to blitz the place, working methodically around the house to search for signs of infestation. It was as she was stripping Ryan's bedroom of posters and photos that she found the source of the problem; he had punctured several holes in the wall, each narrowing so that they were almost invisible on the other side. When Liz confronted the 13-year-old he broke down, admitting that he found it impossible to relax unless he was able to keep a constant eye on the people around him.

'Tony goes around filling the holes when he gets in from work but within a day or two the little piles of dust are back. It's driving us round the bend.'

Liz had called me in despair late one evening when her husband was working late and so I had already heard about Ryan's habit but Jenny held her hand over her mouth, shaking her head. 'Why does he do it, do you think?' she asked.

'He's scared one of us will creep up on him when he's not expecting it.'

Jenny dropped her hand. 'Oh, poor love. I can guess what sort of home life he's had then.'

Liz nodded grimly. 'He's beginning to open up so I can sort of understand his reasoning.' She pulled her hands down her face. 'But it's just so hard to keep my patience with him, you know?'

We nodded in unison. All of us understood how trying some days could be, especially when a problem seemed to be irresolvable. If any of us embarked on our fostering 'careers' seeking perfection we had long since abandoned the aspiration, each of us content to get through the day with the children in one piece and our reputations intact. None of us ever tried to pretend that we found it easy. Fostering is a great leveller in that way. I'm not sure whether it attracts the sort of person who doesn't bother to put up a front or whether it quickly strips away the usual façade that people construct, but I felt completely at ease with Jenny, Rachel and Liz; I hadn't felt as comfortable amongst a group of people since my school days.

We fell silent for a moment while we sipped our tea. 'How about Levi? How's he settling?' Jenny asked Rachel. After moving little Katy, a girl of 18 months, on to adoption, Rachel had accepted a new placement, a young lad of 11, even though he was outside of her approved age range.

'Hmmm, good days and bad,' she said, rocking her hand one way then the other. 'See what he did the other day when I tried to stop him taking his phone to bed?'

Rachel pulled up the hem of her jeans to reveal her shin. There was a huge bruise the size of a pineapple between her knee and ankle, the skin mottled red, purple and blue where Levi had kicked her. We shook our heads in stunned silence. 'He's got an unfortunate fascination for animal intestines too,' she added with a grimace.

There were occasions when one of us would come up with a suggestion or strategy we may have used in the past that had been helpful, but sometimes there wasn't a lot we could say other than offering the support of listening. I felt a rush of admiration for them all.

'And how are the boys doing?' I asked Jenny eventually, finishing the last of my tea.

'Well, I suddenly feel like I've got it easy,' she said, laughing. 'Kane doesn't say much. Carl's the demanding one. He's been diagnosed with ADHD but I must admit he's calming down since I got really firm with him. I'm not sure he even has ADHD. I think he's just another child who's never been taught that life has rules.'

'Shhh,' Liz said in mock horror, peering over her shoulder theatrically. 'You're bordering on inappropriate.' Any foster carer harbouring the view that ADHD was a medical diagnosis of naughtiness would be swiftly sent for retraining.

A flash memory surfaced from the last local authority course I had attended. The tutor had told us of the many bizarre techniques desperate parents and doctors had employed in the past to 'cure' children of their bad or defiant behaviour. I had been shocked to hear that until 1930 frazzled parents of over-energetic children had been able to pop to their local apothecary and buy a bottle of Mrs Winslow's soothing syrup, a cocktail of morphine and opium powders. Intended to soothe restless youngsters, it was so potent that it often killed them instead. Even more extreme, some children were lobotomised at the request of harassed mothers or sometimes step-parents who found them difficult to live with.

Jenny flapped her hand. 'Can't say anything these days, even if it's true.'

'And?' I prompted. 'Any news on Billy? Did the adoption team get back to you?'

The amused light in Jenny's eyes dimmed.

'Oh no, what have they said?'

'They've got adopters lined up. My rights only kicked in a few weeks ago and they said they'd already told the adopters about him.' She sighed, drawing her lips into a thin line. 'The handover starts at the beginning of next month.'

I had heard of several cases where foster carers were discouraged from adopting the children they were looking after. If a foster carer adopts it means that they have less capacity to offer the local authority in the future and, with such a shortage of carers nationwide, social workers are often reluctant to support their application. I could understand the temptation to keep experienced foster carers in the system but it seemed unfair on the individual children, particularly when someone like Billy was clearly so settled and attached. Rachel, hopelessly soft, flattened her hand to her chest in sympathy.

Jenny stared into the garden, her eyes misting over.

'How long have you known he was going?' Rachel asked.

'They told me a couple of weeks ago. Until then I thought it was just a case of completing the paperwork so that I could adopt him.'

'No,' Liz said, lowering her chin and giving Jenny a meaningful stare. 'You knew he'd be going the day he arrived. You shouldn't have allowed yourself to get so attached.'

Liz had a point. Strictly speaking she was absolutely right, but when it comes to children, emotional responses are automatic. It can be difficult and sometimes impossible to rein in such a natural instinct. Jenny pulled a face but it was good natured; there was enough affection and respect between us to talk frankly, and I knew that, when I moved much-loved children on to adoption, trying to see things from Liz's practical perspective had helped to ease the heartache. And if the truth be told Liz wasn't so very different from the rest of us, when it came down to it. I remembered when she had cared for a newborn baby a couple of years earlier; she came out with her usual rhetoric about how it was the basic duty of a foster carer to move children on, but the weepy expression and grainy voice hadn't been lost on me. When I had draped an arm around her shoulder and gave it a squeeze, a little sob had escaped her throat, her head lingering on my chest a touch longer than it would normally have done.

'So did you ask Des why he hadn't mentioned anything to you?' Liz asked, angling herself to face me from the other end of the sofa.

'He planned to mention it on his next visit,' I said lightly with a wave of my hand, hoping to move the conversation swiftly in another direction. I felt I could say anything during one of our meet-ups, knowing it wouldn't be met with shocked gasps or awkward silences. It was a relief to be somewhere you could lay all your cards on the table and not have to pretend to be anything other than fallible. Having said that, there were still some cards I preferred to keep close to my chest.

Some chance of that with three perceptive women around.

'You know, I always got the feeling that you two might get together one day,' Liz said, giving me a significant look.

Betrayed

'Me and Des?!' I shrieked with exaggerated shock. 'Goodness, no. I don't know why you'd think that.' I held my tea out at an angle and swept imaginary crumbs from my lap with the other hand. When I looked up, everyone still had their eyes on me. 'What?'

'Erm, let's see now, why would we think that?' Liz scratched her chin theatrically. 'Because he's funny and kind. Because your kids love him. And because you're lonely ...'

'Really, I'm not,' I insisted, aware of the heat rising in my face. Liz was a straight-talker, one of the reasons she was so well suited to fostering teenagers, but sometimes her blunt approach left me a little breathless. 'I don't know why you keep saying that.'

'They don't believe anyone can manage without a man in their life,' Rachel joked, though I sensed a sour undertone. Rachel's husband ran off with a hairdresser during an extended trip to the US and she could always be relied upon for a bitter remark if our conversation strayed towards men. Like me, she was fostering as a single carer, although she had recently started a low-key relationship with a physiotherapist. I sometimes wondered whether he was ever subjected to some of the scathing comments she made when she was with us.

'He's got a soft spot for you,' Jenny added a little more gently than Liz, a teasing smile on her face. 'We can see it a mile off, even if you can't.'

'Don't be daft,' I said, dismissing them with a strained laugh.

'It certainly won't be the same without him around,' Rachel said, kindly taking the heat away from me. 'He's one of those rare guys that actually listens to women. I really like him.'

High praise indeed, I thought.

'Yes, I wonder what the Americans will make of him, though,' Liz said. We all chortled.

'Oh, they're very welcoming,' Rachel said acidly, and our smiles withered a fraction.

Of all of them, Rachel was the foster carer I was most in tune with. Jenny and Rachel both had a different supervising social worker, but Des, being a live wire, was one of those staff members that everyone got to know well. We all agreed that he would be missed.

'She seems lovely,' Rachel said, tilting her head towards the patio doors. In the garden Zadie was on her knees rolling a ball across the neatly trimmed grass. The boys sat opposite and she had them taking turns to bowl it back to her, Bobby the puppy bounding excitedly between the three of them. The teenager was beaming at them, no trace of the frozen smile she reserved for everyone else.

'Oh she is, absolutely,' I said, grateful that the conversation had been steered away from me. 'And she's so helpful. It's like having a live-in au pair and virtual assistant rolled into one. I only have to mention something that needs organising and she produces a colour-coded spreadsheet for me. She's intelligent, polite and *so* quiet. In fact if it wasn't for all the cleaning and tidying up she does I'd hardly know she was there.'

'But?' Jenny asked, her head cocked.

'There's something not quite right,' I said in a hushed tone. 'She's hinted at some problems at home but …'

'No, don't do that, Kingsley!' Liz yelled, already on her feet and charging towards the garden. All of us were used to disjointed conversations, one or the other of us regularly leaping up to head off a tantrum or avert some other drama.

Jenny and I followed closely behind. 'What happened?' I asked Zadie. She was sitting with Billy cradled gently on her lap, a mortified expression on her face.

'I'm sorry,' she said, almost in tears.

'It wasn't your fault, honey. I saw what happened. Kingsley whacked him on the head with this,' Liz said, brandishing a metal toy car in the air. 'What do you say to Billy?' she demanded, kneeling in front of Kingsley. The toddler wore a thoughtful expression, then blew a raspberry in Liz's face.

Leaving Liz to talk to a now prostrate and screaming Kingsley, we came back into the house. Billy was in Jenny's arms and Rachel and I watched as she sang softly to him. Billy gave her a watery, loving smile and she gently ruffled his hair. Watching my friends showing such tender care to other women's children has always restored my faith in human nature and a lump rose in my throat. Rachel tilted her head and pouted, her expression saying ah-bless-them.

On the way home we made a detour via the post office to collect some parcels for my mother. Several large companies had donated their off-cuts to the WEPH's quilt-making project and Mum had asked if I would mind picking them up and taking them to the church hall. At the collection depot there was a pile of boxes labelled 'Project

Congo'. Zadie's eyes brightened with interest, her sallow skin temporarily aglow.

As I lowered the back seats of my car to make more room in the boot, Zadie chattered animatedly about how the members of the group would feel when they found out exactly how much material they had to choose from and whether they would be surprised to see it all. As soon as we pulled up outside the hall she jumped out, keen to see Mum's reaction.

Mum greeted us at the door, clapping her hands in delight when she saw the boot so heavily laden. Zadie, bless her, insisted on helping me to carry the boxes in and when Mum brought out some sample quilts that had already been made she and Zadie were chatting away like old friends. It was lovely to see.

And then a strange thing happened. Just as we were carrying the last box into the hall there was a bright flash behind us. Spinning around, I caught a glimpse of the tail end of a dark-blue car before it disappeared from view behind a hedge. At first I wondered whether the car had been travelling too fast and triggered a speed camera, but then, with an uncomfortable jolt in my chest, I began to suspect that someone had taken a photo of us.

That evening Zadie sat with the rest of the family and played board games. I was delighted that we seemed to have forged a new understanding but my worries stayed with me and I was particularly bothered by the thought that our photo may have been taken. I had heard stories of birth families putting pictures of their children's foster carers on Facebook in the hope that their whereabouts could be located. It was an unnerving thought. I kept telling myself to forget it but my mind seemed unwilling to tidy it away. The flash might have been headlamps from the car but, equally, it could have been a member of Zadie's family wanting to let us know that they were watching.

If Zadie had reason to be afraid of them, I reasoned, perhaps we did too.

Chapter 11

It was early in June when Peggy called with details of Zadie's first LAC (looked-after child) review. When a child is taken into care, the local authority is legally required to hold a meeting, inviting everyone involved in looking after their welfare, including their parents. The purpose of the LAC review is to ensure the child's needs are being met and that there is a suitable care plan in place. The child's education, health, conduct and any contact arrangements are usually discussed, as well as any problems they may be experiencing.

The first review often takes place within the first week of placement but it can sometimes be tricky to arrange a time that fits in with all the professionals involved as well as finding a suitable venue. With a shortage of meeting rooms at the civic centre, the local authority sometimes resorts to hiring private rooms, and on this occasion Peggy had arranged for us to meet in a disused classroom in a local private girls' school.

Zadie, though she was far more comfortable in our company, still seemed reluctant to leave the house, and on the morning of the review she was visibly shaken. She knew that her father had been invited to the meeting, and though she had nodded politely when I told her and made no comment other than 'Thank you, Rosie,' I got the feeling she was terrified of facing him.

The day of the review was bright and clear and so we sat outside to have our breakfast; well, Jamie, Emily and I ate, while Zadie pummelled her wrist with the bands. I sat in my favourite wicker chair gazing at some overgrown bushes near the stone wall at the bottom of our garden, the ragged, untended leaves glistening from earlier rainfall. A light breeze played with the apple blossom that had fallen from our tree, sweeping the delicate petals up then casting them adrift over the garden. Some fluttered across the table like tiny butterflies.

I reached out to touch one as it floated past. 'We need to have a chat later about what we're doing in the summer,' I said to no one in particular, trying to ignore the regular ping as another band hit her skin, 'or everywhere will be booked.' If Zadie was still with us by the time Emily and Jamie broke up from school it would be nice for her to get away and have a break from staring at the same four walls.

Zadie, distracted, gave a half-hearted smile.

'We can't go the first week of the summer holidays,' Jamie said as he shovelled the last of his cornflakes into his mouth.

'Slow down, Jamie. It's not a race,' I said, grimacing, only half-aware that Emily had stilled, her hand hovering in the air so that the piece of toast she was about to bite hung an inch from her mouth. 'Actually, if I can find a finishing school for boys I'll book you in there for the summer. The rest of us will go on holiday.'

Jamie chewed quickly, then wiped his mouth on the sleeve of his blazer. 'Fine by me,' he said, throwing me a disarming smile.

Zadie hid her amusement under lowered eyelids. Emily's brows were drawn in a frown.

'What is it, Ems? What have I said?'

'Nothing,' she said instantly, though she kept her eyes averted.

'She's upset about Dad,' Jamie blurted out. 'You mentioning the holidays probably reminded her about it.'

'What about Dad?' I asked, stirred with curiosity.

The change in pitch around the table seemed to cut through Zadie's mental fog and I noticed that her eyes were now darting between Emily and Jamie with the same intensity as mine.

Jamie eyed Emily hesitantly. Colour rose to her cheeks and she gave him a sharp look.

I felt my pulse quicken. 'What is it?' I repeated, running my fingers over the latticework arm of my chair. My tone was demanding, though I wasn't sure I was ready to hear whatever they had to say. 'Tell me, one of you. What's wrong with Dad?'

'He and Debbie are getting married in July,' Jamie said, eyeing Emily with a touch of defiance. 'He told us last week.'

I felt a twinge low down in my stomach as I looked at Emily. Her mouth was pinched closed and there was both embarrassment and sadness in her eyes. A ripple ran through my throat. Swallowing it down, I reached for her hand. 'Why didn't you tell me, honey? Is that why you've been quiet lately?'

She shrugged.

'Jamie?'

'She told me not to tell,' he said, thumbing Emily over his shoulder and helping himself to some toast.

Emily shot her brother another sharp look. 'I didn't exactly say that.'

'She did, Mum.'

'Shut up, Jamie,' Emily hissed.

'You shut up,' he returned.

'Be quiet, not shut up,' I said, realising that I sounded like I was talking to a couple of toddlers. My gaze slipped across to Zadie, wondering what she must think of us. She cleared her throat and lowered her gaze.

'I didn't want to upset you,' Emily said, her eyes misted over.

'Honey, I'm not upset,' I said airily, managing a wan smile. 'I think it's nice.' I must admit that I had to concentrate to get the words out without clenching my teeth.

'Really? Well, I don't,' Emily said, twisting her face into a grimace. 'I think it's weird. He's a bit past it for all that romance stuff, isn't he?'

I laughed. 'He's only a couple of years older than me.'

'Exactly,' she said with disdain.

I stroked her cheek. 'You'll get used to the idea, honey.'

Emily swiped at her damp eyes briskly and glanced around the table. Zadie, who had been watching our exchange with interest, offered Emily a tender smile. It was a simple act but one born of kindness and Emily smiled gratefully back. It was touching that Zadie, with all she had to cope with and the changes in her life, took the time to consider the feelings of Emily. Not for the first time, I got the sense that her gentle presence would help to solidify her place in the family.

We left home at 1.30 p.m. and by that time the sun was shining so brightly through the windscreen that I lowered the sunshields and rolled the windows down. The warm breeze floated through the interior of the car laden with a twin scent of exhaust fumes and freshly cut grass. In the rear-view mirror I could see Zadie bobbing nervously up and down, lifting her arms every few seconds to adjust her headscarf. By the time we reached the outskirts of town she had pulled it down so far that it resembled a hoodie and was almost touching her eyebrows.

I was actually surprised that I had managed to get her into the car at all. Besides the review, Zadie was overdue for her LAC medical, a compulsory health assessment for looked-after children that was supposed to take place within 28 days of coming into care. In the last three weeks I had booked two appointments but had to cancel both at the last minute because Zadie had worked herself up into such a tizzy, physically sick with nerves. I was beginning to suspect that fear had been the narrative of her life so far, to such an extent that it would take a long time to overwrite.

Pulling up at a red light, I stretched in my seat and gave a heavy sigh, wondering for the umpteenth time why she was so afraid. Still, I thought, at least the mystery over Emily's recent doldrums was finally solved. I pictured her troubled expression at breakfast with a twist of sadness but I reminded myself that children manage to adjust to all sorts of situations. I had seen it many times and Emily and Jamie were, on the whole, happy and well-adjusted individuals with strong moral compasses. I tried to tell myself that I couldn't really ask for more than that.

Riverdene School for Girls was screened from view of the road by a sweeping line of tall fir trees and so it was only as we pulled into the narrow drive that its full finery was revealed. The main school was a building caught in time with high turrets, ivy-covered stone walls and an ancient-looking clock tower. Surrounded by impressive lawns with meadows beyond and bordered by woods, it was an idyllic place and I thought what a joy the school run must be for Riverdene parents, knowing their children were passing their childhood days in such a beautiful place.

I nudged my car into a space at the bottom end of the car park between one of the school minibuses and a row of tennis courts, watching as a group of girls about Zadie's age, dressed in white shorts and polo shirts, bobbed lightly around the astroturf practising their serves. 'Come on then,' I said cheerily. 'Let's go and find Peggy.' The fresh air and beautiful surroundings had lightened my mood, so much so that I'd almost forgotten my dislike of formal meetings.

When I opened the door for Zadie and caught the look of anguish on her face my own stomach performed a lazy half-roll. As she climbed out she made a little noise and then, straightening, she rubbed her hands roughly up and down her face. She looked a little queasy and drew in a shaky lungful of air but it didn't seem to help. I draped a steadying arm around her shoulder. 'I'm here for you, honey,' I told her. She gave me a wan smile and smoothed her robe in that way she always did.

We made our way around the sprawl of other buildings, the windows of each echoing those of the main school with tall arches and glass of leaded light. Across the grounds I could see a cricket pavilion surrounded by neat flower beds and, beyond that, a chapel. The air was softly fragrant, alive with the faint buzz of insects and distant, excited chatter. Zadie gazed around in awe and I felt a sudden pang of pity for her – an intelligent girl with a thirst for learning, and yet even our local comprehensive was forbidden ground. 'What a place,' I said.

'Yes,' she breathed, 'it's like Hogwarts.'

I smiled at that, remembering what Emily had said about Zadie probably being too sheltered to have even heard of Harry Potter. She spoke without a trace of resentment – she just didn't have it in her.

Eventually we found what we were looking for: a building known as the Dene, where Peggy said the meeting was to be held. The interior of the Dene itself wasn't quite as impressive as its surroundings; paint was peeling from the walls of the narrow stairway we climbed and the floors creaked beneath our feet, but the crumbling brickwork and dead flies collecting along the windowsills seemed to add to its enchantment.

Betrayed

On the second floor the dusty oak boards seemed to sag a little, so much so that I found myself tiptoeing, as if that would lighten the load. Our footsteps echoed around the place and I felt a twitch of anticipation, imagining what stories the old building had to tell. Standing beside Zadie on the landing, a large space about ten feet square with large boxes stacked high against the walls and several doors on three sides, I turned one way and then the other, unsure where to go.

I crept across the hall and opened one of the scarred doors, aware of Zadie's reticence; I got the sense she would have liked nothing more than to turn tail and run back to the sanctuary of the car; a feeling I could sympathise with. A combination of mustiness and damp drifted from the room, the stale hot air spilling into the corridor. Against the far wall stood an ancient photocopier with one of the little white doors hanging on its hinges and, behind, the ornate window was cracked in several places. To my surprise, in the middle of the next room was a large Victorian bath and I guessed that at some point the Dene would have housed dormitories for borders.

'Look, Zadie,' I said. 'A bathroom.'

Zadie leaned around me. Peering in, she made a rising noise of surprise.

'Tempting to lock ourselves in there and skip the scary meeting, isn't it?'

She shot her head around and took in a sharp breath, her eyes widened with hope. 'Can we?'

'I'm afraid not, sweetie. As much as I'd like to.'

Her brow furrowed. 'Don't you want to go either then?'

I shook my head. 'Not really. I don't like meetings. When it comes round to my turn to speak my tongue swells.'

'Your tongue?'

I nodded. 'When all the attention is on me my tongue feels too big for my mouth, then it won't bend. It gets so stiff that I can't talk properly.'

For a moment she just stared at me, her eyes shining. And then she convulsed, her whole body racked with laughter. It was a real belly giggle, the loudest noise I had ever heard her make, and it tickled me so much that I burst into a fit of uncontrollable laughter as well. For the next half a minute or so we couldn't stop, both of us doubled over and convulsing, our arms clutched to our tummies. Every time I straightened, gasping as I tried to catch my breath, she looked at me and we dissolved into fresh paroxysms. The sound of scraping chairs from inside the room at the far end of the hall finally sobered us and we looked at each other, a little surprised and disorientated, as if we'd forgotten where we were and why we were there. A low hum of conversation from inside the room drew me over and Zadie followed, both of us exchanging smirks and trembling with suppressed giggles, like chastised school-girls. I rapped softly on the door before opening it, noticing that Zadie was wiping her fingers beneath her eyes – she had been crying with laughter.

Peggy was sitting on one of a group of half a dozen hard-backed chairs that had been arranged in a semi-circle in the small room. She smiled and stood up as we entered, tucking a wad of papers into her armpit and clamping them there with her arm. 'Hello, Rosie. You found it then? Bit of a rabbit warren, isn't it?'

'Certainly is. What an amazing place, though,' I replied, my jaw stiff and eyes watery from our laughing fit. Zadie hung her head low, hiding the vestiges of a smile. I looked from Peggy to the gentleman sitting two seats away from her own chair. Unmistakably Zadie's father, his eyes were the same deep brown but slightly sunken, surrounded by dark circles. A thick beard covered his cheeks and chin but the area above his lip was closely shaven. He was wearing a long beige-coloured robe that reached his ankles, shiny black shoes visible beneath and a round hat on the top of his head. He was staring at a point beyond my shoulder where his daughter hovered, using me as a human shield. Parents are often unsure how to behave towards their child's foster carer and, not wanting to appear partisan, I smiled, even though he wasn't quite looking at me.

'Yes, marvellous, isn't it?' Peggy said, her breath rattling as she turned and gestured to her right. 'This is Diane Howell, our Independent Reviewing Officer.' A woman dressed in a smart black trouser suit nodded towards me, her auburn hair spun into a high bun. She smiled warmly.

'And this is Mr Hassan, Zadie's father.' The gentleman stood and shuffled a few paces towards me, giving me the once-over then, for the first time. The expression he wore echoed that of his son when we met at the Lavender Fields and I folded my arms, my smile freezing awkwardly on my face. His scrutiny got me wondering how I must look to others and I suddenly wished that I wasn't such a low-maintenance woman. Vowing to replace the low lighting with a 100 watt bulb that would force me to face reality and conduct a complete overhaul, I wrapped my arms further around myself; at least with them entwined I couldn't make the same mistake as I had with Chit by offering a friendly hand to shake. 'Hello. Nice to meet you,' I said, feeling myself shrink a little under a current of unease.

'Hello,' he said with a stiff nod before removing his hat and shuffling sideways to confront his daughter. His face was heavily lined and there were deep crevices running vertically from the downturned corners of his mouth to his chin, giving him a sad look that I imagined would remain, even if he were feeling happy. 'Zadie,' he mumbled.

'Papa,' Zadie whispered. I half-turned, discreetly offering them some space. Zadie kept her eyes downcast, her whole body trembling.

'What is this nonsense about?' he asked gruffly. I tried telling myself that any parent would feel a mixture of emotions if their child ran away, and anger was bound to be one of them, but there was a fury in his eyes that I found extremely unsettling; it wasn't surprising that Zadie looked intimidated.

She parted her lips as if to reply but then she made a gasping noise instead, casting a beseeching look in my direction.

I rested my arm on her back. 'Are you OK, honey?' Her eyes flicked to her father and then back to me. A tiny twitch near her eye gave me the feeling that tears weren't too far away.

'I feel a bit sick,' she said, her voice wobbling.

'Sit down,' Mr Hassan barked, though his features remained serene.

Zadie looked startled and shuffled towards a chair, but Peggy held up her hand. 'You don't have to stay if you don't feel up to it, Zadie,' she said firmly, her eyes flicking to Mr Hassan. I got the feeling she was daring him to challenge her. He didn't.

Zadie's eyes flitted from Peggy to her father. She stood frozen, petrified. 'Would you prefer to wait outside?' Peggy was nodding as she spoke as if underlining Zadie's right to make her own decision. It was a sensitive gesture that I hadn't expected. I was beginning to realise she wasn't as unfeeling as I'd first thought.

The teenager gave the tiniest nod. 'Very well,' Peggy said in a clipped tone as she turned to open the door. Zadie dived outside, her face yellowish and sickly looking. At least there was a bathroom out there for her, I thought. She looked like she might need it at any moment.

'Right, shall we get started?' the IRO said, opening the manila folder balanced on her knees. And when we were seated she said, 'If you could give us an overview of things so far please, Peggy.'

Peggy walked her fingers over the wad of papers on her lap, finally settling on one with a little 'hmph' in her throat. 'Zadie was found by police on the Tuesday 3 May,' Peggy began, giving the few scant details she knew about the days when Zadie went missing. When she told the IRO that Zadie had pleaded not to go home Mr Hassan's expression didn't change but I noticed his hands gripping the brim of his hat so that his fingernails glowed white. 'And that's all we know at the moment. Mr Hassan has kindly agreed for Zadie to remain with Rosie under a Section 20 but Zadie herself hasn't given us much to go on, as yet.'

'She's playing games and you're indulging her,' he said in a low voice, agitatedly feeding the brim of his hat through his hands. 'She's mentally unstable and manipulative. What she needs is discipline and –'

'Sorry, Mr Hassan.' Diane held her pen in mid-air. 'We will move on to your thoughts in a moment but I'd like to hear how Zadie is coping in placement first.' Mr Hassan sniffed and I noticed that the whites of his eyes were bloodshot. I was surprised by his words. I didn't recognise her in his description, not Zadie. Even so, this wasn't easy for him, I realised, not at all. Unlike some of the parents I had met before, he did seem to care, very much; he looked like he hadn't slept in days. Diane turned to me. 'Rosie? Would you mind?'

I thought about how Zadie had cried when she told me about her early memories and tried to push my growing sympathy aside. It was good that Mr Hassan was showing a thread of discomfort, I told myself. His daughter was sad and he needed to react, to feel something.

'Well, she's very quiet but she's coping well on the whole,' I said, then went on to tell them about Zadie's night terror. When I mentioned the cuts on her tummy I paused for a moment to register their reaction. Diane winced but Mr Hassan wore the same mask of serenity as Zadie had in her early days with us, his face marbleised except for the smallest of twitches at the corner of his mouth. Outside, I could hear the stilted conversations of girls as they passed by and, trying to gather myself to continue, I held on to the sound for a moment. It's never easy to confront parents, especially for someone like myself who, as a girl, would feign a nosebleed if called upon by a teacher to read out in class. Feeling steadier after a moment's pause, I went on to explain that Zadie was reluctant to tell me why she ran away out of loyalty to her family. Mr Hassan made a steeple with his fingers and raised his hands to his lips, his gaze growing more intent.

'And she's mentioned her mother a few times. I know she misses her,' I said, angling my knees towards Mr Hassan before continuing. 'She doesn't seem to know what happened to her.'

His chin slackened with surprise and his eyes grew darker. I hesitated for a moment, unsure how he would react if I continued.

'I think it would really help her if she knew more about what happened to her,' I ventured, noticing Mr Hassan's raised eyebrows, the vein pulsing at the side of his neck.

'I agree,' Peggy jumped in. 'I know you say it's a private matter, Mr Hassan, but the girl needs to know her background, however painful you feel it might be. Children usually find the truth easier to deal with than the unknown.'

A flash of shame passed over his face and he swallowed loudly. 'I've tried to do my best with her,' he said, nodding in my direction as if he suspected me to be the one who was most likely to agree with him. 'I've had to bring up four children alone. Their mother ...' He paused, licking his lips.

I took the opportunity to interrupt. 'Don't you mean three?'

He frowned. 'What?'

'You said four. Four children. Don't you mean three?'

He gave a small flick of the wrist. 'Yes, yes. Three. But four with my young nephew. He's around most of the time. Anyway, their mother, she walked out before Zadie started school. I had to work *and* keep a roof over our heads.'

He looked directly at me, his face rippling with a curious fragility. 'It's not been easy.'

I felt sorry for him then, despite myself. He looked suddenly old, his eyes tired. Tilting my head, I gave him a mild smile.

'What is it you do, Mr Hassan?' Peggy asked.

'I run a fuel station. My brothers are involved as well. When they were little Zadie and her brothers played in the back room while I served customers. It wasn't ideal but I've always made sure they're in clean clothes and well fed.' There was an angry undertone to his voice; aggressive defensiveness.

I nodded again, this time with an openly sympathetic smile. I understood how difficult it could be to feel solely responsible for earning a living alongside caring for the family.

'Well, we'll see what support we can put in place if Zadie returns home. It's a shame you didn't ask for help before now. There is a lot we can do to help families going through –'

'*If* she returns home? What do you mean, if?' Mr Hassan cut in sharply, rising to his feet. 'She's *my* daughter. I'm not allowing this to go on much longer, especially with where she's been placed.' His eyes flicked in my direction. 'With all due respect, you've sent her to a most unconventional home.'

I felt my cheeks pinkening up. Peggy had been reading through her notes but she glanced up at that comment and our eyes met. She raised an eyebrow minutely. Mr Hassan continued, 'I was having trouble with Zadie before. What's it going to be like after she's been exposed to such different values?'

Embarrassed, I searched my mind for a response. What sort of people did he think we were? Peggy gave an impatient snicker. 'Zadie comes from a one-parent household, Mr Hassan, and she's been placed in another one. I don't see the difference, quite frankly.'

I felt a swell of gratitude towards her. There was something honest and child-like in her manner, despite being middle-aged. It was reassuring to be in the company of someone who had no pretentions, no inhibitions. Mr Hassan remained silent for the rest of the meeting. He stood stiff-shouldered at the window and stared out at the grounds, although as it was wrapping up and Diane asked if there was anything he wanted to add, he reiterated his wish for Zadie to return home as soon as possible.

On the way home I told Zadie most of what had been said, though I held back on her father's insistence that she go back. When we arrived home she drifted up to her room and soon after dinner she showered and went straight to bed. I read a crime novel into the early hours that night, trying to overwrite the now ever-present nagging in my mind.

I fell asleep with the book still clutched in my hand and when I woke to the sound of screaming at first I thought I was dreaming about the protagonist in the story who real-ised she was being followed as she returned home after a night out. I sat up with a jerk, blinking in the inky black-ness. Emily and Jamie emerged from their rooms, their faces white and confused, as I blundered along the hall trying to find the arm of my dressing gown. 'It's all right,' I said, giving their arms a quick squeeze. 'You go back to bed.'

The expression on Zadie's face was a shock to witness. Her mouth was gaping in horror and her skin was a pasty grey. I crouched beside her bed and ran my hand over her forehead and down through her thick hair, whispering gently. She turned and stared directly at me, clamping a clammy palm around my wrist. 'What have you done with Nady?' she asked in a raspy voice.

My stomach rolled. I leaned away from her and let my hand fall from her hair to rest on the duvet. My hand clenched tightly. 'Who's Nady?' I asked, unsettled by her glassy, vacant stare and the urgency in her tone.

Her eyes clamped tightly closed and she began to whim-per. 'Nady,' she repeated, as if there was someone hovering just out of her reach. 'Nady, Nady …'

I sat beside her until she fell quiet, then returned to my own room, filled with a feeling of disquiet. Picking up my book, I tried to continue where I'd left off but I found it difficult to concentrate. I just couldn't help wondering what was going on in the Hassan family, what had led to Zadie's night terrors and just who on earth was Nady?

Chapter 12

Having finally managed to submerge myself in the complicated plot of my book, I couldn't remember dropping off and even slept through Zadie's early morning wash, only waking when my alarm went off at 6 a.m. When I came down to make coffee, the answering machine was flashing with four messages. I went through to the kitchen to flick the kettle on then came back to the hall and pressed 'play'. The first message began with the words, 'Have you been mis-sold ...' so I quickly hit the delete button. The next sounded robotic so I gave that one short shrift as well. And then a woman's voice floated through the hall, brisk and firm: 'Something has come up, Rosie. I need to come and see you urgently. Tomorrow if possible.' It was Peggy.

The message had been left at 10.32 p.m. I felt a stab of pity for the social worker, so overloaded with cases that she had to work late into the evening. The last message was from Des, saying sorry that he hadn't checked in with me since the ball and asking whether everything was going well. I played the message again, listening to the hesitancy in his tone. It was unusual for him to call so late in the day. Unsettled, I pressed delete and walked slowly back to the kitchen, the name Nady playing over and over in my mind.

Two coffees and one shower later I felt more relaxed and a little after 10 a.m. Zadie was standing beside me in the kitchen, ready to make a honey-drizzled farina cake, one of the specialities that she used to make at home. It had been tempting to ask about her night terror as we ate our breakfast but I resisted the urge, unwilling to distract her from eating. Now, as I took a pack of eggs from the fridge and handed them to her, she seemed so tired and far away that I asked her, for the third time that morning, how she was instead.

'Well, thank you,' she answered with habitual politeness.

I leaned my hip against the worktop and let her words float in the air. After a moment she asked, 'How about you?'

My thoughts flicked back to breakfast, Emily singing as she danced around the kitchen with a piece of toast in her hand. She seemed to have adjusted to the news of her father's remarriage, perhaps partly relieved by my own mild acceptance. I think that seeing how fearful Zadie was about meeting her own father helped to give Emily some perspective, grateful – as we all were when reminded how unsettled some lives can be – for the steadying certainties of a warm bed and loving family. So, with Emily back to her usual effervescent self and Jamie ticking along cheerfully, albeit with a touch more sarcasm than ever before, the only one for me to worry about was Zadie.

'Oh, you know me, always the same. If my little brood are happy then I'm happy.'

She gave me a long assessing look, breaking into a smile when I started jigging from foot to foot and singing 'The Kids Are Alright'.

'You're a little mad, Rosie,' she said, giggling freely as she reached for the scales. My heart swelled at the wonderful sound, as delicious as the abandoned chuckle of a young baby. She didn't have a recipe to hand; she seemed to know all the measures and ingredients by heart.

'That's what they tell me,' I said, pulling a large glass bowl from the low cupboard in front of me. She gave me another genuine smile. We worked side by side for the next half an hour or so. She didn't join in the conversation much after that but I could tell she was enjoying herself, or was, at least, content.

When the mixture was ready and she was scraping the golden thick liquid into greased tins I decided to start up a conversation about her disturbed nights in what I thought would be a gentle opener. 'I know what I've been meaning to ask you. Who is Nady?'

I hadn't realised just how pale dark skin can fade to when the blood runs out of it. Zadie froze, her skin blanching to resemble the washed-out tone of the cake mixture in the bowl still balanced between her fingertips. My heart quickened at her reaction.

'How do you know about Nadeen?'

I stared at her for a moment before answering, still taken aback by her instant mortification. 'Well,' I said slowly, 'it's just that you kept saying "Nady" over and over when I came to your room last night.'

She said nothing, her eyes fixed on me with a mixture of wariness and irritation.

I put my hand on her shoulder. She was trembling. 'You were calling out. I came up to see what was wrong.' I fell silent for a moment and then said, 'Who is Nadeen, honey?'

She swallowed loudly and licked her lips. 'My sister,' she answered eventually, lowering the spatula and bowl to the worktop with an air of finality, as if it was all over for her; she'd finally been caught out.

'Your sister?' I exclaimed, louder than I had intended. 'I had no idea you had a sister. Why have you never mentioned her before? Why did your father not say anything about her? Does Peggy know? Where is she then, this sister?'

Zadie, probably not expecting such a barrage of questions, looked at me with alarm. I could have kicked myself for not being gentler. 'I don't know,' she answered with a wail. And then she burst into tears.

Some time later, when she had recovered a little, we sat side by side on the sofa. Zadie, a tissue clutched in each hand, was still regarding me warily, as if she thought she might be punished for revealing the existence of her own flesh and blood.

'Zadie, you do trust me don't you?'

'Of course I do,' she said, her voice still nasal from crying.

'So you must know that all I want is to help you?'

She nodded, then dabbed her nose with a bunched-up tissue.

'Do you think you could tell me about Nadeen? I won't say anything to anyone else except Peggy, if you don't want me to.'

'What do you want to know?'

'Well,' I said, trying to organise the dozens of questions floating around in my head into some sort of rational order, prioritising them too in case she clammed up before I got to the end of the list. 'How old is she, for a start?'

'Three years older than me,' she replied economically.

My head bobbed involuntarily. 'So that would make her 16?'

Zadie shook her head. 'She's actually nearly four years older. So she's 17.'

'When did you last see her?'

'Last year.'

'Did she run away too?'

She sniffed. 'I woke up one morning and she was gone, just like with Ma.' Tears began to spill from her eyes again and she clamped them tightly shut, bunching the tissue in front of her eyes with both hands. 'That's what I try to do when I use the computer,' she choked out, her voice thick with tears. 'I've tried Facebook and all the networking sites but there's just no sign of her anywhere.'

'Oh, I'm so sorry, honey,' I said, placing my hand gently on her knee.

Peggy arrived a little after 4 p.m., just as Emily was raiding the cupboard for chocolate biscuits and offering some to Zadie. Rather than hiding away when they came home, Zadie now seemed to look forward to their company, moving towards the hall as soon as she heard their key in the lock. Zadie had said nothing more about her sister. After our conversation she had drifted to her room and spent most of the afternoon there, quietly reading. Jamie had brought two of his friends back with him so the hallway floor was littered with rucksacks, PE bags and trainers. I have always told my own children and those I foster that their friends are welcome any time, but today really wasn't a good day for unannounced visitors. I made a mental note to add a caveat to my open invitation so that they checked with me first.

'I'm gasping,' Peggy said wheezily, wrapping her fingers around the door jamb for purchase as she tackled the front step. 'Oh, I didn't realise you had someone else in placement,' she puffed, walking through the living room. She withdrew a tissue from her sleeve and blew her nose loudly. 'I should have been informed of that.'

'This is my son, Jamie,' I said as he crossed in front of me, heading for the kitchen. 'And these are his friends.' I waved a hand over the two teenage boys lolling back on the sofa. They glanced up with blank expressions before returning their attention to the gadgets clasped in their hands. It always puzzled me why they bothered to spend time with each other after school when the majority of it was spent staring at their phones and texting absent friends.

'You only just met me,' Jamie called out over his shoulder as he retrieved several bags of crisps from one of the cupboards. 'Can we have these, Mum?' he asked, popping several bags open before I even managed a nod. My son's capacity for diplomacy knows no bounds. Since fostering I have found myself increasingly unsettled by the layers of deception that people hide beneath and so I've learnt to appreciate Jamie's unflinching honesty, but there were times when it lost its charm.

Peggy's jaw dropped in her customary way and then she smiled, perhaps appreciative of someone as straight talking as herself.

'So I did. Well,' she said, her chest heaving, 'that certainly put me right. Rosie, can we go somewhere private to have a chat?'

The girls, armed with snacks, had gone into the dining room, Zadie at the computer and Emily with her school books spread over the table. 'There's only the garden,' I said, 'unless you want to sit on my bed?'

'I wouldn't trust myself not to drop off,' Peggy said, hammering towards the garden. 'It's been mad, these past few weeks. Not that it's ever much different. I'll need a drink if I'm to make it to that swing, Rosie.'

After making her a quick cup of tea we sat on the swing. Well out of earshot, I told Peggy what Zadie had said about her sister. This time, her jaw dropped and stayed where it was. 'Well, I never did.' Stubborn grey hairs snaked themselves above the rest of her hair and stood defiantly still in the breeze. 'The father never mentioned anything about a sister. How old is she?'

'Nearly four years older than Zadie, so around about 17 or so.'

Peggy sucked in a lungful of air and made a whooshing sound. 'Hmmm, that's worrying.'

'I know. To think of a girl that age trying to survive on the streets, it's –'

Peggy harrumphed. 'If that's what she's doing.'

I frowned, shaking my head.

'If you knew the number of girls from Zadie's sort of background who go missing every year.' Peggy grimaced and looked straight at me. 'Forced marriage is what I'm worried about.'

'Ah.' I nodded slowly. I hadn't thought of that at all.

'It just strikes me as odd that I've spoken to the father several times and he's never mentioned a missing daughter. Mind you, he didn't even report Zadie missing when she ran off. I'll see if I can do a bit more digging and let you know if I find anything out.'

I thanked her, my mind running over the possibility of forced marriage. It seemed unbelievable that such a thing could happen in the UK in the twenty-first century. I felt a slither of discomfort at the thought of such disturbing secrets lurking underground, out of the radar of the authorities.

Peggy was still frowning, deep in concentration. I could tell that the news had unsettled her. 'So what did you want to see me about?' I asked after a moment or two.

She lifted her eyebrows as if making an effort to shift her mind back to the present. 'Ah, yes,' she swallowed, licking her lips. 'There's been a complaint.'

I closed my eyes and groaned. 'Oh dear,' I said wearily, my mind flicking through all the possibilities I could think of. Bracing myself, I asked, 'What about?'

Peggy sighed. 'I find it difficult to believe that you would have actually done this but I'm duty bound to ask you about it. It's been said that you've been indoctrinating Zadie, trying to convert her to Christianity.'

I laughed, shaking my head. 'Who told you that?'

'The brother. So it's not true then?'

'No, of course not.'

Peggy nodded decisively. 'I didn't think so. I know how experienced you are but he claims to have photographic evidence and —'

Gasping, I suddenly remembered the dark car slowing as it passed by the church hall, the unexpected flash of light. I dropped my face into my hands. 'Oh no, Peggy,' I groaned, 'now you come to mention it, there was one time …'

Her jaw dropped in alarm. 'What do you mean?'

I hesitated. 'I suppose I did take her to a church, sort of,' I said slowly, my face flushing.

Peggy's lips stretched into a thin line and she made a little noise of disbelief. 'Why would you do a thing like that?'

I explained about Project Congo and the quilt-making group at the church hall. 'But we just dropped the packages off and then left. There was no service or worship. We didn't even go into the actual church. I would never have done that. I was just doing a favour to help my mother.'

'Rosie, I —'

'I'm not even sure I have a faith of my own,' I went on, not letting the social worker get a word in edgeways, 'so why would I try to indoctrinate Zadie when I'm unsure of my own beliefs?'

That's what really got my goat. I had conflicted feelings towards organised religion, sceptical despite my upbringing. While hopeful that there was someone compassionate watching over us and admiring of the foundations that underpinned many faiths – personal responsibility, humanity and kindness – whether Christianity, Islam or Buddhism, I wasn't utterly convinced by any of them, certainly not enough to recruit others into sharing my hope. *And* I hadn't even taken Zadie into the church. The hall, which was acting as a store room, was a building like any other. That's the way I saw it anyway.

My stomach churned as I remembered another foster carer from Bright Heights who was disciplined and almost struck off for telling a child whose mother had died that she was in a better place, safe in heaven with Jesus. At the time I had thought it unfair to take action against someone who was only trying, in her own way, to relieve a child's sorrow.

'I see,' Peggy began. 'Well –'

'And when you think about it,' I jumped in, only half-aware that I still wasn't listening to Peggy, 'that church is used by Muslims for worship anyway.' I knew that the local minister, dismayed at Muslims having to pray in the street because their mosque was too small to accommodate their number, had offered use of the church during weekdays. 'If the Islamic community leaders are happy with it I don't see that just visiting the car park is that offensive and –'

Peggy reached out her hand and rested it heavily on my shoulder. 'Rosie,' she said, 'if you'll hold your horses for just one minute and let me speak.'

I had been so frantically defending myself that I hadn't noticed Peggy's mild manner. When I finally drew breath I registered that her lips were curled in a smile. 'Rosie, my pet. I didn't think for one minute that you would disrespect their faith. I know how dedicated you are.'

I let out a breath and gave her a sheepish smile. 'Sorry. I wasn't sure how far it would go.' I knew that some complaints were blown out of all proportion and sometimes foster carers were made an example of.

Peggy held up her hands. 'It stops here as far as I'm concerned. I'll write a report and feed back what you've said, but that's the last you'll hear of it from me.'

I nodded gratefully. Peggy was turning out to be a gem.

'So now that's sorted, I just have one more piece of news.' Peggy bit her bottom lip. 'Mr Hassan is insisting on contact. And soon. I've had to arrange it for tomorrow, I'm afraid.'

I blew out some air.

Peggy tucked her hands deep into her armpits and hoisted up her chest, wheezing faintly. 'Judging by Zadie's reaction yesterday, it's not going to be easy for her.'

I blew out my cheeks and looked at her. 'Hmmm, that's an understatement,' I said.

That night I couldn't sleep for worrying that Zadie might harm herself again. Deep down I was painfully alert to the likelihood that hurting herself was a coping mechanism she had come to depend on. I hadn't actually seen any physical injuries as she kept herself so carefully hidden away but most of her clothes were lightly bloodstained so I knew some form of self-harm was going on, albeit mild. I had heard somewhere that a child in care was ten times more likely to die than those living with their own family, and knowing that Zadie was a self-harmer left me feeling even more fearful for her well-being.

Chapter 13

The next morning I waited until Zadie had finished her breakfast before I broke the news about contact. She had managed to finish a whole bowl of cereal and was helping herself to toast, something she hadn't done before, and so I didn't want anything to put her off. It was as she began clearing the table that I said, as gently as I could, 'Zadie, Peggy said that your father is keen to talk to you as he didn't get to see much of you at the review.'

She had been stacking our bowls into a pile and her hands froze around them as if she was afraid they might topple over, though her expression remained serene. 'OK,' she whispered quietly without meeting my gaze.

'We need to be ready to leave the house around half past nine.' I waited a moment and then said, 'We're meeting him at ten.'

She drew a sharp breath. 'Today?!' she exclaimed, clutching the bowls to her chest like armour and wrapping her arms around them. She was staring at me, her eyes wide in alarm. 'Today?' she repeated, quieter this time. 'I'm sorry, I didn't realise it would be so soon.'

'I know. It was a surprise for me too.'

Zadie gave me a long look and then spent the next hour in her room while Emily and Jamie got themselves ready for school. I was about to call her when I heard a click as her bedroom door opened. Standing at the bottom of the stairs, I watched her make her way down with what I hoped was an encouraging smile on my face. She walked slowly, her rucksack draped over her shoulder and the fingers of one hand brushing against the wall in a thoughtful way. 'I can't go,' she said as she reached the bottom stair. She flattened her hand against the wall as if the action would give more weight to her decision.

I looked at her, surprised by the boldness in her voice. I could tell her refusal had nothing to do with teenage defiance, though; her eyebrows were arched in panic and her bottom lip was quivering. My heart squeezed in sympathy. 'I know you're scared, honey, but I'll be with you the whole time. There's nothing your father can do but talk.'

She sank down on the second stair and rubbed her forehead roughly with a clenched hand. 'Oh, you don't understand, Rosie. They'll take me. I'll never be found again.' She leaned her elbows on her knees and dropped her head onto tight fists. Her shoulders twitched as she began to cry.

I sat down beside her and rubbed her back. She was trembling. 'What do you mean, you'd never be found? How could they take you anywhere, if I'm right beside you?' I stared at her headscarf; it was all I could see of her. My thoughts were swirling and I took a moment to try and make sense of what she was saying. Tentatively, I reached out and touched her headscarf, gently drawing it to the side so that I could catch a glimpse of her expression. She raised her face but the shutters were already down, her face closed up.

'Who do you mean when you say "they"?'

She rolled her lips inwards and clamped them shut as if she thought they might break ranks and give up secrets without her permission. With a little hiccup, she lowered her head again.

'I'm sorry, Zadie, but this has gone on long enough. You can't keep me in the dark any longer.' I could hear that my voice had lost its usual softness, but I was beginning to feel rattled. I reached for her hands and gave them a gentle squeeze. 'If I'm to keep us safe you must tell me what's going on. And I mean *everything*.'

The change in my tone had an effect on her. At first she stared at me in surprise, then she began picking at invisible threads on her sleeve and then moving on to the bands on her wrist. Her fingers plucked at them agitatedly. It was difficult to watch her so tormented and the last thing I wanted to do was cause her more stress but I had let things drift long enough and so I stayed firm, silencing the ache for her in my chest by biting down on my lower lip. After a moment or so she cleared her throat and I clenched my own nervous hands between my knees in anticipation of what she was going to tell me. What followed took me completely by surprise.

'My father, my uncles, the whole family. They want to cut me. It's time, you see. That's why I ran away. That and ...' her voice trailed off into silence and she sat motionless, as if movement might encourage more words to stream from her mouth. She seemed to consider everything so carefully before she spoke. *You're worried about getting caught out again,* I thought silently, wondering just what else she might have to hide.

'Cut?' I repeated, buying some time to process what she had said. I assumed she was referring to FGM, female genital mutilation. 'Circumcision? Is that what you mean?' I asked, couching the question in softer terms. Mutilation was such a shocking word and I didn't want her to clam up on me, just when she was beginning to open up.

She nodded but angled herself away so that I couldn't see her face. Being such a private person, I knew how embarrassed she must feel discussing something so intimate, poor girl. 'Did they tell you that's what they were going to do?' I asked. I couldn't imagine the terror a child must feel knowing that they were going to go through something like that. My own children made enough fuss about routine vaccinations; so much so that I would wait until the day they were due before mentioning anything about it.

'No. I overheard my brother talking with Papa. And Nady was a bit younger than me when she had it done so I knew it was coming.'

'Your sister?'

Zadie nodded and gave a hiccuping sob. She half-stood but I grabbed her arm. 'No,' I said, surprised by the brittle edge to my tone. 'Sit down. We're not finished.' Contrite, she quickly sat down again and drew a shaky breath.

'How do you know Nadeen had,' I paused, clearing my throat, 'the procedure? Did she tell you?'

Her brow furrowed and a shadow crossed her face. 'I heard it going on,' she said, her voice trailing off with a wail. And then through her tears she told me the whole dreadful business. It seemed that when her sister was about 12 a man known locally as 'the dentist' came late one night and 'cut' her. Zadie heard her screams from upstairs but was power-less to do anything to help. 'Nady was ill for a couple of weeks afterwards, too weak to get out of bed. One minute she would shiver and the next she was burning hot.'

'I expect she had a nasty infection,' I said, deciding not to voice the thought that her sister was probably lucky to have survived. 'It must have been very hard for you to see her suffering like that.'

Zadie nodded. 'Papa wouldn't fetch the doctor. The dentist came back and gave her some pills but they didn't help. Mostly I took care of her myself.'

My heart was speared with a sudden grief for Zadie, her poor sister and all the other girls who had ever experienced the trauma of being cut. I rubbed my hands briskly through my hair, unsettled by the thought that, somewhere in the world, that sort of violation was undoubtedly happening right at that very moment. What a heavy responsibility Zadie must have felt, caring for a dangerously ill child at such a tender age herself. 'That's just awful,' I said out loud, unable to keep my feelings to myself.

'It is,' Zadie agreed, her voice tremulous. 'I just kept hearing the sound that the girls make when they have it done. They all sound the same, like a wolf crying out.'

Slowly lowering my hands to my lap, I turned towards her. 'How do you know that?'

Her eyes flitted from me to the wall.

'Zadie,' I said with a warning tone, strong and purposeful. I had had enough of secrets.

She chewed her lip and turned back, a worried look on her face. I locked my eyes on hers, refusing to allow my expression to soften. She tugged on her headscarf, fidgeted on the stair, ran her hands one over the other. 'I've seen clips of it online,' she said eventually.

I tried to disguise my shock but I'm not sure I did it skilfully. 'Why would you watch something like that?'

Again she looked anguished. 'Chit said it would be a good idea for me to see how it was done.'

'A good idea,' I repeated flatly, lost for words. Chit again. I was beginning to form a firmer picture of Zadie's brother in my mind, and so far he wasn't looking too good. Something wasn't right there, not right at all. 'Why on earth would he do that?'

Zadie looked at me warily. I tried to smooth the frown from my forehead and said gently, 'It's all right, Zadie. I'm not cross with you. I'm sorry I sounded sharp, I'm just trying to make sense of it all.'

She gave a little nod of understanding. 'He was trying to prepare me.'

I looked at her doubtfully, pincering my lips together to hold back a harsh snort. Zadie moved her mouth to speak and I wondered whether she would try to defend him, but instead she shut it again. After a moment or two she spoke without further prompting, her words tumbling out in a flurry. 'Sometimes they do it with scissors or glass. I think my father had arranged for the dentist to come and see me, but then he was arrested. I was so relieved, but then I overheard one of my aunties saying she would do it instead.'

I gasped out loud at that. It was shocking enough that her male relatives were involved, but that a woman would be complicit in causing such harm was beyond belief. 'Your auntie?'

She nodded. 'My dad's sister. I was so frightened, Rosie.'

'Of course you were.' I rested my hand firmly on her leg. 'You did the right thing, running away.' My voice was grainy with emotion, mostly anger. There was so much more I wanted to say but I forced myself to stay silent. Instead I reached out and put my arm around her. She cuddled into me and wept in silence, her shoulders hunched over, trying to make herself as small as possible. Every so often she gulped down a sob and held her breath, caught herself under control, then apologised, as if comforting her was such a hardship for me.

As soon as Zadie had retreated to her room, swollen-eyed and exhausted, I telephoned Peggy. She answered her mobile after the first ring and when I explained why contact needed to be cancelled she gave a weary sigh instead of the shocked gasp I was expecting. 'I've checked around and we have absolutely no record of the sister,' she said mildly, 'but at least that sheds a bit more light on the matter, though it doesn't explain where she is now.'

I grasped a handful of hair from my forehead and held it in a bunch at the top of my head. The mystery surrounding

Zadie's missing sister was now firmly in the back of my mind. 'No it doesn't, but anyway, I can't believe her father would do such a thing, can you?'

Peggy heaved a doubtful sigh. 'If it's part of his culture he's unlikely to want anything different for his own daughter. He would naturally want Zadie to fit in and be accepted. To find a husband one day.'

'So you're not shocked?' I asked, incredulous. 'Am I overreacting here?'

I could hear a light tapping, as if Peggy's fingernails were strumming the handset. 'Shocked? No, Rosie, sorry but I'm not shocked. We have a number of similar cases. Teachers report it, you see, when girls return to school after the summer holidays. Often their families take them back to their own birth country for the procedure and when the girls return to school they show signs of discomfort. Sometimes they can't sit down for weeks.'

I winced, feeling a little sick in my stomach. 'So what do you do about it?'

'Very little, I'm afraid. It's a dilemma, weighing up what will do the most damage. If the child is in an otherwise loving home and we remove them, they end up being cast out by their entire community. What would you do?'

'But surely it's against the law?' I pressed, ignoring her question with one of my own.

'There's nothing British police can do if the procedure is done abroad. Although things are changing, so I believe.'

'Ah-ha,' I said, grasping onto the possibility that social services might now have enough concerns about the family to secure an interim care order, 'but if you knew that plans were being made for FGM to be done in this country …' I let the words float in the air. It was shocking to think that families were still getting away with committing such an abuse on young girls, but what mattered more to me at the moment was protecting Zadie.

There was silence. All I could hear was the soft whirring of computers and a low hum of distant voices.

'Peggy?'

'As I say, I'm sorry, Rosie,' Peggy said. 'We've been told to keep meticulous records of any girl we believe has been cut. Apparently the police are clamping down on anyone who has helped to organise it, but, as far as I know, no child has ever been removed from home to prevent FGM.'

That night after the children had gone to bed I sat in the dining room and did some online research. It seemed that FGM began as an African tribal practice but was later adopted by Muslims. One site even suggested that the procedure was becoming popular with Western women.

What Peggy had said about other girls in similar circumstances resonated with me and my mind drifted to think of the women all over the world who suffered because of the dictates of male preferences, like those poor Chinese women from years ago with their feet bound so tightly that they were left disabled. And then I thought about women in the West – with so much freedom and all of the choices available to them, some still felt the need to subject themselves to surgery as if fettered to pleasing a man and keeping him happy. I sat strumming my fingers on the desk, silently ranting against the unfairness of it all. I suddenly imagined how furious Rachel would be if she knew. If she was caring for Zadie I wasn't sure she would be able to contain her wrath.

While I understood the importance of recognising the strengths of other cultures and the danger of dismissing traditions just because they were outside of my own experience, I couldn't see how cutting a young girl in such an intimate place was anything other than a brutal violation.

One positive out of it all was that Zadie's actions seemed to make a lot more sense and I could see that the fear of what was about to happen was enough to drive such a gentle, peace-loving girl into rebelling and running away. Some things still didn't add up, though: the manic exercising, the sudden affection for her robe, the domineering actions of her older brother. I would have expected the disappearance of their mother to bring out his protective side. Instead he seemed to want to torment her. I could hardly believe that Chit had shown her videos of such a disturbing procedure, knowing that she would one day have to endure it herself.

And in that instant it occurred to me – it was her brother who had emailed the link to the pornographic video to Zadie. There was no doubt about it in my mind. Chit Hassan had form.

Chapter 14

In the morning Peggy called. 'I've spoken to the father,' she said, in that distancing way of hers. *The* father, *the* mother, *the* sister. It made Zadie's relatives sound anonymous, like faceless cardboard cut-outs from a report rather than living, breathing people sharing the closest of blood ties. I wondered if it was her way of dehumanising them, perhaps making it easier for her to do her job. 'He wouldn't admit to making plans for Zadie to be cut, although when I pushed him he told me that a small procedure for girls is considered necessary for their own well-being in his culture. According to him, cutting girls is seen as the duty of loving parents and part of the job of raising a girl properly. Islamic law forbids brutal behaviour of any kind, apparently. British people know the practice as clitoridotomy, he tells me. All perfectly legal, so he says.

'I've had a little look online and the thing is, he seems to be correct on that, Rosie.' There was a pause, a rustling of papers. 'Yes, here we are,' she said, sounding satisfied, like she'd just solved the last clue in a particularly tricky cross-word. 'There are doctors on here describing the procedure. It sounds to me like circumcision, only under a more palat-able guise.' Peggy snorted. 'I've even downloaded a price list from Harley Street.'

She paused. I didn't say anything in reply. I was too incensed. Grown women making a voluntary decision to take themselves off to London for a cosmetic procedure was hardly on a par with the enforced cutting of a young girl. It struck me as an attempt by Zadie's father to mini-mise the brutal act. I must have been breathing harshly or something. Peggy seemed to sense that I was livid and her tone softened. 'Look, Rosie, all I'm saying is that there are too many unknowns at the moment, so much we don't understand. My advice is to hold fire for a while, until we know more. Let's not judge the father too harshly.'

'So that's it. We do nothing?'

'I didn't say that,' Peggy said slowly, with exaggerated patience. 'I've asked for an Emergency Strategy Meeting to be arranged so we can go through all the concerns.'

'Oh good,' I breathed, relieved that some action was being taken.

'Meanwhile, you keep up the good work. And remem-ber, Rosie, I'm only interested in Zadie's best interests. We simply don't know enough about her culture to ride rough-shod over her relatives' wishes.'

It was only when Zadie asked if she could spend some time on the computer later that day that I remembered why she had been so keen to use it. She had said that she regularly trawled ancestry and social networking sites in an attempt to locate her sister. It had been such a frantic few days since our chat that I hadn't really absorbed it all. Now, as I watched her leaning close to the screen with an intense expression, I wondered whether there was anything I could do to help her.

Nowadays it must be easier than ever to locate missing people, I thought, unless what Peggy feared had actually happened: Nadeen being forced into a marriage and sent abroad. Leaning against the worktop and nursing a cup of tea in my hands, I determined to do some detective work of my own. I had a mountain of chores that needed doing – the pocket of Jamie's school blazer was torn and needed sewing, he'd been squeezing himself into his old one for two weeks now, I hadn't filled in my fostering diary since the previous Thursday, and on top of that the contents of the airing cupboard were spilling out over the bathroom floor in their desperation to be ironed – but tracking down missing relatives was more important than running an orderly household, I told myself, and definitely more intriguing.

As soon as Zadie's hour of screen time was up I took her place at the computer desk, the swivel chair still pleasantly warm. There was nothing to lose in making the effort, and if I had no luck I thought that I might even consider employing a professional. I remembered walking past the offices of a firm of private detectives on one of our riverside walks, my attention drawn by the small windows shaded with aluminium blinds and tall pot plants. If I'm honest, the thought that I might have a case to take to them filled me with a sense of excitement and mystery.

Half an hour later and I had worked my way through the electoral register and all the genealogy and social networking sites I could find, probably only repeating what Zadie had already done countless times. I sat for a moment tapping my foot lightly against the desk and then it occurred to me that there might be a specific site for people from minority backgrounds. If there was, I reasoned, it would certainly narrow down the numbers; there seemed to be thousands of friends and relatives desperately searching for long-lost loved ones. Quite quickly, I came across an organisation called MEWC, the Middle Eastern Women's Centre, a support organisation for women living in fear in the UK. The blurb on their site said that they existed to help all women who found themselves being oppressed, threatened or abused, although they specialised in supporting women from minority cultures. I went to find my phone and was pleased to see that Zadie had tucked herself away in her room, reading. With her safely out of earshot I sat back at the computer and dialled the advice line number.

The voice that answered was rich and warm. I had already half-prepared a mental script, imagining that I would reach a switchboard and expecting to be transferred several times before possibly finding someone who might be able to help and so I was surprised to find that the director of the charity, Sofia Omar, was manning the lines.

She listened attentively while I ran through some of what I knew about Zadie, although, keen to protect her identity, I mentioned no names. Sofia only interrupted when I told her about Zadie's self-harming.

Betrayed

'Asian women are twice as likely to self-harm and three times more likely to commit suicide,' Sofia told me in impeccable English, although her accent was richly exotic.

'Really?' I said, picturing Zadie's blood-stained pyjamas with a shudder. 'I had no idea.'

'No, most people don't, isn't it? That's why we have such a mountain to climb. It's such a hidden problem.'

'Yes, I see. The thing is, I was wondering whether there was some way I could locate her sister, or at least find out what happened to her. It might just give Zadie some peace. I've tried all the obvious searches but ...' I hesitated, feeling a little foolish. Sofia was running a women's centre, not a missing person's helpline. 'Well, I was wondering whether you might be able to offer any suggestions, with you having expert knowledge of her culture and –'

'Yes,' she said immediately. 'I have a number of ideas, but it would be much easier to have a discussion face-to-face. How easy is it for you to get to London?'

After talking to Sofia on the telephone I found I couldn't wait to meet her in person to find out if there was anything she could do to help me in the search for Nadeen. Fortunately, Peggy agreed that it would be a good idea to consult an expert for cultural advice and gave permission for me to share some of Zadie's personal information. My mother, always easy to sweep up into a flurry of excitement despite her advancing years, agreed that there was no time to be lost. She arrived at my doorstep early the next morning with her new iPad tucked under her arm like a clutch bag, more than happy to spend the day with Zadie.

The journey down to London was long but, taking the opportunity to finish the book I was reading, time passed quickly. Bustled along by a sea of commuters at King's Cross station, it felt strange to be alone without teenagers mooching a few steps behind or little ones skipping beside me, clutching my hands. How funny it was, I thought, as I allowed myself to be swept along again – it wasn't unusual for me to long for an hour to myself away from the unrelenting needs of children, and yet there I was, set free for the whole day, and already I was missing them.

When I finally turned the corner into King's Avenue it was just before 1.30 p.m. – exactly on time. Not bad considering the distance I had travelled. I almost walked past the offices of the Middle Eastern Women's Centre. Number 57 King's Avenue wasn't the sort of venue I had been expecting at all. As I walked up the path of the three-storey town house I screwed up my eyes to decipher the engraving on the small bronze plaque fixed beneath an intercom. The letters MEWC were tiny, about half an inch high and indecipherable to outsiders. Passers-by would probably have no idea what went on inside the unexceptional building.

I pressed the buzzer and was surprised when a smartly dressed man of Asian appearance answered the door. Silently, he stood aside and welcomed me into the large hallway. A woman in her forties appeared from one of several doorways and walked towards me with her hand outstretched. She was wearing a black tailored, expensive-looking jacket over a smart dress with horizontal black and white stripes and her long straight hair was pulled back at the sides, held in place by thin silver grips.

Betrayed

She was petite, barely two inches taller than me, even in the heels she was wearing. As I shook her small hand I wondered why I was so surprised by her appearance, but then she introduced herself and I remembered the commanding impression she had made over the telephone. 'So nice to meet you, Rosie,' she said. Her voice was deep and carried a tone of confidence, incongruous with her delicate vulnerability.

Sofia led the way past a room with several desks and computers, through to a large lounge diner with a kitchen at one end and patio doors overlooking a small paved garden at the other. Her movements were slow and self-assured. She was the sort of woman who would draw the attention of men, I imagined, whatever her age.

'Please, sit down,' she said, gesturing towards a large dining table. In the centre of the table was a cafetière filled with dark liquid, a milk jug and several mugs on a woven mat. Sofia sat opposite me and began to pour, smiling warmly as she offered me the steaming mug of coffee. Her eyes were brown with golden flecks that seemed to light up her face but they were also heavily lined, as if she'd endured more in her life than she should. But there was a youthful, eager watchfulness in her countenance and a way about her that some people have, of establishing an intimate connection with a tilt of her head, a warmth of expression.

Immediately comfortable, I thanked her for the drink, took a few tentative sips then briefly repeated what I had told her over the telephone. Showing interest by settling back in her chair and giving me her full attention, I felt encouraged to go into more detail and told her exactly why Zadie ran away.

'So the FGM, it was imminent, yes?'

I lowered my cup gently to the table and nodded. 'Zadie thought so. She overheard the family making plans.'

'They were going to take her overseas?' Sofia raised her mug and blew softly over the hot liquid, narrowing her eyes against the rising wisps of steam. She rested the rim of the mug against her lips and looked at me expectantly. I could tell she was totally immersed in Zadie's story and, eager to find out what she would make of it all, I spoke quickly.

'No. It seems that an auntie was willing to do it.'

She rolled her eyes but didn't appear to be at all surprised. 'Many women, they support the cutting of their own daughters. They build the girls up, telling them that something special is going to be done to them, as if it's some sort of rite of passage. The matriarch then, she cuts them, while other members of the family hold them down. Traditionally, mothers would perform the procedure on a kitchen table using what they have to hand: scissors, glass, sometimes sharpened bamboo. Girls often end up with fractured arms because they struggle so frantically to escape.'

My hand, halfway to raising my mug to my mouth, froze in mid-air. I lowered it gently to the table, then pushed it a bit further away. 'How could a woman do that?'

Sofia lowered her mug to the table and lifted her arms, resting one over the other on the top of her head. She let out a heavy breath. 'Mothers around the world enforce the status quo. They want to marry their daughters into good families as much as fathers do. When you think about it, FGM is just a more extreme form of the chastity belt. Parents have always tried to control their daughters, to own them and keep them pure. Trouble is, the procedure is still so badly performed that the girl ends up mutilated when that was almost certainly not the intention, leaving the girls with a lifelong sense of loss. Many cultures, they believe cutting will bring their daughters good luck and happiness so they close their eyes to the reality. I heard recently of a woman who was shunned by her community after the birth of her first child because she developed fistulas, one of the many complications of FGM. She leaked faeces and urine wherever she went and ended up a pariah.'

I shook my head in disbelief. 'Zadie told me that her sister was very ill afterwards. The poor girl had the responsibility of nursing her.'

Sofia grimaced. 'They call it the three feminine sorrows, you know.'

'What?'

'The pain a woman goes through after her surgery. One is the extreme pain when she is cut, but that's not the end of it. She then has to endure the agony of her wedding night, when she is reopened. And the third, I'm sure you can guess ...'

'The day she gives birth?'

Sofia nodded grimly. 'The surgery has lasting effects for a woman. Sometimes, when they've been cut as an infant, they don't even realise they're different from other women. They think everyone suffers in the same way. It's only as they go through life that they realise what's been done to them. I've had women coming to see me, totally distraught after attending clinic for a smear test, only to be told that they've been disfigured. It comes as a huge shock to them.'

I shook my head, my stomach churning. What Sofia was telling me was awful. 'Zadie's father told her social worker that they don't practise FGM. They approve of female circumcisions, he says, and he claims the procedure is legal in this country. That we practise it here under some other name.' I frowned and rubbed my head. 'The name escapes me at the moment.'

Sofia snorted. 'The cutting of genitalia is mutilation, however much some try to couch it in softer names. And it is most definitely illegal, has been since 1985, although no one here has been convicted of the crime. France has had some successful prosecutions but that's because strip medical examinations are routine in schools over there so it's picked up quickly.'

She reached for her cup, tilted it towards her, drained the dregs of her coffee and set it gently down again. 'Did you know that there is no requirement in Muslim law for a girl to be cut? These people give our religion a bad name.'

'You're still Muslim?' I asked. Sofia wasn't wearing a headscarf and so I was a little surprised. 'Yes.' She gave a half-laugh. 'Do I not fit the stereotype?'

I suddenly remembered reading about the young Saudi women who simultaneously rip their headscarves off when flying west, once safely in international airspace. I felt my cheeks redden and began blustering apologies for my ignorance – of course, not all Muslim women cover their heads. Sofia waved a hand through the air, brushing the awkwardness away with a smile. 'I get the same reaction all over the country. For a start I don't feel the need to wear a veil, but then, like FGM, the practice of covering women up comes from culture, not religion. I'm still very much Muslim, only these days it's on *my* terms. You know, Rosie, men in your own culture have had decades to adjust to the idea of equality between the sexes and still some struggle with it. Look how long it has taken for the Church of England to accept women as preachers. I long for the day when I can walk into a mosque and worship alongside my brothers.' She examined her fingernails then looked up, giving me a rueful smile. 'When it comes down to it, many women suffer, not for their god or religion but because of men.'

I tapped my forefinger on my lip, thinking. 'What I don't understand is why women still support it.'

Sofia gave a grim smile. 'Women have fallen into line for centuries. I don't think you would believe the lengths some of them are willing to go to, in order to please their husbands. I've had to hold a woman's hand while she let her baby die inside of her.'

I put my hand over my mouth. It was hard to take it all in.

'Yes,' Sofia said, her voice softening to a loud whisper. I leant further towards her, drawn into her confidence. 'It was a few years ago. A Muslim mother of three went into labour and it was a difficult birth. After an hour of pushing midwives told her that the baby was trapped in the birth canal and would need to be delivered by caesarean section.' Sofia looked straight at me, her lips drawing thin with the memory. 'The mother refused a caesarean and one of the midwives called me in desperation, hoping I might be able to reason with her.'

'But why would she refuse help?'

'Because she knew that the maximum caesareans a woman can have is three. After that she would be able to bear her husband no more children. She let the baby die so that her husband would not be displeased with her. To maximise her chances of giving him more children.'

I pulled my hands down my face, my heart squeezed with emotion. 'That's terrible. That poor baby. To think something like that could happen in this day and age.'

'Yes,' Sofia said bitterly. 'And I stood by and watched it. It was so horrific. The midwives were distraught, even the doctors were close to tears. They tried to section her but the baby died before psychiatrists could agree on whether she was of sound mind. I felt so utterly helpless.' Sofia stared at a point beyond me, her mind drawn into the past.

'You'd think it would be against the law to allow that to happen.'

She shook her head, as if she was trying to escape the memory. 'There are no laws to protect the unborn child.'

'No,' I said, 'but there should be.' Having seen the effects of alcohol and drug abuse on tiny infants, I've often felt that mothers who've caused such damage should be charged with grievous bodily harm. 'It sounds like something that would happen in the third world. But this was in England?'

'In a London hospital,' Sofia pursed her lips. 'It is hard to believe but I have to say the UK leads the world in matters of human rights. I wouldn't be alive today if it weren't for your wonderful country.' Sofia went on to tell me about her past, her tone warmly confidential. She fled Iraq over a decade earlier, her life having been threatened because she dared to speak out for a woman who had been sentenced to death for adultery. 'There is still an order for my execution,' she said, gesturing across the room where two heavily set Asian men sat at opposite ends of a leather sofa, playing cards. 'Hence my friends over there. I can't leave the house without security. I tour the country making guest appearances at high-profile events and trying to raise awareness, but I can't even go to buy a pint of milk without two bodyguards accompanying me.'

I was blown away. 'You're so brave,' I said. 'I don't think I could do it. Aren't you ever tempted to hide away?'

'There's too much to be done. Women need to know that we're here to help. And besides,' she said, 'where better to hide than in plain sight?'

'You're an inspiration,' I said with conviction. She was such a driven, sassy woman. Sofia pressed her lips together in a self-effacing smile. 'Thank you. Anyway, please continue.'

I told her more about Zadie's self-harming and my suspicion that her brother was sending her violent and pornographic material to watch. When I mentioned the online clips of FGM she merely sighed and bobbed her head. Clearly she'd heard it all before. I spoke for over half an hour. Sofia chipped in occasionally to ask a question but apart from that she listened and sipped her coffee. It felt so good to share my fears for Zadie with such an insightful, knowledgeable woman.

'So how do you know all of this?'

'It's just what I've managed to piece together from Zadie. She's been reluctant to talk and I get the feeling she hasn't opened up fully yet but we're getting there' – I gave her a rueful smile – 'slowly.'

Sofia raised her thickly defined brows. 'I think you've done very well. Many women and girls from Zadie's background are terribly suspicious, mistrustful of everyone. I know that some people consider Asian women a bit aloof and uncommunicative,' Sofia pursed her lips and rested her hands on the table. 'Often they're just scared.'

I nodded. Zadie was scared all right. Scared of everyone.

'I'm guessing that's why Zadie's sister ran away. Because of what they did to her. Although Zadie's social worker thinks there may be more to it. She's worried that she may have been forced into a marriage and sent away.'

'It's possible. Forced marriage is not illegal at the moment in the UK, although there are high-level talks about making it so in the near future. It's something we've been campaigning for since 2005. Child marriage goes against Islamic teaching, just as FGM does. The Qur'an is clear that intellectual maturity is the basis for deciding age of marriage, not puberty. Attitudes towards the abuse of children changed during Victorian times over here, but in many societies marriage to a child is still seen as a badge of honour. Like the Catholics did until recently, many Muslim societies sweep the issue under the carpet. If Zadie's sister was sent away to be married, it's unlikely anyone in the community would come forward and report it.'

We sat in silence for a moment, both of us lost in thought. I wondered how Zadie managed to cope so well, having to bear the weight of two unresolved losses – her mother and her sister.

'Social services have no idea what happened to the sister?'

'No, they don't have any information at all. It's almost as if she never existed. You'd think that school would have reported her missing or –'

'Does Zadie attend school, then?'

'Actually, no. Good point,' I said, realising that there was probably no one to miss her sister, apart from close family, and they were never going to say anything. 'She was keen to continue studying but her father pulled her out.'

'Sadly that's often what happens. Many Muslim families value education but they feel that the benefits of going to school are outweighed by the risk of being corrupted by lax western values. We have so many teachers contacting us about pupils who literally seem to vanish from the face of the earth once they hit puberty. It's a phenomenon that's rarely acknowledged openly. The British are so fearful of being accused of racism.'

'What about the police? Isn't it reported?'

'All the families have to say is that their daughters have been sent to study abroad. That's often the end of it. The police are so desperate to maintain good race relations that they put political correctness before justice.'

'So what really happens to these girls?'

'Some spend the rest of their days at home, like Zadie. Cooking, cleaning, looking after the men and then being married off at an early age to live a life full of regret. Some are sent abroad in early puberty for marriage to someone they've never met.' Sofia topped up her mug with more coffee. Its rich scent drifted across the table. 'You know, I'm very concerned, Rosie.' She looked at me with quiet intensity. 'There's no way Zadie's whereabouts have been compromised, is there?'

'No, the family don't have my address.'

'Good. On no account must it be disclosed. You will make sure of that?'

'I will do my best. Zadie's social worker was going to let her brother have contact with her at my home. I didn't feel comfortable with it so I refused, but –'

Sofia groaned, interrupting me. 'That makes me so cross,' she snapped. 'There have been so many cases of families executing their daughters for the slightest of misdemeanours. The authorities know this and yet they're still reluctant to acknowledge the dangers in case they offend anyone.' She made a fist and tapped it on the table. 'Listen, Rosie, please. On no account must Zadie be allowed home. Tell her social worker. She would be sent abroad within a matter of days, I'm almost certain of this. Her family will be desperate to put things right. To atone for all the shame.'

My pulse quickened. I was beginning to realise just how precarious the situation was. I chewed my lip. 'Zadie's social worker said that her father is pushing very hard for contact. Because she's in voluntary care I'll be the one supervising it.'

'I tell you what you need to do.' Sofia swallowed and looked at me with gravitas. 'When you get home you must sew something metal into the hem of Zadie's clothes.'

Confused, I frowned and gave her a half-smile.

'I'm serious. If they manage to abduct her – and believe me, they will try – the metal in her clothes will set off the detector at the airport. This will give her enough time to alert the security staff. Rosie, believe me when I say these people will stop at nothing to preserve their honour.'

I felt the blood drain from my face.

'So the authorities can't tell you any more about her mother?' she asked, her deep, smoky voice interrupting my thoughts.

I threw my hands into the air. 'They don't seem to know anything about her either. Do you have any idea what I can do to find out about her or Zadie's sister? I think it would really help her to find out what happened to them. Even if it's bad news.'

Sofia nodded. 'I'll make a few discreet enquiries if you give me their names and anything else you know about them. But, Rosie,' Sofia wrapped her hands around her mug, interlocking her fingers, 'we must tread very carefully. If her sister ran away she may not want to be found. We mustn't compromise her safety in any way, and you'd be amazed just how strong the community is. A few months ago I was visited by a woman terrified for her life. Her husband became convinced that she was having an affair and had made threats against her. I convinced her to report it to the authorities and the next day she walked into a police station 50 miles from home. One of the officers called an interpreter in, and do you know what happened?'

I shook my head.

'The interpreter was a distant relative. The woman nearly died of shock when he walked into the room and sat opposite her.'

I gasped and my hand flew to my mouth. 'So what happened?'

'The officers removed him, but of course her husband discovered where she was and so the police had to make urgent arrangements for her to be moved. These families have all-seeing eyes – amazing networks enabling them to keep control. It's not unusual for male family members to become interpreters for that very reason.'

I stayed with Sofia for nearly four hours and, though I was tired, I was sorry to leave; she was a woman cut from different cloth. After the meeting, rather than catching the first train home, I took a ride on the Tube to Victoria and then headed on foot towards Oxford Street on the lookout for a café or sandwich bar. Usually my day is circumscribed by children and so it felt slightly hedonistic to walk past Pizza Hut and McDonald's without a backward glance. I ended up in a little café down in the crypt of Westminster Cathedral where I sat in peaceful silence, amazed to find that, despite the flock of people milling around above ground, the place was almost deserted.

What Sofia had said about Zadie being in danger reso-nated with me as I made my way back to King's Cross. I kept playing her warnings over and over in my mind during the train journey home and began to feel increasingly edgy. So much so that when my mobile rang I started violently and the woman sitting opposite leaned over to ask if I was all right. It was Peggy. As soon as I heard her voice I took a deep breath, ready to repeat some of Sofia's dire warnings.

'It's all right, Rosie,' she said quickly, before I had a chance to speak. 'We've had our meeting. I'm taking this to court in the morning and I'm certain we'll secure an Interim Care Order.'

'Oh thank goodness,' I said, releasing the tight hold on my handset and sinking further into the seat.

'It's the pornography that worries us – I think that's what will secure it, rather than anything else. We've had a surge in the number of cases where teens have become reliant on it, with some disturbing consequences. I won't go into it on the phone but I'm sure you can imagine. Anyway, I'll let you know the outcome in the morning.'

It was gone ten o'clock when I finally arrived home and the children were already in bed. Mum and I sat together on the sofa, both of us clasping a hot drink in our hands. 'So how was your day?' she asked, leaning back into the cushions. I told her what a revelation it was to meet some-one like Sofia. Usually a good listener, Mum seemed a little distracted as if she was only half-listening. 'What is it, Mum? Have they worn you out?'

'No, love, I'm all right. It's just, well, I worry, that's all. What with you here on your own and all this going on. What if –'

'Mum,' I held up my hand, feeling more than a little guilty about my thoughtlessness. Mum was so energetic that it was easy to forget she was nearly 70. I was relieved I hadn't yet told her about Sofia's concerns. 'There's no need to worry,' I said, sounding much more confident than I felt.

'There's no way they can find out where we are. It's all absolutely fine.'

She raised her eyebrows. 'Well, let's hope so,' she said with a sighing yawn, removing her glasses and pinching the bridge of her nose between thumb and forefinger. 'But this is social services we're talking about.'

By the time we'd finished talking it was getting late so Mum took my bed and I settled myself on the sofa with a spare duvet and my sewing box. There was nothing like taking practical action to soothe the mind, and so, with a DVD of *Pride and Prejudice* playing in the background, I sat up until nearly 3 a.m. sewing tiny spoons into the hems of Zadie's robes.

Chapter 15

Towards mid-July, after Zadie had been with us for over two months, I realised that I was growing used to her silent soundtrack. Despite her restless fingers endlessly twirling the bands on her wrist, she was a gentle presence and our days passed companionably. I always hesitated to use the 'Q' word but things were so quiet that I agreed to cover the out-of-hours rota for zero to ten-year-olds. It was strange, then, that I still wasn't feeling relaxed around Zadie. With the threat of her imminent return home removed by the Interim Care Order there was no reason for tension, but I was still dogged by the same sense of urgency, the clock in my head gaining momentum with each passing day. All I could think of were missed opportunities, as if I was ignoring something vital.

For her part, Zadie finally seemed to register that we all wanted her around. She apologised less and sat with us in the evenings to read or watch television, becoming obsessed with one film in particular – *The Parent Trap*. It's a film about identical twin girls who plot to reunite their estranged parents and it had been a firm favourite with all the children I fostered. The twins in the story sought what children covet most, a loving and united family, and Zadie watched it at every opportunity, perhaps because it appealed to her longing for the family she had lost.

There were still days when she seemed far away, her sadness keeping her distanced from our everyday banter, but physically she looked much better. Despite her poor appetite and frequent nervy tummy, her cheeks were filling out and her skin had lost its sallow tone. In the middle of the third week of July and the arrival of Ramadan, Zadie was only allowed to eat two meals: one before sunrise and the other after sunset. Determined that she should keep her strength up, I got up with her at 4.30 a.m. each morning to make sure she ate a decent breakfast, secretly willing the month to pass quickly.

Sofia kept in touch, calling every few days to see how Zadie was and updating me on the moves she was making to try and find her sister. About six weeks after my visit to the Women's Centre Sofia rang to tell me that they were making some progress; it seemed that a Nadeen Hassan had signed a petition against forced marriage that was organised by another women's centre south of the river. I didn't mention anything about it to Zadie in case it turned out to be a dead end but I felt my own hope rising.

Sofia also told me about a school not too far from where we lived that had a high Muslim intake and special provisions respecting the Islamic faith; single-sex sports, segregated changing and prayer rooms with washing facilities. It sounded ideal for Zadie and, if she did go back home, was somewhere that her father was unlikely to object to. I thanked Sofia for her help and immediately gave them a call. The admissions secretary told me that there were no places available immediately but the summer holidays were fast approaching. She was almost certain that some of the children in Zadie's year would not return for the autumn term and so there was likely to be a vacancy for Zadie to start in September.

Hurrying upstairs to give Zadie the good news, I knocked on her bedroom door, then froze halfway over the threshold. She was sitting on her bed reading one of my favourite books – *Jonathan Livingston Seagull*, a spiritual story that I was almost certain her father would disapprove of. She misinterpreted the look of horror on my face. 'I'm sorry, Rosie,' she said, her face crimson. 'I didn't think you'd mind …' Her voice trailed away as she held the book aloft.

'No, of course I don't mind,' I said, reasoning that it was hardly offensive material and I hadn't encouraged her to read it. I walked further into the room and crouched beside her bed. 'Anyway, I've got some good news for you,' I said, smiling up at her. 'There's a school nearby that I think your father would approve of. They've got a place for you to start in September, if you're still with us by then, that is.'

Knowing Zadie as I did, I hadn't expected cheers or air punches. Those reactions usually came from Jamie. But I watched her face eagerly, expecting her to break into one of her rare smiles. So I was taken aback when she burst into tears and buried her face in her pillow. To say I was bemused was an understatement. I stayed by her side for a while, stroking her back and trying to get her to talk.

After ten minutes I decided to give her some time alone and went downstairs shaking my head.

The phone rang as I reached the bottom stair. 'How are you fixed at the moment?' Peggy asked before the receiver reached my ear. 'Things still peaceful?'

'Y-es,' I answered hesitantly. 'Relatively.'

'Good. Look, I'm not really supposed to get involved in this but we've just had a newborn come in and I'd like to send her in your direction, if that's OK with you? All of our in-house carers are full and we need someone experienced with this one.'

Peggy went on to explain that baby Megan had been born early that morning with a cleft lip. Her birth mother had recently fled from her violent partner and was living in a refuge but was also suffering from severe depression. Overwhelmed by the prospect of having a baby who would need special care and grieving over her lost relationship, she had reluctantly agreed that her baby daughter could be taken into temporary foster care. 'So, what do you think?'

I thought about my previous struggles to separate after caring for young babies but my heart was already quickening as I wondered what Megan looked like and anticipating the soft warmth of a newborn in my arms. You're really never going to be very good at the last bit, I told myself, the most important part where you have to give them back. My head was reminding me of the stark pain of letting go and the heartache of loss. But my heart was already wondering whether I still had a steriliser tucked away in the loft. 'Yes,

I'd love to,' I told Peggy, in spite of myself. 'How soon can we pick her up?'

Remembering Emily and Jamie's excited reactions whenever I had announced the imminent arrival of a young baby, I rushed back up to Zadie's room to tell her, hoping that it might be just the distraction she needed.

Zadie paled as soon as I gave her the news, staring at me goggle-eyed as if had told her we were going to share the house with a pack of wild animals. 'What's wrong? Don't you like babies?' I asked.

Leaning against the headboard, she drew her knees up and tucked her arms beneath them. 'Yes, I do,' she whispered.

'It doesn't affect your stay here,' I told her, wondering whether she was worried she might have to move on, as if it was a case of out with the old and in with the new. 'I was hoping we might look after her together,' I added, hoping to make her feel included.

She nodded and stretched her face into a sort of panicked smile.

I waited until Emily and Jamie came home to order the equipment I needed. I told Peggy that I still had Sarah's crib, bedding and baby bath tucked away in the loft, but Peggy insisted that Megan should have everything new. When Emily was born I hadn't been able to afford anything that wasn't second-hand and so she and I had a wonderful time, sitting side by side at the computer and flicking through the pages of an online baby superstore.

Zadie eyed us warily, politely declining my invite for her to join us. She was withdrawn for the rest of the evening, joining us for dinner (we all ate after sunset to save the bother of cooking twice) but retreating back to her room as soon as she had helped with the washing up. Even the next day when the delivery arrived, she gave us a wide berth. It was Saturday and so Emily and Jamie were home. They tore into the boxes, helping me to organise everything, but Zadie wouldn't be coaxed from her room.

I was certain that once the baby arrived Zadie would brighten, realising that by accepting Megan as a new placement I was not severing the final safety rope and accelerating her downfall.

Megan was such a dear little thing. The first thing I noticed when I picked her up from her hospital crib was her downy hair, almost black in colour and so long that it fell in soft wisps around her ears, her delicately fine fringe brushing the tops of her barely there eyebrows. Tracing an index finger over the soft skin of her cheek, I took in her round forehead, her tiny nose and the large hazel eyes that swept over my face. Her pupils were dilated, inquisitive, as if considering the unfamiliar hands that cradled her, weighing them up. Swaying her gently in my arms, she fixed me with an unblinking gaze and I felt a rush of tenderness. A sudden flare of recognition passed between us, a silent accord, as if she was accepting of her fate.

She actually reminded me of Emily in her early days and I wondered where all the years had gone. How could it be that Emily, once tiny enough to fit snugly on my forearm, was almost at the end of her school years? It was a reminder to savour every moment I got to spend with little ones.

Betrayed

Every baby deserved to be adored. Even though Megan's mother was unable to cherish her daughter, there were thousands, actually probably millions, of women around the world who would be more than happy to do it for her, and I was lucky enough to be the one holding her in my arms.

For one brief moment my stomach rolled as I questioned the wisdom of taking another baby home with me, knowing how quickly a strong attachment can form. Babies have a way of nestling into your heart and mind, however many courses on undermining attachment a foster carer may attend. Taking her wrinkled hand in my own, I examined her pearl-like fingernails and planted a kiss on each one, brushing the anxiety away.

Running my forefinger softly over the neat row of dimples between each tiny knuckle, I marvelled how something so tiny could be so perfectly formed. And then my eyes took in the small gap, about a centimetre or so, in her top lip – not nearly as extensive as I had feared when I had spoken to Peggy on the telephone.

Megan's birth mother was being supervised in the relatives' waiting room, the midwives reassuring me that she wouldn't be allowed to roam the hospital corridors until I was safely away. Social workers suspected that Megan's mother had smoked throughout pregnancy, though they were most concerned about her drinking – she had turned up to ante-natal checks barely able to stand.

'If they're intent on having some sort of fix while they're pregnant,' the midwife said as she took me into a side room to show me how to feed a baby with a cleft lip, 'they'd do

far less damage with Class A drugs than a glass of wine.'
Her lips drew into a tight, wearisome line. 'Why can't they
think about anyone else but themselves?'

Not for the first time I realised how vulnerable little
ones were, at the mercy of their parents from the moment
of conception.

Chapter 16

Maybe it was my unsettled mood or the unfamiliar snuffles and sighs coming from the crib beside my bed, but I found it impossible to sleep during the nights following Megan's arrival. It was several days before I mastered the technique of giving her a bottle and I think at first I was a little anxious about that. The gap in Megan's lip meant that it was difficult for her to create enough suction to get any milk so I had to hold her upright to avoid any liquid running into her nasal passage while stretching my arm round far enough so that my fingers could hold her lip together to create a tight seal. It was a tricky manoeuvre, especially as I also had to keep a bulb suction close by for those times when she jerked back, alarmed when too much milk pooled in her nose. But the sound of those clicking noises, the ones that meant she was getting the milk she needed, was a rich reward.

Since it took so long to feed her there was barely two hours between her finishing one bottle and needing the next and so, in that small window of opportunity, I should have gone out like a light. Instead, every time my mind drifted towards sleep my limbs tensed, snapping me back to full alert. I kept thinking about Zadie's strange reaction to the baby when I first brought her home – she took one look at Megan, then paled and fled back to her room. I knew that some cultures shunned babies with birth defects and wondered whether Zadie had been told that dark forces were responsible for something like a cleft lip. As much as I loved caring for Megan, I couldn't help feeling a little guilty that I had imposed a new situation on Zadie that she wasn't comfortable with.

About a week into the placement, Megan woke a little after 2 a.m. for her feed and it was half an hour later, after I had settled her back in her crib, that I was drawn to check on Zadie. As I neared her room I felt an intangible clawing deep in my stomach and by the time I tapped on her door I knew there was something badly wrong. Perhaps it was sixth sense or my imagination but there was something unnatural about the cold silence answering my increasing vigorous taps. Half-frightened that I'd find her lying lifeless in bed I threw the door open and strode into the room. Worryingly, her duvet remained still even though I called her name over and over. Flicking on the light, I took a deep breath and caught hold of the top of the duvet, almost crying out as I flipped it back.

Zadie was lying still on her side, her stomach covered in blood. I clamped my hand over my mouth and strangled a moan, my eyes running over the length of her body trying to absorb the extent of her injuries. Her arms were by her side, her left hand curled loosely around a knife and her pyjama top was bundled up around her chest leaving her bloody abdomen horribly exposed. Her eyes were half-open with an awful glassy stillness and she seemed to be muttering feverishly under her breath.

'What's happened, Mum?'

Emily was at the door. When she caught sight of Zadie her mouth dropped open in horror.

'Emily, bring me my phone and then go back to your room, honey. Make sure Jamie doesn't get up.'

Moments later three luminous nines glowed on the screen of my mobile phone, the handset on loudspeaker as I tore into the bathroom. As I wrenched open the medicine cabinet door I remembered that children in care were far more likely to die than their peers in the general population. Please, I repeated over and over again, don't let Zadie become another of those statistics.

The operator's calm but insistent tone floated across the landing. 'Help is on its way, Mrs Lewis. Try to stay calm.'

It's strange how in moments of panic my brain seems to constrict, sharpening its focus on small details and crowding everything else out. All I could see as I pulled the contents of the cabinet to the floor and rummaged through the boxes of painkillers were those dreaded numbers – 999 – the ones I hoped I would never have to dial again after Phoebe left us.

I had known something was wrong. The feeling had dogged me for weeks and I sensed that some main event loomed in the future, waiting for me. Even so, I had to admit – I hadn't seen this coming. It was almost a blessing that I didn't realise at the time that the most shocking event still lay several months into the future.

Armed with bandages and padded gauze I raced back to the bedroom, hesitating for a fragment of a second in the doorway. Zadie began to shiver uncontrollably, her eyes fluttering towards unconsciousness. She let out a strangled gasp and I sprang into action, kneeling beside her bed. With timorous fingers I did my best to stem the flow of blood coming from her stomach.

'Mrs Lewis?' The emergency operator was still on the line.

'I've done what I can,' I said, my voice quivering, 'but I can't seem to stop the bleeding.'

Pacing the floor of the relatives' waiting room, I clenched my hands together and prayed with full concentration so that I said all I wanted to without my mind drifting off in other directions as it usually did. Wherever I was in the room, my eyes were trained continually on the small rectangle of glass in the door, watching for a nurse to pass by so that I could pounce on them for some news. When the door clicked open I darted across the room, my heart beating so hard that I could feel the pulse reverberating up to my neck and deep down into my stomach.

The doctor was young but tense and tired looking. He entered the room with a grave expression and I felt a jolt of panic; he didn't look like a man about to deliver good news. Meeting my anxious stare with a sympathetic smile, he seemed to hesitate for a fraction of a second before saying anything. I steeled myself. 'We've managed to stop the bleeding,' he said in a soft voice. 'A couple of the wounds were fairly nasty but nothing too alarming.'

I let out a huge breath, thinking that the doctor, being young, was probably still perfecting his bedside manner. Zadie's injuries were not alarming. As far as I was concerned that was good news. He probably needed to lighten up a little bit, I thought, wondering if he'd had a particularly difficult shift. 'Oh thank goodness,' I said, immediately tensing when I saw that the young man still looked gravely concerned.

'But?' I said, my stomach beginning to perform a slow churning somersault.

He ran his forefinger around the inside of his collar, pivoting his head as if it was too hot in the room. 'I understand you've been Zadie's foster carer for a while?'

'Yes,' I said quickly, my alarm growing by the second. 'What is it? What's wrong?'

Another pause. 'Were you aware that she's pregnant?'

I didn't register what he said instantaneously, my mind taking a few moments to process the words. When it did my eyes widened and I stared at him agog, blinking rapidly. My arm flew out to rest on the back of a chair and I held on tight, my legs suddenly unable to hold up my own weight, as if the floor had suddenly become soft.

'I'm so sorry. I can see this has come as a bit of a shock to you.'

'No,' I said firmly, recovering my wherewithal. 'She can't be. It's not possible.'

He cleared his throat and locked eyes with me. 'I'm afraid there really is no doubt.'

I began spluttering, then gasping for breath as if someone had clamped a hand over my mouth. There was a humming noise in my ears. 'But how can that be?' I asked, searching his face. He moved his mouth but didn't manage to produce any sound before I shook my head and said, 'I'm sorry, that was a stupid question.' I rubbed my hand across my forehead. 'I just don't understand.'

He nodded patiently, then cleared his throat. 'I'm afraid I must ask – how long has she been in your care?'

I felt the heat rise to my face, the implications beginning to dawn on me. 'About ten weeks, I think,' I said, a new wave of panic coursing through my stomach.

He nodded and relaxed a fraction, seemingly satisfied. With my hands on my cheeks in a futile attempt to shield myself from the answer I asked a vital question, my voice weak. 'How far gone is she?'

'I can't say for certain. We're organising a scan at the moment but I'd guess somewhere between 20 and 25 weeks.' He patted my arm. 'This must be distressing news for you, I'm sure.'

I nodded vaguely, my mind still catching up with events. When I actually thought about it, it simply wasn't possible that Zadie had become pregnant in my care; she had hardly been out of my sight since she first arrived. 'Does she know?' I asked suddenly.

'It's difficult to tell. One of the nurses tried discussing it with her but she seems to have completely withdrawn. I suspect she has known for a while. It's not unusual for girls to bury their heads in the sand. The reality is too frightening to acknowledge.'

Betrayed

Of course she knows, I registered with a jot. Of course she does: the manic exercising, the nausea and tiredness. Suddenly it all made sense and I felt incredibly, ridiculously stupid. How could I not have noticed? But then, she was only 13 years old and from a devout, religious home. It was the last thing I should have expected, surely?

As I walked along the corridor to the accident and emergency department, I gazed at the stark white walls, wondering what I could possibly say to Zadie to reassure her. While fostering I have supported lots of children through difficult times but in Zadie's situation I knew that there was simply no easy solution. Whatever happened, whatever decisions were to be made, her life from that moment had changed irrevocably. The thought made me a little dizzy and I slowed my step as I neared the double doors of the emergency treatment area, the sight of her waxen face through a circular glass observation panel making my pulse play even louder in my ears.

Partly because social services needed to be informed but mainly, I think, to give myself more time to gather myself, I slipped through the exit doors and dialled the number for the emergency, out-of-hours duty social worker. The stench of stale tobacco hit me, the brown droopy plants in a nearby flower-bed festooned with hundreds of cigarette butts where petals should be. Wrinkling my nose, I moved several metres away and leaned against the cold concrete wall for support as I rattled off a summary of the night's events to a man with a heavy foreign accent who yawned several times during the largely one-sided conversation.

While he thanked me for letting him know, he said very little else and offered nothing in the way of advice. Still, my duty was done and the fresh cold air had cleared the fuzzy feeling from my head.

Zadie was propped up on several pillows on a hospital trolley pressed against the far wall of a large treatment area. Three other trolleys were lined up along the space, each of them surrounded by canisters and tubes but all empty of patients. A nurse was crouched beside an open cupboard on the other side of the room, filling the shelves with small boxes. She gave me a brief smile as I walked in and nodded in answer to my quizzical look, waving permission for me to come in with her free hand.

Zadie's arms were tightly folded over the white sheet covering her, her hands clamped around a white cellular blanket as if she was afraid someone was going to snatch it away. She looked so young and vulnerable without her headscarf that my heart squeezed at the sight. Looking up, her face clouded with apprehension when she saw me. With a smile from me the muscles in her face softened and her lip quivered. Still several feet away I whispered, 'Oh, Zadie.' That was enough. Her eyes crumpled and she began to cry, unravelling her arms and holding them out to me. It was a childlike gesture and I was immediately undone. Welling up, I closed the space between us and through the haze I leaned across the bed, taking her hands in mine. 'It's going to be all right, you know,' I said, planting a kiss on her hair. 'We'll take care of you.'

* * *

Betrayed

When I got home Mum greeted me at the door. I had called her on the way home from the hospital, unable to keep the news to myself, and, with Megan fast asleep in the crook of one arm, she draped the other around my shoulders and guided me into the hall. While Mum settled Megan in her crib I walked through to the dining room and as I lowered my keys to the table I noticed signs everywhere. They hit me with full force, making me feel even more ashamed of myself than I had at the hospital. I had wanted so much to help Zadie, but now the seemingly innocuous incidents all connected up to make me feel like the worst foster carer in England. I pictured Zadie sitting down to meals, her drained face edged with a tinge of green.

And then, standing at the patio doors and staring into the garden, I remembered how Zadie had thrown herself around on the trampoline as if she were representing her country in the Olympics and then, coming in, her robe held out in front of her with nervous fingers that never kept still.

I had wrongly attributed it all to anxiety instead of a burgeoning tummy. I covered my face with my hands, incidents playing hazily over in my mind like poor-quality podcasts. I replayed our conversation on the swing when Zadie had slipped up and told me that she preferred to wear school uniform to school. I had thought it strange that when I took her shopping all she wanted was robes. She hadn't preferred the anonymity of the burqa at all; she had been hiding her growing tummy. Zadie hadn't said much at the hospital. She had cried and clung to me but after that she seemed to be exhausted, her voice so deep and slow with tiredness that I hadn't pressed her to talk.

I clapped my hands to my face, trying to push aside a rush of angry frustration. The clues had been dangled in front of me and I had been blind to them all. If I had realised the truth sooner, Zadie may have had more choices. None of them would have been easy but she would have had more control over what happened to her. At this late stage it was possible that there would be no way out: it was likely that she would have to carry the baby to term.

'She's off and dreaming somewhere peaceful,' Mum said behind me. Turning, I gave her a weary smile and she sighed. 'It never rains but it pours,' she murmured. 'Come on, you.' And she slipped her arm through mine, steering me towards the kitchen. I sank down onto one of the stools and watched her bustling around the place.

'I do wish you'd get yourself some proper cups and saucers,' she said as she flicked the kettle on and draped a tea towel over her elbow, the red and white striped cloth occupying the soft space Megan had just vacated. It was such an everyday, ordinary thing to say that if I'd had the energy I would have got up and hugged her. It had been a horrible night and so to hear that Mum was still disturbed by the prospect of tea served in a mug was strangely comforting. Being gently nagged took me right back to my childhood where decisions were made for me, my responsibilities limited to making my own bed and remembering to take my packed lunch for school.

Registering with a start that Zadie would be craving such solidity, especially in her time of crisis, I resolved to be her bulwark, supporting her through the tough months that lay ahead. Mum tutted as she examined my mismatched crockery, curling her lip and sighing with resigned exasperation. 'It just doesn't taste the same in these things,' she moaned, dropping a tea-bag into my chunky bright red mug.

I smiled to myself, filled with gratitude for her presence.

Zadie sat quietly in the back of the car as I drove towards home the next day, but when I pulled the car into our street she loosened her seat belt, leaned forward in her seat and slipped a hesitant hand over the head rest behind me. 'Rosie,' she whispered in a shaky voice, 'do Emily and Jamie know?'

She sagged in grateful relief when I reassured her that I hadn't mentioned anything and my heart went out to her, knowing how humiliated she must feel. As soon as we got in she wanted to go to her room, and after transferring a sleeping Megan from the car seat to her crib I followed Zadie upstairs, noticing a faint swell beneath her robe as she reached for her dressing gown. Though it was barely there, in my mind it became fluorescent, neon letters spelling the message, HOW ON EARTH DID YOU MANAGE TO OVERLOOK THIS?

My insides swirled with fury and disappointment in myself. I think most foster carers worry that they might miss signs of illness or other conditions when caring for other people's children, which is partly why they can often be found sitting in doctors' waiting rooms. I remembered the previous year when the local authority had given Rachel a hard time over the head lice in Katy's hair. Her birth mother had reported that the child was 'running alive' with them and made a formal complaint. Rachel was mortified that she hadn't noticed, but how I envied that scenario now. Zadie's situation was infinitely harder to fix.

Supporting Zadie by the arm as she eased herself gently into bed, all I could think of was how terrified she must have been, keeping such a secret shut away in her young mind. Tucking the duvet up beneath her chin as I would with a much younger child, I felt fresh bubbles of anger surfacing. Children like Zadie seemed to have the chance of living a normal life removed from them when they were so young. All the teenager had done was obediently follow the plans mapped out for her by the adults she was supposed to be able to trust, and that path had led her to a place of turmoil, where every apparent choice would lead to more heartache. She was so young; her head should have been full of dreams. I blinked a few times, trying not to think about it. Sometimes, when fostering, you just had to put on a virtual set of blinkers and get on with the job.

'Thank you, Rosie,' she said, dabbing at her damp eyes with a tissue. She was still trembling slightly from the trauma of the day.

'Please don't thank me,' I said, biting down the words. I don't deserve it, I told myself silently, but I didn't say anything. The last thing she needed burdening with was my own feelings. Sitting down beside her, I brushed back a tendril of dark hair from her face. 'Are you ready to talk?'

She gave a little resigned sigh. I think she realised that the days of ignoring it all and hoping it would go away were over.

'How long have you known?'

Tears ran from the outer corners of her eyes and down towards her pillow. She shrugged, her fingers working over the damp tissue so that it began to crumble. Tiny particles fluttered down to rest on the duvet. 'I'm not sure. It feels like I've been worrying about it for months. My monthlies stopped and I felt sick all the time but I just kept hoping there was something else wrong with me, like cancer or something.'

I put my hands up to cover my mouth and left them there. 'Oh, Zadie,' I said, 'how can you say that?'

'Papa wouldn't be angry with me if I was ill, would he? But if he finds out about this –'

I let out a loud whistle of air, nauseous with the thought that a child would rather face a serious illness than upset her family. Dropping my hands to cup my chin, I locked eyes with hers. 'I'm sorry you didn't feel able to tell me. I should have noticed something.' I released my hands and left them dangling, as if trying to clutch hold of an explanation for my blindness.

'I wanted to,' she said earnestly, taking one of my hands and giving it a little squeeze. 'But I didn't want to say the words. I just kept hoping that if I …' she stopped, a wariness crossing her features.

'You thought that if you starved yourself and threw yourself around enough it might all go away.'

She nodded and bit down on her lip.

'Can you tell me who the father is?' I asked as gently as I could. Neither of us had the stomach to put words to the final attempt she made to rid herself of the problem.

She froze, her fingers closing around the shrinking ball of tissue. Her eyes flicked from me to the wall and back again. 'A boy from school,' she whispered, holding herself very still.

I tilted my head and gave her a doubtful look. She glanced away. However much I thought about it, I just couldn't imagine the girl in front of me even voluntarily holding hands with a boy, let alone conducting a secret sexual relationship. It hurt that Zadie still didn't feel able to confide in me. That was my responsibility and it was a failing that didn't sit easily. I thought back to the foster carers' ball and the award I had received for my work with Phoebe. You're certainly not in the running for any commendations this time around, Rosie Lewis, I chided.

It was only then, as I was berating myself for being such a fraud, that I remembered what had been troubling me on the night of the ball. Picturing myself as I climbed up onstage, I remembered the cold rush of unease as I puzzled over Chit's preoccupation with Zadie's sleeping habits. And then the truth was refracted through that night with such force that I felt stunned, as if I'd been staring, unprotected, into bright sunlight. I closed my eyes, my thoughts scattered and scorched. I rubbed my temples and took a deep breath, trying to slow everything down. And then my eyes popped open, a tide of fury surging through my veins and making my face glow hot. Zadie was staring at me in alarm but I got to my feet and paced the room, knowing that I should allow my thoughts to settle before confronting her. Rubbing a hot hand over my forehead, I stood still for a moment, making myself count slowly from one to ten.

I think it was the look on my face as I turned around that told Zadie there was no use in pretending any more. With all of her secrets finally stripped away she immediately dissolved into tears, the sound of her sobs and the naked shame on her face confirming the truth as clearly as if it was written on her bedroom wall.

And then, as we sat side by side on the edge of the bed, she told me everything; how Chit began his slow grooming of her by showing her pornography. Revolted, she tried to avoid him, but there were so many times that she was left in his care while her father worked that there was no escape. 'It got worse after Nadeen left,' she spluttered. 'He made me watch films and stuff on the computer. He couldn't stop; it was like he was possessed.'

By the time she fell silent she looked so fearful, so vulnerable and lost that my anger melted away, for the moment at least. I gathered her in my arms and held her, my mind running over events haphazardly.

'Does your father know?' I asked.

'Oh no. No, no,' she said, shaking her head manically. 'He mustn't ever know, he'd be so hurt.'

That was it. A fresh wave of fury hit. I remembered Chit's refusal to shake my hand and an ice-cold fury slivered through my chest. He was so chaste that he couldn't shake the hand of a woman, yet he was somehow able to justify the rape of his sister. What appalled me most was her quiet acceptance, her desire to protect her family after all that had been done to her. I wanted her to rage, shout and scream but instead she twisted herself gently away from me, raising her head and wiping her face on the arm of her robe. Dark blotches were left behind by her tears.

Still gripped by a fierce anger, it was several minutes before I could trust myself to speak. 'I should have realised. I'm sor —'

'Please don't,' she said, moving closer and lowering her head to my shoulder.

'We have to report him, Zadie,' I said after a moment or two.

She jerked her head away from me, flinching as though she'd been slapped. Her body began shaking.

'I can't,' she said, crying again. 'Papa will never forgive me.'

'I'll support you,' I said, trying to keep my tone soft and reassuring as I explained that I had no choice but to report her disclosure to Peggy. I traced a path from her cheek to her forehead and back again. She closed her eyes and let the tears come.

'I want to die,' she said, opening her eyes and fixing them on mine.

My stomach did a somersault. I remembered reading in the newspaper years earlier about the child chess prodigy who was so tormented by the prospect of giving evidence against her own father, who had been accused of raping her, that she drank heavily and fell to her death from an eighth-floor balcony. Her family had known she was under stress but never suspected that she might try to harm herself.

Betrayed

I stared at Zadie. It wasn't her words that speared my chest with ice so much as the tone she used. There was no hysteria or self-pity. She spoke calmly, in a flat, non-attention-seeking monotone. I got the feeling that she was informing me of her intention, and after what she did to herself yesterday I had every reason to believe she was capable of it.

I took her chin in my hand, holding firmly. 'I don't ever want to hear you say that again,' I said briskly, realising that the tone I was using sounded just like my mother's. 'That's just panic talking.' The soft skin of her neck rippled against my knuckles as she gulped. 'This is as bad and as scary as it gets, honey. And you're not alone in this. I'll be right here with you, every step of the way.'

'I can't …'

'Listen to me,' I said, interrupting her. 'What I need you to do is think of one thing that makes you happy. Just one thing. It doesn't have to be anything big. Just something you enjoy doing or a place you like to go. And then I need you to hold on to that thought for the next few hours. Can you think of something?'

She nodded. 'I like being with Emily and Jamie.'

'Right,' I said, blinking back my own tears. 'Then think about being with them and nothing else. Can you do that for me?'

She nodded bravely, brushing away her tears with the back of her hand.

Filled with a longing to gather all of the children to me, safe and snug, when evening came I dragged a camping mattress upstairs and set it on the floor beside Zadie's bed.

Even though her subconscious had perhaps known for a while, I think that acknowledging the pregnancy was a huge shock for Zadie. She was certainly in no condition to heed my warnings against harming herself again, so I decided to keep vigil at her side for as many nights as it took for her to accept the situation. After a while emotional exhaustion and the trauma of the day overtook her and she fell asleep, one small hand lying protectively across her stomach. Megan slept in a carry-cot on the other side of me, blissfully unaware of all that was going on around her.

I woke before dawn the next morning. Zadie was still asleep, her breathing slow and regular, so, with Megan's carry-cot tucked under my arm, I crept out of her room on tiptoe. As she was pregnant Zadie wasn't obliged to continue fasting and so I decided to leave her to sleep, after what she had been through. Downstairs I tucked Megan in the corner of the living room and then sat at the computer and wrote an incident report, firing it straight off in an email to Peggy.

With the task done, I sat back in the chair, thinking so hard that my head began to thud. Feeling top heavy, I leaned my elbows on the desk and, closing my eyes, I rested my head in my hands. Fostering has the power to catapult carers into a world that doesn't make sense, and as I sat in the dining room cradling my head in my hands I felt as if there were just one too many things for Zadie to cope with. I kept picturing Chit at the Lavender Fields, his non-chalance, the arrogant tilt of his chin. Nausea rose as I chronicled each hurdle Zadie would have to face because of him and I blew out an angry gasp of frustration.

Being able to work from home, particularly for carers who have a family to fit around, is a great advantage, but sometimes it can be a drawback. Most people can forget about their job when they leave their place of work, but when tensions are high and placements aren't running smoothly there is no clocking-off time, no haven to escape to.

Forcing my thoughts away from her brother, I made myself work through the tasks of the day: packing lunches, sterilising bottles, putting on a wash. It felt calming to go through the motions of everyday life and gave me a bit of breathing space to see things more clearly. I decided not to mention anything about Zadie's troubles to Emily and Jamie. Zadie had a follow-up appointment at the hospital later that day and I wanted to wait and hear what her options were before involving anyone else.

Megan woke on the dot of 6 a.m. and with her bottle warmed and ready I gathered her blanketed form in my arms, and settled myself on the sofa. Pressing gently on her chin so that I could position the teat over her tongue, there were a few noisy clicks until I managed to form a tight seal with my fingers and then, as the milk began to flow and I relaxed, there was the sound of footsteps on the stairs. I could tell it was Zadie by the careful hesitancy, as if she were walking on tiptoe. Skirting the walls of the room in her apologetic way, cardigan sleeves pulled down over her knuckles and clamped between tight fists, she drifted softly towards us.

'Morning, honey. I hope Megan didn't keep you awake?' The baby had woken twice during the night for a feed but I had swept her quickly out of her cot in the hope that Zadie wouldn't be disturbed.

Perching on the edge of the sofa, she glanced at Megan, then looked quickly away, as if the sight scorched her eyes. When I came to think about it, the timing for taking a new placement couldn't have been worse. But Megan was such a dear little thing, I hoped that the powers that be wouldn't decide to move her. 'No, it was fine.'

'How are you feeling this morning?'

'Fine, thank you,' she said, bobbing her head and forcing a smile.

Zadie toyed with her breakfast and scampered back to her room quickly afterwards, too embarrassed, I think, to face Emily and Jamie. Peggy called soon after they had left for school, even more breathless than usual.

'I'm so sorry I haven't been in touch sooner,' she said. 'I was on leave yesterday and no one passed the message on.' I pictured Peggy's jaw dropping as she received the news, staying there instead of recovering.

'That's OK,' I said. 'Things have been a little hectic here anyway.'

'Oh dearie me, I can imagine. I got your email. Poor Zadie. How far gone is she?' she asked, sounding so concerned that I felt an immediate flare of affection for her. She had shown such unquestioning support. Sometimes fostered children can divide foster carers and social workers just as other children may play one parent off against the other. But I felt confident that Peggy and I were united in our determination to take the best care we could of Zadie. It was a relief to feel that I wasn't a lone voice as I had been when caring for Phoebe.

I ran my free hand through my unruly curls. 'We'll know for definite later today but the doctor thinks around 20 to 25 weeks.'

Peggy groaned as she realised what the late stage might mean for Zadie. 'Oh dear. She'll have to go ahead with it if she's past 24 weeks.'

'Yes I know, Peggy. I know.'

We fell silent for a moment.

'Her father will have to be told, of course, but not before I've taken some advice from the police. I have a meeting with them later on today. I'm expecting that the brother will be arrested. Can you imagine how the father will react?'

'Hmmm,' I said, the muscles in my neck tensing at the mere thought. We fell silent again and when I asked the next question I found myself holding on a little tighter to the receiver. 'What's going to happen about Megan now?' I knew there was every chance that Peggy would want to move her, given the circumstances.

There was a pause, Peggy making a low humming noise as she gathered her thoughts.

'I know what you say about Zadie's reaction to Megan, but do you know what, Rosie? If she's keeping this baby I think it might just turn out to be the best thing that could have happened.'

I wasn't sure whether I was relieved for Megan or for myself but I relaxed my grip on the telephone and let out an audible breath, knowing that she wouldn't have to go through yet another disruption in her early life. And Peggy was probably right, I realised as I wound the curly telephone wire around my index finger. Perhaps, by watching us care for Megan, Zadie might feel a little less afraid of what loomed in her future.

As soon as I replaced the receiver I picked it up again. Des needed to be updated on the turn of events. He answered a few seconds after the call connected. 'Des, there's a problem,' I said. It wasn't the first time I'd started one of our conversations in this way and he replied with a calm, 'A-ha?'

'Zadie's pregnant.' I thought that was probably enough information to be going on with so I waited a few seconds before adding, 'She cut her stomach and I had to call an ambulance.' I waited another moment. 'It was awful, Des. And I've just found out that her brother is responsible.'

'A-ha,' he said slowly. 'OK. I'll try and get over in the next few days so we can have a wee chat.' I realised that while I saw Zadie's situation as alarming and tragic, in Des's world it was just another unremarkable day at the office. At first his under-reaction was welcoming and my pulse must have plummeted by at least a third. But then I thought of all of the other Zadies across the country and, though calmer, I felt terribly, unreservedly sad.

In the ultrasound department I settled Megan's car seat on the floor at my feet and turned just as Zadie was pulling up her robe to reveal her belly. It was so smooth and taut that I could hardly believe she was pregnant. I tried not to stare directly at her bareness, concentrating instead on the sonographer – a woman in her thirties with spiky blonde hair and sharp, angular features – as she squeezed some gel onto Zadie's skin. The name on the staff badge hanging from a lanyard around her neck read 'Helen'. 'It's all been a big mistake,' I was willing her to pronounce. 'The doctor must have been at the end of a very long shift.'

'There we are,' Helen said, smiling down at Zadie. 'Can you see that movement? That's baby's heart beating.'

My own heart responded to those words by sinking a little further in my chest. Zadie, who was lying rigid on the trolley, glanced at the screen, then squeezed her eyes shut and turned her head away. Since our arrival at the hospital she had answered all questions awkwardly, with one- or two-syllable whispered words and a pointed look in my direction, willing me to take over. She was pale and looked like she might throw up at any second. 'Well, goodness,' I said, pressing Zadie's hand as I responded on her behalf.

Helen continued a running commentary. 'Aw, the little cutie is sucking its thumb,' she said, running her index finger over the screen.

It really was a beautiful sight and, mesmerised, I stared at the silvery form, squinting a little until it came into focus. Floating serenely against a backdrop of black, the baby held a tiny fist to its mouth. Despite the circumstances, I found myself smiling, just for a moment. But then I glanced at Zadie's face. Her eyes were still screwed tightly together and she was grimacing as though in pain. I thought of all she would have to endure in the coming months and of all the decisions that would have to be made and my heart was swept away on a wave of pity.

'Can you tell how far along things are?' I asked gently, stroking Zadie's hand as I did so in an effort to cushion the reply.

'Absolutely,' Helen said, her tone still chirpy but gentler. I could see the sympathy in her eyes as she took in Zadie's anguished expression. She glanced at me and shook her head slightly as she clicked the button on a probe in her other hand. 'I'm just doing some measurements and I'll let you know.'

I took a few deep breaths, bracing myself.

'Baby's due date is predicted for 6 November, so that puts you at around 25 weeks by my reckoning.'

I'm not sure if Zadie realised the significance but she let out a muffled sob. Helen looked at me and tilted her head to the side, her eyes soft with compassion. I had worried that the medical staff might not be able to conceal their disapproval of such an early teenage pregnancy, but everyone, from the receptionist who registered us, to Suzanne, the midwife who had checked Zadie's blood pressure and weight on arrival, treated her no differently than I imagined they would behave towards a woman in her twenties.

After the scan we returned to the antenatal unit to see Suzanne. The midwife was somewhere in her thirties, with a high, bouncy ponytail and deep dimples, visible even when she wasn't smiling. She was wearing a light-blue uniform with a white plastic apron over the top and moved with a purposeful cheeriness. 'Right, lovely,' she said brightly as she ushered Zadie into a small side room. 'Now we've got your dates confirmed we can get you booked in.'

Zadie hovered in the doorway, bewildered. 'Can you do the rest for me, Rosie?' she asked tearfully. 'I need to go to the bathroom.'

She raced off before I'd managed a nod. My eyes met Suzanne's and she shook her head in pity. 'Poor girl. You realise it's too late to consider a termination?' she asked in hushed tones.

I nodded, pressing my eyes together and opening them slowly. 'What will it do to her, putting her body through childbirth at her age?' To me, what Zadie was going to have to endure was too awful to think about.

'You'd be surprised,' the midwife said with a grim smile. 'Girls much younger than Zadie have gone through labour. Somehow nature sees them through.' She looked at me, pursing her lips. 'It's not unusual to find girls in Africa who are grandmothers before they reach adulthood.'

'Oh no,' I said, waving the information away. It was heartbreaking. My eyes pricked with tears and I cleared my throat, choking a little cough.

'We'll take the very best care of her we can,' Suzanne said, placing her hand on mine. 'I think she's very lucky to have someone like you on her side.'

That evening the children went to bed early and after giving Megan a dream feed I ran a bath, hoping to soak my anxiety away. On the way home from hospital Zadie had retreated into a daze, going straight to her room as soon as we got home. I thought about the difficult decisions that lay ahead, strangely relieved that the option of a termination wasn't open to her. What would I have advised? I wondered, not even certain myself of the right thing to do. And even with that option removed, there were still some tough decisions to be made. Whatever Zadie decided might resonate with her for years to come, perhaps even for the rest of her life. Some girls Zadie's age kept their babies, I knew that – there were lots of them in mother and baby placements up and down the country – but this conception was so different. Zadie's baby would be born, not only out of rape but incest as well. What would giving birth do to her young mind, in those circumstances? I heaved a heavy sigh with the thought that, after going through labour, she would then have to decide whether to try and keep the baby herself, with all the conflicting emotions that might stir up, or offer the baby up to strangers.

My thoughts circled and eventually the tension in my neck eased. By then the water was barely tepid. Shivering, I climbed out and, hearing the telephone ring, I dried myself quickly and pulled on my long flowered dressing gown. Running down the stairs hoping that the shrill tone hadn't woken Megan, I snatched up the receiver and whispered a soft 'Hello', surprised to hear Sofia apologising for the late hour.

'That's OK,' I told her. 'I wasn't in bed.'

'Oh yes, very good,' she said in her deep velvety voice. 'I had to call. You see, I have some news.'

What she said took my breath away.

'We've found her, Rosie. We've found Nadeen.'

Chapter 17

The timing couldn't have been more fortuitous. The morning after Sofia's call I heard from Peggy. The social worker had passed news of Zadie's pregnancy on to her father, although he hadn't been told that Chit was responsible, and his reaction was to pronounce her 'dead to him'. Astonished and furious with him, Peggy and I had decided that Zadie should only be told the barest of details, and only if she pressed for information. I could understand that her father must have been shocked, but how could he possibly abandon her, just when she needed him the most?

But at least she might be on the way to having one close family member on her side, I thought, almost bursting with the longing to tell Zadie. I held myself back, having promised Sofia that I wouldn't mention anything until I heard more. Sofia had located Nadeen through a women's rights organisation but hadn't spoken to her directly – we needed permission from Peggy to share Zadie's personal information with anyone, even her sister – and so had no idea whether she had any desire to reconnect with Zadie. Peggy agreed that Nadeen could be contacted and suggested that she be pre-warned about the pregnancy before any face-to-face meeting was arranged. We already knew how strongly Zadie felt about finding her sister but the longing wasn't necessarily mutual. It was possible that the teenager would prefer to sever all ties with the past, and if that was the case we wanted to shield Zadie from the rejection.

There was another piece of news that needed to be shared, though. With Zadie's due date confirmed and the possibility of a termination removed, I had waited for an opportunity to tell Emily and Jamie that someone new would soon be moving into our little house. It came the following evening, when Zadie went up for a shower.

'Woowha, I didn't see that coming,' Jamie said, mouth gaping. 'I didn't even know she had a boyfriend. How did she keep that quiet?'

Behind him, Emily simply stared in silence, lips parted in shock.

I looked down, my lips pressed together.

'Zadie's far too shy for anything like that. I don't think she would ...' Emily stopped in mid-sentence, the implications sinking in. She looked at me and her eyes misted over. 'Oh no, Mum. Why would anyone do that to her? She's younger than me!'

'Do what?' Jamie asked, blinking. 'Oh,' he said, his eyes rolling as the penny dropped. 'You mean someone made her do it?'

'Shhh,' I said, waving my hand between them. 'Keep your voices down. All you two need to know is that she's going to have a baby. You mustn't question her about it or anything,' I said, looking pointedly at Jamie.

'Why are you looking at me?' he asked, nursing an injured expression as he flumped himself onto the sofa and picked up the TV handset. 'As if I would …'

'Sick, that's what it is,' Emily growled under her breath as she stormed after me into the kitchen. Nostrils flaring, she was staring at me in disbelief as I rifled around in the cupboard for a bag of flour. 'Mum, what are you doing?'

'Bright Heights is having a cake sale at the weekend. I promised to make some jam tarts.'

'Jam tarts?' she screeched. 'I don't get how you can just stand there and make jam tarts! How can you be so calm about this?'

Her fury counterbalanced Zadie's quiet acceptance and I listened to her tirade with an unexpected feeling of satisfaction as I pulled a pack of butter from the fridge. She was expressing the outrage I myself was feeling, and as I measured out the ingredients for the pastry and cut the butter into small squares my own anger began to quell.

Emily was still ranting when the doorbell sounded about ten minutes later. Checking my watch with sticky fingers, I walked to the door, wondering whether Des had decided to carry out one of his unannounced checks – we were supposed to have at least two surprise visits a year and I was well overdue for one. It was gone 7 p.m. though, a bit late, even for Des.

'I'm so sorry,' Jenny said, looking bereft as she stood on my doorstep. 'I just didn't know who else to turn to.' Even before she stepped into the hall I could see that she was trembling. 'Aiden's away and …'

'What's happened?' I asked, slipping my arm around her shoulder, being careful to keep my flour-covered hands away from her expensive-looking black shawl. She looked awful, her fine-boned features speckled with blotches, so unlike her usual immaculate self. Her eyes were rimmed with dark splodges of mascara, there was a heavy crease in her brow and her wavy hair was almost as crumpled as my own. 'My goodness, you're shaking like a leaf,' I said as I drew her into the kitchen.

The sight of Jenny seemed to take the wind out of Emily's sails. She stared at her for a moment, then lifted a hand to say 'Hi,' before discreetly leaving the room.

'I'm sorry, Rosie. It's just such a shock,' Jenny said as she sank down on one of the stools, breathing into a tissue.

'What is?' I asked, hastily washing my hands under the tap and reaching for a towel. I wondered what on earth could have happened. Perhaps Aiden had walked out on her, I thought, quickly dismissing the idea. Whenever I saw them together the affection between them was almost tangible. Maybe there was something wrong with one of her children?

'It's Billy,' she managed to croak before breaking into a sob. 'He's g-gone.'

My heart lurched with fear as I took the stool opposite her, remembering those forbidding statistics about the vulnerability of children in care. But Jenny was one of the most dedicated, attentive carers I had ever met. She wouldn't allow any child in her care to come to harm. If my own children had to be taken into care, Jenny was the foster carer I would be hoping for. An uneasy knot formed in my stomach. 'Gone where?'

'Gone,' she repeated, a little hysterically, flapping the sodden tissue through the air. Her nose was now a deep mottled red. 'They've taken him.'

'Who has?' I asked, trying desperately to keep up with the conversation. I had only spoken to Jenny a couple of days earlier, and although the siblings had moved on to long-term carers Billy's case hadn't even been listed to be heard by the adoption and permanency matching panel.

'Social services,' she wailed miserably. Between sobs, Jenny went on to tell me that the couple who were being considered as adopters for Billy had plans to emigrate to Australia. Jenny, knowing how attached Billy was to her, had decided to apply to make an Annex A application directly to the court, a right that foster carers gain once a child has been in placement with them for over a year. 'I told his social worker what I intended to do the day before yesterday,' she said, wrapping her arms around herself and shivering again, 'and so they came before he had his tea this evening and removed him so that I wouldn't have a chance to make my application.' She continued crying softly into her tissue.

'Oh no,' I said, my fingers touching my lips. I rubbed her knee with my other hand. 'What an awful shock for you.' And for him, I thought to myself, but I didn't say anything. Instead I asked, 'How did he react?'

She looked up at me. 'Oh, Rosie, you should have seen his face. He was so bewildered, clinging to me as I packed up his things. What must he have thought? They wouldn't even tell me where he was going. I asked if he could come to you but they looked at me as if I had no business even suggesting it.' She gave a bitter snort. 'Now I understand how birth parents feel.'

'I'm so sorry.' As I drew her into a hug I thought of the wine hidden away at the back of the top cupboard, still untouched from last Christmas. Brushing off the dried noodles clinging to the bottom of the bottle, I remembered the lengthy process I went through to register as a foster carer and my desperation to avoid saying the wrong thing.

My assessing social worker was a serious woman in her late thirties with mousy hair and a permanently stern expression. During one of our counselling sessions she asked me about my drinking habits and where alcohol is stored in the home.

'Oh, it never lasts long enough to need storing,' I joked. Her thin lips drew so tight they became almost invisible, and since then, if anyone ever brought a drop of alcohol over the threshold I would scurry away with it, burying it somewhere dark and out of sight.

I watched Jenny as I poured us both a small glass. She looked so bereft and my heart went out to her but the cold hard fact was that, however strong the bond, foster carers have no say in what happens to the children in their care. The best social workers consulted foster carers and took their feelings into account but they certainly weren't obliged to and it often didn't happen.

We talked until the early hours and Jenny slept the rest of the night on the sofa. By the time she left early the next morning she seemed calmer, though I sensed that letting herself into an empty house would revive the shock of Billy's removal.

It was as if the stars had aligned themselves to give Zadie an extra special gift on the most perfect day possible. The moment I had been waiting for came towards the end of August, on her 14th birthday. Zadie wasn't allowed to celebrate her own birthday since it went against her faith, so I made no reference to it out of respect for her. It had been a struggle to stop myself doing something special in celebration of the day she was born, and so when Sofia called, around lunchtime, I couldn't have been happier. It seemed that Sofia had personally met with Nadeen, who had been delighted to hear news of her sister. Shocked at the news of her pregnancy, she was desperate to meet up with her and offer some comfort.

And so it was a gloriously warm day in August when Nadeen walked up the path and knocked hesitantly on our door. It had been two days since I broke the news to Zadie and she had barely sat still since. Leaving her in the living room, quivering with anticipation and anxiously twirling her fingers around the bands on her wrist, I answered the door with my own stomach performing mini-somersaults in excited anticipation.

Nadeen was standing on the front step, her eyes already glittering with tears. Being older than Zadie, her face was leaner and her cheekbones more prominent; she was striking to look at, beautiful even, despite the grey smock top she was wearing over plain black trousers and absence of any make-up. She stood with her hands clasped in front of her, one wrestling with the other in the same way as her sister. The agonised openness in her face and her resemblance to Zadie melted my heart so that instead of standing aside to welcome her in I lurched forwards and pulled her into a bear hug. 'It's so lovely to see you,' I said, a little choked myself. Separating her hands, she hugged me back. As I pulled away there were tears streaming down her face.

'Thank you,' she spluttered, her eyes drifting behind me, towards the sound of light, hesitant footsteps coming down the hall. I turned to see Zadie standing a few feet away, her face alive with emotion. There was a moment of hesitation and then the two girls flew together, their arms wrapped tightly around one another, each sobbing on the other's shoulder. Sidestepping the pair of them as I passed them in the hall, I patted their backs and went quietly into the living room.

Eventually they pulled apart and followed me, their hands tightly interlinked as they walked to the sofa. Sinking down in unison and clasping hands tightly at their knees, they both stared at one another in wonder, as if they'd just woken from a wonderful but rather bewildering dream.

'I'm going to make some drinks,' I said softly. 'I'll leave you girls to chat for a while.'

Zadie nodded gratefully, her face streaked with tears. Nadeen brushed them away with the pad of her thumb. It was strange to see a young woman interacting with her sister in that way, as if Zadie was one of her own children. I guessed that the responsibility of looking after the family had fallen onto Nadeen's shoulders, as the eldest girl, a habit that hadn't been broken by their separation.

In the kitchen I took my time as I made some hot chocolate for the sisters and tea for myself, grateful for the chance to try and regain my composure. Above the sound of the microwave I could hear the soft burr of voices but when I walked back into the living room they fell silent, both regarding me shyly. They were still holding hands, releasing each other only when I offered them their drinks.

'I'm so grateful to you for trying to find me,' Nadeen said as I sat in a nearby armchair, my tea balanced on my lap, hands resting either side of the mug.

Freeing one hand I waved it through the air. 'No need to thank me. Sofia did all the hard work.' I hesitated for a moment, my eyes flicking to Zadie. 'We weren't sure how you'd feel about hearing from us.'

'Oh, I was so happy. It's been agony having to stay away, but I had no choice.' Nadeen set her hot chocolate down between her feet and grabbed Zadie's free hand. 'You do realise that, don't you, Zadie?' Again, she spoke tenderly, like a doting parent to a child.

Zadie frowned as if she didn't, but nodded anyway out of politeness.

'I couldn't put Zadie at risk by trying to contact her,' Nadeen explained, turning to me. 'Unless you've ever lived under the sort of complex code of honour we ...' she trailed off, the muscles around her jaw tensing with the memory. She lifted her chest and took another breath, trying to find the words to explain herself. 'Soon after I ran away I rang home to try and talk to Zadie but Chit wouldn't let me. He told me that our uncles had held a meeting. If I tried to take Zadie away with me there would be consequences for both of us.' She turned back to Zadie, her eyes brimming with tears again. 'If I'd known what was happening to you,' she whispered, her eyes falling to Zadie's rounded belly, 'I would have ...' She stopped, her voice trailing into a sob.

'Don't,' Zadie said, wiping away a tear of her own. 'It's all right.'

'No, it's not,' Nadeen spat out. 'It's not all right, Zadie.' She turned to me again. 'She's always been the peacemaker,' she said with a teary, rueful smile. 'Ever since Mama ...' She paused, her eyes flicking to Zadie again. She licked her lips and continued, '... left.'

'Do you know what happened to her?' I asked gently.

Again her eyes strayed to Zadie and she shook her head. 'Soon after she left Papa brought us to England. I was seven and you had just turned four, do you remember, Zadie?' She touched her chin, another tender, motherly gesture.

Zadie tilted her head to one side, considering, then shook it.

'No, I think you blanked a lot of it out. It was all so bewildering, coming to England, and without our mama. We all missed her so much.'

About half an hour later, when Zadie went to the bathroom, I got the chance to talk to Nadeen alone. I was about to ask her where she had been living when she turned to me and opened her mouth to say something. Stopping herself, she glanced towards the door, then shuffled along the sofa, only speaking when she was close enough to talk under her breath. 'It wasn't exactly true, what I said about our mother,' she said, twisting her mouth into a grimace. 'There was some sort of trouble back in Egypt. Mama displeased the family in some way and ...' she hesitated, took a breath '... the community attacked her. Zadie was there when it happened. By the time we got home she was alone, traumatised, and Mama was gone. We left for England soon afterwards.'

'Oh, Nadeen,' I said, my hand migrating to my mouth. It sounded to me like their mother hadn't turned her back on her family at all. I had a feeling that the truth was a lot more shocking than that.

'I'm afraid they killed her,' she said sadly, echoing my own thoughts. 'Papa said that she abandoned us but Zadie is the only one who believes him.'

My heart ached with pity for their mother and for them. When Emily and Jamie were small I became acutely aware of my own health, worried that they might be left alone without the love of their mother. If that had happened I would have wanted someone to do all they could to take care of them and I determined to do just that for Zadie, and her sister, if she wanted me to. 'Have you ever thought about reporting it?'

Nadeen shook her head. 'We were too young when we left Egypt. I've spoken to a legal advisor at the women's centre but she said that the police here have no jurisdiction to investigate anywhere else but the UK. I'm not sure we'd ever be able to find out what happened to her. One thing I do know, though – she would never have left us by choice. I was only young but I know that much. The boys never talk of it but I think they know the truth. Chit was never the same after she left: he's always been so angry.'

For the first time, I felt a glimmer of sympathy for Zadie's brother, although I quickly brushed it aside. I looked at Nadeen. 'Is that why you ran away? Because of your brother?'

She tucked her chin in. 'No, I never would have left Zadie there alone, not unless I had to. Papa had arranged to send me back to Egypt to be married. It was all arranged. The man was wealthy, well connected and 36 years old. So you see, I had to leave. I had no choice.'

I listened mutely, my only response a half-shake of the head. My thoughts drifted, quickly interrupted by the sound of a door opening upstairs, then light footsteps on the stairs, followed by heavier ones. I recovered my where-withal. 'You were very brave,' I said under my breath.

She smiled, grateful, but quickly grew serious when Zadie came back in the room, closely followed by Emily.

'This is my daughter, Emily,' I said. Emily smiled and perched on the arm of my chair. Zadie returned to her place next to her sister. Almost as soon as she had sat down Nadeen turned to her. She reached out for Zadie's robe, pinching some material from the sleeve and stretching it outwards before letting it drop. 'Why are you still wearing this?' she asked with an undertone of annoyance. 'There's no need for you to dress like that any more, Zadie. You're letting men trample all over your rights, just like Mama did.'

'It's to keep the patriarchy alive,' Emily piped up beside me. I threw her a meaningful hard stare but she either didn't notice or chose to ignore it. 'We're analysing *A Doll's House* in school and Mrs Roberts says that men love to objectify women because it gives them a feeling of power. Telling a woman how to dress is a man's way of removing her identity. Your robe is a symbol of oppression, Zadie.'

I glared at Emily in silent rebuke but she held my gaze, unrepentant. Whenever she sensed an injustice she would go off on a rant and there would be no stopping her until she either burnt out or ran out of words. Zadie's sister could say whatever she liked but I knew we could get into no end of trouble for putting forward our own opinions. Foster carers are supposed to remain neutral.

'She's right, Zadie,' Nadeen said, picking up the thread and continuing. 'Men buckle in the presence of attractive women, everyone knows that. If women cover themselves up, men feel less threatened because they're always in control. I'm not saying you should start wearing mini-skirts, Zadie. The Koran tells us that we should dress and behave modestly, but that doesn't mean we have to cloak ourselves from top to toe in black.'

Zadie's brow furrowed as she looked between Emily and her sister. Even though her pregnancy was no longer a secret, Zadie chose to keep wearing her robes. I suspected that it was more a case of hiding behind them than a conscious choice, but, even so, I didn't want her to feel pressured into turning her back on them. After a moment her eyes fell on mine and she asked, 'What do you think, Rosie?'

'Don't get me involved,' I said with an evasive laugh. 'It doesn't matter what I think.'

'Oh, but I really want to know.'

I thought of all the magazines in the newsagents that made me cringe when I had little ones in placement, particularly those that had come from an abusive background and then the over-sexualised adverts on television that were so difficult to avoid. I pursed my lips. 'I don't think you're being oppressed by your robe unless you're being forced to wear it,' I said, trying to take a mild line. 'And I think western culture is as guilty of objectifying women as anyone else. Having said that, it takes courage to question what your parents taught you, Zadie. I think it's important to follow your own heart. If you're wearing a burqa because you truly want to,' I waved my hand between Nadeen and Emily, 'then you mustn't listen to these two.'

Chapter 18

Peggy called just after lunch the next day. 'The brother has been arrested,' she said, launching straight into conversation. 'He's being interviewed at the moment.'

'Oh, goodness,' I said, feeling a little breathless. I hadn't expected things to move so quickly. 'Does her father know why?' I asked, trying to imagine how guilty he must feel, knowing that he had turned his back on his daughter when she was harbouring such an awful secret and all the while protecting the people around her from the knowledge.

'Oh, yes, he knows all right,' she said with a click of her tongue. 'But I'm afraid I can't tell you what you're hoping to hear, Rosie.'

I frowned. Surely her father would be horrified by the news, I thought, expecting him to plead for Zadie's forgiveness and beg her to return home.

'Don't get me wrong, I get the feeling that he's genuinely shocked. I don't think he had any idea what was going on. But he feels that Zadie is tainted by sin for allowing it to happen.'

I gave a little disbelieving laugh, pressing a hand against my cheek. 'She was 13 years old, Peggy,' I said, astonished.

'I know, Rosie. I know. You're preaching to the converted, remember? But he sees her as culpable and blames western culture for influencing her.'

To think that her brother had taken the life of his young sister and changed it irrevocably and yet it was still Zadie who was thought of as indecent beggared belief. How, in the twenty-first century, was it still possible for a woman, no, not even a woman, a child, to be blamed for rape? I was so incensed that I hardly listened to the rest of the conversation and when Peggy rang off I replaced the receiver with a flourish. My mind flashed back to a history lesson at school and the women condemned to burning in the thirteenth century by the Inquisition, their sin – having sexual intercourse with Satan. To my mind, tarnishing Zadie because of her brother's abuse was as skewed as burning 'witches'. It was hypocrisy beyond the pale.

I felt a sudden, overwhelming gratitude to Sofia for her tireless efforts to locate Nadeen. Since visiting, the teenager had emailed Zadie at least once, sometimes two or three times a day, her messages supportive and uplifting. Still strong in her faith, Nadeen encouraged Zadie to make the best of the hand she had been dealt. I got the feeling she was devastated about the pregnancy but also pragmatic. Her positivity would be invaluable to Zadie, I was certain.

Betrayed

My rage over the injustice shown by the rest of Zadie's family was still simmering as I loaded some bed linen into the washing machine that evening. I felt so frazzled that when the doorbell went I started, spilling a few flakes of washing power over the floor. Emily answered the door and before I even realised that it was Des he had picked Megan up from her carry-cot. Seconds later she was in his arms, her head tucked into his neck, a crocheted blanket tucked around her back. 'She's a wee cutie,' he said, bobbing from one foot to the other.

'Lovely, isn't she,' I said from the kitchen as I turned the dial on the washing machine. Ever so gently, Des transferred Megan to the crook of his arm, faintly humming an uncatchable tune. Probably one of his rock songs, I thought, twisting round to get a better view of the pair. There was something appealing about the sight: Des bobbing his head and smiling, Megan reaching out a tiny hand to touch his bristly chin.

'Look, Mum,' Emily called out. 'Des has been humanised.'

Des stopped humming and laughed. 'Watch it, wee lass.'

Just after 7 p.m., when Megan had finally managed to take a couple of ounces of milk, I prised her away from Des and tucked her up for a sleep. It was a lovely evening so I abandoned the washing up and, barefoot, we wandered into the garden to talk, closing the patio doors so that we couldn't be overheard. Warm air infused with a hint of honeysuckle drifted towards us as we sat at the patio table, but the beauty of the day and the vivid colours felt wrong somehow. After my earlier discovery I felt that it should have been stormy, the flowers jagged and strewn across a windswept lawn.

'It's just not fair, Des,' I said, as Emily had so succinctly put it when I told her the news. The words felt childish on my lips but fitting all the same. It simply wasn't fair. 'She's so lovely,' I said, my hand picking at the wickerwork on the seat of my chair. 'She doesn't deserve this.' My voice cracked and I cleared my throat. I had spent all day trying to keep my emotions in check and I wasn't sure I could hold out until later, when I would be alone. I tucked my hands at the nape of my neck and scrunched my neck back against clasped fingers, telling myself that I really didn't have a right to be so self-indulgent when Zadie was being so brave.

Des scratched his stubble, studying me intently.

'I just don't know how to help her,' I said. 'What is she supposed to do for the best?'

He gave a little shrug, then leaned across the table and touched my hand. 'It's difficult to know what the best thing would be. For now I think we just have to get her through the next few months. Put the big decisions on hold for a wee while.'

I sucked in an impatient breath. 'I just wish I'd noticed sooner. It might have simplified things.'

Des pouted, considering. He tilted his head. 'You mean a termination? Making a decision like that wouldnae be simple, Rosie. And I'm almost certain it would go against her faith.'

I rubbed my left hand over my nose so firmly that my eyes smarted. I swiped a few tears away. 'I know. I know you're right. I just feel sick to my stomach that I allowed

Chit near her at contact. He was leaning over her, being intimidating, and I sat on a bench reading a book.' I leaned my elbows on the table and grabbed at my hair, pulling it roughly back from my forehead. 'Why wasn't I stronger? Why didn't I stand up to him?'

'Supervising contact isnae easy, Rosie,' Des said softly, shunting his chair around the table until it was next to mine. 'Spotting the moment to intervene is something even social workers struggle with, and you havenae even had any training on it. Don't be so hard on yourself.'

'I just feel so angry.'

Des let out a little snort and shook his head. 'Sounds like a perfectly normal reaction to me.'

'Then how come you're so composed?' I asked with a touch of fierceness, wanting him to mirror my own rage. It was almost as if his stillness was acceptance, and acceptance was offensive.

He let out a humourless laugh. 'Social workers visit families in the aftermath of abuse, we type up reports containing the most sickening information and we read them out in the witness box, but seeing the effect it has on a child's life from the perspective of a foster carer, that's tough, Rosie. It's normal to feel the way you do.' Des paused for a moment. 'If it makes you feel any better, I feel exactly the same.' He made a fist and landed it in the palm of his other hand. Slap. 'I've just learnt over the years to contain it. If you don't,' he said softly, 'it might just break your heart.'

My head banged with the effort of holding myself together and I pressed my index fingers into my temples, releasing the pressure. Abruptly, Des stood, took me by the hand and pulled me into a bear hug. At first I was so surprised that I laughed out loud but the steady heat from his hands on the small of my back and the soft breeze brushing the back of my neck were so soothing that I closed my eyes and laid my head on his shoulder. Almost a foot taller than me, he stood at the perfect height, just right for me to relax into him. With the grass soft and warm beneath my feet and my ear pressed against his chest, so that all I could hear was the low thump of his heart, all the problems of the day were momentarily absorbed. I was filled with a warm rush of gratitude.

Chapter 19

By August, once Zadie really started to show, we barely made it 50 metres to the shops before someone had their hands on her belly or their head in Megan's pram. It's funny how the promise of new life seems to draw people in, inspiring genuine warmth even in complete strangers. I think many people long to reach out to their neighbours but fear of rejection keeps them locked up in their own solitary world. Perhaps the presence of little ones provides an immediate talking point, an opening. Whatever the reason, pregnancy certainly seemed to bring out the best in people.

There were occasional unpleasant vibes from passers-by, lips pursed in disapproving pouts, low whispers or prolonged stares. Zadie would freeze under all the attention and once or twice I felt like taking them aside and telling them the full story, asking them how disapproving they were then, but I would never have embarrassed Zadie in that way. I just wished that people would realise that things weren't always as they seemed.

The shock of acknowledging that she really was pregnant seemed to fade with each passing day, releasing Zadie from a tight grip of anxiety. Though she would obviously never have chosen to be in the position she found herself in, she was learning to cope with it so well, bearing the discomfort of pregnancy with a stolidity I could barely believe. Our relationship was definitely closer after all she had been through since coming to stay with us. As a consequence she was learning to confide in me instead of bottling everything up. It should have felt weird, discussing heartburn, sciatica and sore ribs with a 14-year-old girl, but it was easy to forget that Zadie, with her tummy ballooning and ankles swelling, was still a young girl and not a grown woman.

Towards the end of the month when Megan had just turned six weeks old, she blessed us with her first, fleeting smile. Dressed only in a pink cotton vest and nappy, she was laying on a rug in the conservatory, her arms batting the air as if trying to catch the light breeze drifting in from the open door. Kneeling at her side, I leaned over and she reached out a dimpled hand, extending her tiny fingers as she tried to touch my hair. I shook my head gently from side to side so that my curls swayed above her and her eyes widened in wonder. 'Swish-swish,' I said softly, smiling as she finally managed to clamp her fist around a lock of hair. 'Ow! That actually hurts,' I squealed, easing a forefinger into her palm to release her grip. 'You rascal,' I said, smiling and tickling her tummy.

And then it happened, and it was sheer luck that we all had our eyes on her at the time. Emily and Jamie cheered so loudly that Megan startled, her bottom lip jutting out with the threat of tears. Zadie was on her knees in an instant. 'There, it's all right,' she cooed, taking Megan's tiny hand in her own. I turned to Emily and she met my meaningful glance with a raised eyebrow. I began to hope then that Megan's arrival was going to be a blessing in disguise.

All being well, the baby, once born, would share Zadie's room. We decided to redecorate the space to suit both of them and Zadie chose a neutral, pale-yellow colour scheme. Jamie helped me to paint the walls and Zadie stencilled a border of white ducks just below the picture rail. Though I was sure that I should be feeling a little guilty about it, I was beginning to enjoy myself. I couldn't help but feel a little excited about the prospect of having another new baby around, particularly as Zadie was beginning to relax and show an interest in Megan. Two babies in the house would certainly keep us busy, but I didn't mind; if it were up to me I would have filled the house with little ones.

Sometimes my mother would join us in the evenings and the conversation would drift to her younger days, the wartime years growing up in Merseyside and then moving away to marry, and, inevitably, her own experiences of childbirth. 'Of course, back in those days we were given an enema as soon as we got to hospital. I told the midwife I'd rather not but they said I was being difficult and called the matron, a terrifying woman. One look from her and I told them they could do what they liked. That was the worst part of the whole experience. It was all plain sailing after that.' With the gentle wisdom of an older woman, she embellished the wonder of it all and glossed over the gruesome reality. There was only so much grit a girl in Zadie's position could take. Mum seemed to have a knack of saying just the right thing and I would often find the pair huddled together on the sofa, chatting, every so often breaking into soft laughter.

'Will it hurt, Rosie?' Zadie asked me one evening in early September as I sat beside her on the sofa and reached for her feet. Planting them to rest on the cushion on my lap, I rubbed the tender skin around her swollen ankles and tried to arrange my face into a non-committal expression. I blinked a few times, taking my time to answer. 'I mean, really badly hurt?'

Propped up against several plumped-up cushions, she leaned her head into one of them and awaited my reply with serious, searching eyes. I should have anticipated the question and prepared an answer in advance. Faking a yawn, I summoned a casual tone. 'It's all over with so quickly,' I said, noticing that Jamie had swiftly left the room. He probably sensed a conversation looming that he wanted no part of. 'Before you know it you'll be sitting up and drinking a cup of tea.' It was the line my mum fed me when I was pregnant with Emily, but I should have been more inventive because Zadie looked doubtful.

'Why does everyone say it's so bad then?'

'Erm. Well, everybody's experience is different,' I said, wondering how far I should go in glossing over the harsh reality. 'But they'll give you something to help that anyway.'

'I don't think I'm allowed pain relief,' she said mildly. My hand fell still on her foot. I stared at her and she looked back without a hint of gravitas. 'That won't matter, though, will it? If it's not that bad?'

I hesitated for a moment. 'Er, no, not really,' I said weakly. I stared into the distance for a moment, then rubbed her leg briskly. 'You must forget all your worries and trust me,' I said with an absolute certainty that I didn't feel. Naturally, Zadie had asked me to stay with her throughout the labour and of course I had agreed but the thought of what she was going to have to go through was already keeping me awake at night. In truth, I wasn't sure my squeamish stomach would survive the drama. 'You are going to be fine and so is the baby.'

Half-nodding, she allowed her eyes to close and asked no further questions. I suspected that she was afraid of what she might hear if she prodded me for more details. However was she going to find the courage she would need when the time came? I wondered. But then, she'd been through so much already. I hoped that her strength of character and quiet resilience would be enough to get her through.

Chapter 20

Peals of laughter and happy shouts floated in from the garden the next day as I stood at the hob, blinking against the rising steam from the home-made vegetable soup I was stirring in a large saucepan. Curious about what was unfolding in the garden, I turned the gas down and, leaving our lunch to simmer, I pulled some freshly laundered sheets from the washing machine and headed for the back door, a sweet fruity fragrance rising as I draped them over my arms.

Pulling up short in the doorway, I watched Jamie hammering down the path on his skateboard with my heart in my mouth. There was nothing unusual about his kamikaze spins but what stopped me in my tracks was the sight of Zadie, tearing along in his wake. At the end of the garden Jamie stopped and with a deft flick of the heel the board flipped upwards, into his outstretched hands. Handing it to Zadie like a baton, he jogged backwards up the gently sloping path and tilted his hand in the air, demonstrating his technique.

Betrayed

Clutching the damp sheets to my chest, I rolled backwards on my heels and then up on my toes, readying myself to intervene. My lips moved to shape the words but the expression on Zadie's face held me back. Her features were alive; skin glowing, eyes bright and carefree as she smiled at Jamie and positioned the board in front of her. I faltered, hesitant to deny her a few last moments of childhood. Encouragingly, Jamie supported her hand as she climbed on the board and before I could muster a shout she was away, sailing along the paving stones, her arms outstretched for balance, my son whooping and laughing behind her. A light wind tugged at her robe, pulling it back to reveal the tight ball of her tummy.

Moments later the board wobbled and her arms jerked manically up and down as she staggered, struggling to stay upright. Dropping the sheets, my hands flew to my mouth as I watched Zadie lean forward, her hand clutching her swollen belly. Jamie was at her side in seconds, his arm supporting her elbow, his face clouded with concern. She grimaced as she half-limped to the swing, Jamie gently guiding her along. She's barely half a year older than him, I thought, the sight causing something to shift in my chest.

Becoming aware of a sore spot at the back of my throat, I wasn't sure I could trust myself to hold it together. Suddenly cold, I went to my bedroom to retrieve my oldest, most comfortable cardigan, tucking it beneath my chin on the way downstairs. In the kitchen, the soup was thickening and beginning to bubble over. Setting the saucepan aside from the heat, I pulled my cardigan on, wrapped it tightly around myself and lifted one arm to my face, muffling my sobs in the woollen sleeve.

The weeks passed quickly and soon Zadie was in her final month of pregnancy. With no contact between Zadie and her family, the stress of the past months faded and our days were instead filled with a sense of peace. It was as if the soft blankets and delicate cotton sleep-suits dotted around the house were cushioning Zadie, distancing her from the unpleasantness of the past and smoothing her transition to motherhood. Megan had settled into a routine and was feeding well, managing to take more milk. With her sleeping for longer periods during the night, I began to feel less tired myself, my energy slowly returning.

There was now no hiding Zadie's pregnancy, even in her baggiest cardigan, and, as her bump grew, so did Emily and Jamie's excitement. Zadie herself was coping well with the discomfort of a burgeoning tummy, but one Thursday evening in early November, when she was about three weeks away from her due date, she stood next to me in the kitchen and leaned back against the worktop with a heavy sigh.

'How are you doing?'

Staring down at the point where her feet would be, she mumbled, 'Not good.'

Pulling first at one rubber glove and then the other, I draped them over the edge of the sink and put my arm around her. That was it. The floodgates opened and she dissolved into tears. 'Everything hurts, Rosie,' she sobbed. 'My back and my tummy, my legs, my ribs. Even my skin.'

'Oh dear, it does get tough towards the end, honey,' I said, my own anxiety rising with hers. She was so slight and fragile that it was a worry to think of the strain and discomfort her body must have been under. 'But you're doing so well.'

'I'm not,' she wailed. 'Can you get them to take it out?' She clasped my hands, pleading. I could hear the panic in her voice.

'Come here,' I said, leading her to the sofa and supporting her as she lowered herself, palms down behind her to ease the transition. I gave her a hug and when I pulled away her eyes were glistening with tears.

'I'm sorry, Rosie,' she said, dabbing her face on the sleeve of her robe. After a few moments she took a deep breath and buried her face in her hands. 'I can't stand being me,' she said shakily, her voice muffled by trembling fingers. 'I always mess everything up.'

'You haven't messed anything up.' I handed her a tissue from the pocket of my cardigan. She tilted her head up and took it, dabbing her nose as she looked at me. 'None of this was your fault, do you understand that?'

She looked away, then glanced back and gave a half-nod. 'But my life is such a mess. How can it be anything else now?'

I couldn't blame her for feeling pessimistic, with the way her life had gone so far. I wanted to reassure her that the landscape of her past could be altered. Possibly never erased, but brushed over with gentler, softer strokes so that her future could become a blank page, free for her to colour it any way she chose. I rubbed her shoulder. 'We all have times when we drift a little off course, honey.'

Her head shot up. 'Even you?'

She was looking at me in disbelief and I suppressed a laugh. Whatever image I was projecting clearly wasn't accurate. Often I had heard people say how calm I appeared to be and it always struck me as strange; hearing about the awful things that people do to each other scared me half to death. Thankfully, no one seemed to realise how close I sometimes came to *not* holding it all together. 'What I've found is that some of the most special times in life follow the worst.'

She smiled at that and laid her head on my chest.

By the following evening Zadie was calmer, back to her quiet tolerance. We had our dinner later than usual that day as Des had called and was going to join us after his last visit. At the dining table, Zadie had barely started on her dessert when she gently set her spoon on the table and looked at me. 'Sorry, Rosie. I'm so tired. I think I'll go to bed.'

'OK, sweetie. Best you get some rest, if you feel like that. You've had a bit of a day of it, haven't you?'

Smiling around the table as the others said goodnight, she had barely shuffled two steps when she gasped, her hand shooting out to grab the back of Des's chair. We were all on our feet in an instant, me with my hand around the place her waist used to be. 'Are you all right?'

Straightening, she frowned and let out a lungful of air. 'Yes, fine,' she said, her small hand rubbing the underneath of her bump. 'I just had a shooting pain but it's all right. It's gone now.'

* * *

Betrayed

About half an hour after Zadie went to bed I could hear her moving around up in her bedroom. Unusually, Des was still camped out on the sofa playing *FIFA* with Jamie. I thought perhaps he hadn't yet adjusted to going home to an empty house, but I didn't mind. It was nice to have his company and the children loved him being around. I was just thinking about stirring myself to offer everyone a mug of hot chocolate when Zadie came back down.

'Oh what great timing,' I said, half-standing. 'I was just about to make a –' I stilled, my heart beginning to pound. 'Are you all right, honey?'

She grimaced. 'I've got cramps in my stomach. I think maybe I ate too much.'

Straightening, I glanced at Des. He raised his eyebrows. 'I don't think so, sweetie,' I said, using my best soothing voice.

Her eyes widened. 'Oh no, Rosie. Is this it? Do you think this is it?'

'Could be, honey,' I said. 'Very likely, I'd say.'

Emily and Jamie were on their feet in seconds, circling and watching avidly, as if the event might unfold there and then, on the living-room floor.

'Give her some space you two,' I said, laughing. 'Jamie, you go and fetch Zadie's overnight bag, would you?' I had packed everything a couple of weeks earlier and left the bag stowed underneath Zadie's bed. I wanted to have a quick check-through to make sure I hadn't forgotten anything.

Jamie shuffled back a few steps, his eyes fixed on Zadie.

'You're not going to miss anything, Jamie,' I said, waving my hand to hurry him along. 'It might even be a false alarm.'

As if to prove me wrong, the carpet beneath Zadie's feet grew darker, the stain growing outwards. With a look of horror, Zadie leaned over, arching one bare foot and then the other. Tears pooled in her eyes. 'Ah-h, Rosie. What do I do?' she asked in panic, hopping from one foot to the other.

Emily's eyes widened. Jamie spun on his heels and fled. Des, who had been silent until that point, raised his eyebrows again and let out a soft whistle.

A short while later, after Zadie had cleaned herself up and the puddle lay hidden under a thick towel, I reached for the phone to call my mother, rubbing the small of Zadie's back with my other hand. Mum had volunteered to stay over and look after Megan when the moment arrived and I wanted to catch her before she settled herself for the night.

Ten minutes later Mum arrived at my door with a flat wrapped package tucked under her arm and a look of anticipation. 'It's perishing out there,' she said as I took her by her free hand. 'I don't envy you going out in it at this hour.' There was something about my mother's manner that always brought calm to any situation. I was hoping that Zadie would feel it too.

'Do I get a cup of tea then?' she said, kissing Zadie on the cheek and smiling at Des. 'Hello, Des. I was halfway through watching my soaps when you called, Rosie. Zadie, this is for you.'

Betrayed

Mum passed the package around Des and Zadie took it, staring at the plain light-blue paper in confusion, as if we were playing pass the parcel and she couldn't quite believe the music had stopped with her.

'Go on then, open it,' Mum prompted.

With a look of puzzlement Zadie turned the package over in her lap and picked at the tape until it puckered. The wrapping paper rustled with a soft shooshing as she tore it open to reveal a folded patchwork quilt. Pinching one of the bound edges between her fingers and thumbs, she stood up and shook it so that the quilt unfurled, its opposite edge sweeping the floor.

We all crowded around, staring at the fine stitches and intricate patterns in awed silence. The front of the quilt was formed of hundreds of tiny triangles, each complementing the next in pastel shades of pale yellow and duck-egg blue. All the way around the edge, Mum had embroidered the words, *to hope*, *to dream*, *to cherish*, and nestled in the centre, on white linen in the shape of a cradle, was a patchwork Mother Goose dressed in bonnet and shawl. Zadie tucked the top of the quilt under her chin and ran her fingers over the padded top. For a moment she just stared at it and when she eventually looked up there were tears in her eyes. 'You did this for me?'

'For you,' Mum said, '*and* baby, of course.'

'Thank you so much,' Zadie said, still overcome. 'It's beautiful.'

'You're very welcome,' Mum said, patting her on the shoulder. 'How are you feeling anyway?'

'Scared,' Zadie whispered, her lower lip quivering.

'You're bound to be, pet,' Mum said in her most tender voice. A practical woman, my mother was never one to waste much time on sympathy, so my heart melted whenever she softened. I wanted to give her a hug. 'But you've just got to get on with it, girl,' she added, adopting her usual no-nonsense style. And of course, she was right about that. There was no going back now.

By 11 p.m. we were sitting side by side on the sofa, Mum and I reminiscing about our own experiences of childbirth, still whitewashed of course, for Zadie's benefit. Even at their age Emily and Jamie were still fascinated to hear about their own arrivals and my heart ached a little for Zadie as we spoke, wondering whether she had ever heard her own birth story from either of her parents.

Des was only half-listening, his attention focused on the natural birthing leaflet that one of the midwives had given Zadie. I had skimmed through it a couple of weeks earlier and managed to persuade Zadie to practise some of the breathing techniques with me, but the most useful suggestion seemed to be 'Imagine yourself as a flower, slowly opening'. Des was taking it all very seriously, though, his expression intent as he read. When the next contraction hit, Zadie broke into a sweat, her breaths fast and shallow. I could actually see her stomach rippling so I knew things were progressing.

She gripped my hand and I sat beside her, breathing exaggeratedly and encouraging her to do the same. Des grimaced as if the pain was contagious. 'Try imagining that you's lying on a beautiful sandy beach,' he said with strained merriment. 'It's hot and you have all the power of the sun concentrated in your solar plexus.'

My mother gave him a sidelong glance and shook her head.

'Breathe through it, lassie,' Des said, reading straight from the booklet. 'Let the pain wash over you's like a wave.'

'Oh, good heavens,' Mum said, her voice cracking with a chuckle. 'Hark at Miriam Stoppard over there.'

There would have been something vaguely comical about Des's attempts at midwifery if I hadn't been so nervous about what Zadie was about to go through. At least she had escaped FGM, I thought. That was one small mercy to be thankful for. What she would have to endure otherwise, I didn't even want to imagine for a second.

'How about you make us some tea, Des?' I suggested, trying to distract him.

He nodded several times, without taking his eyes off Zadie. 'Tea, yes. Good idea.'

Part of me wanted to delay going into the hospital. I knew once we were there it would mean monitors, internals and all sorts of other interventions. Home was a far more relaxing place to be in early labour, but if I'm honest I was scared. With Zadie being so young, it seemed like such a great responsibility, and besides, watching Des clucking around her with a look of imminent panic on his face was really getting to me. He meant well, bless him. He was so concerned, so gentle and protective, but when he switched the kettle on and offered to make Zadie 'a nice cheese roll' to go with her drink, I'd had enough.

'Cheese roll?' Mum said, looking over her glasses incredulously. 'Bloody cheese roll? Would you fancy a cheese roll if you knew you had to pass something the size of a watermelon before morning?'

Zadie gulped.

'Ssshhh, Mum,' I hissed.

'Well,' she muttered, rolling her eyes.

Des snickered, not at all offended. 'It says here that some women can become exhausted. I thought she might need an energy boost.' He leaned into the living room and angled the leaflet towards Mum so she could see he wasn't making it all up.

Mum scoffed. 'Complete tripe. The people that write that stuff have probably never even had a baby.'

'Mum,' I said warningly, though I needn't have worried about Des's feelings. There was a twinkle in his eyes – I think he enjoyed a bit of gentle sparring. 'Come on, sweetie,' I said. 'I think it's time we went in.'

Zadie was gripped by another contraction. Her face creased in pain. She leaned over the sofa and moaned. Jamie stood in the hall, shaking his hands at his sides and wobbling his knees as if warming up for a race. Emily sat on the arm of the sofa, nibbling her nails. 'Can we come in as well?' Jamie asked.

Zadie's eyes widened in horror.

'I think not, Jamie. I'll keep you all informed. You can take my bed, Mum,' I told her.

'Oh no, don't you worry about me. I'll be on hot coals until I hear from you. It'll be the sofa for me. And remember, Zadie,' Mum called out as Des and I walked either side of her down the hall like doting, expectant grandparents, 'there's nothing more natural than having a baby. Those women that scream and shout are just attention seekers making a fuss.'

When I came to think of it, I remembered Mum trying that line on me, when I called her to let her know that my labour had started. It had worked too, until a midwife clipped a monitor to my swollen tummy and winced. 'Ooh, they're strong ones. You're coping very well.' From that moment the pain kicked in and the howling began. It took three days to get my voice back. 'I thought you said it was no worse than toothache,' I had croaked to Mum with a resentful look, Emily beside me in her crib.

'I never said anything of the sort,' she'd insisted.

Now, as Des and I helped Zadie down the front steps, Mum gave me a complicit smile. Our breath misted in cold air that smelt faintly of smoke. Des guided Zadie into the passenger seat of my car with a gentle hand on her back. 'Good luck, lassie,' he said, leaning over to squeeze her arm. 'You too, Grandma,' he said to me, smiling.

At the maternity unit we were greeted at reception by Suzanne, the midwife who had first booked Zadie in, just a few short weeks earlier. I was pleased to see her; she moved with sure-footed nimbleness, like a tigress, and had the sort of face that babies would respond to: open and doll-like, with big eyes and long lashes.

I had called ahead to let them know we were on our way and to explain the situation, so that Zadie could be spared any embarrassing questions from inquisitive staff.

'Hi, Zadie. Let's get you comfortable, shall we?'

Zadie nodded, her attempt at a smile turning into a rictus of pain as another contraction rippled through her. Gripping a tight hold on the high reception desk, she rested her head on a pile of notes, breathing through another contraction.

'That's what we like to see,' Suzanne chirped, giving Zadie's back a quick rub. 'I can see we won't be sending you home like we do some. Well done, Mum,' she smiled, patting my arm, 'for letting things progress so nicely at home.'

With Zadie's contractions coming quite closely together during our journey, I had started to feel a little more anxious, so it was lovely that Suzanne gave the impression of such brisk efficiency.

In the delivery suite, Suzanne whipped a sheet of blue paper from the bed and laid a fresh one out, her deft moves instilling me with even more confidence. The room was a pale yellow and lit with several lamps, the low lighting casting a gentle glow over everything, even the enamel sink. Sheer white voile hung either side of a slightly open window, flapping gently in the night air. The breeze did nothing to cool the room, though; the heat seemed to shimmer, and, feeling dizzy, I quickly removed my coat.

'Let's get these off,' Suzanne said after washing her hands. Her tone left no room for refusal and Zadie undressed quickly, removing her headscarf first, then her robe. Suzanne helped her into a back-fastening robe, the name of the hospital stamped in tiny pink and blue letters.

Zadie looked even younger and more vulnerable than ever in the large hospital gown, her bump looking alien on her thin body.

Zadie's contractions were coming regularly, every three minutes or so, and Suzanne had hooked her up to a mobile foetal heart monitor so that she could move around easily. The next one had her down on her hands and knees on the linoleum floor, howling like a wounded animal. I knelt down beside her, rubbing her back and repeating soothing words over and over. When it subsided she sank her head into my lap. 'This is bad, Rosie,' she said, her voice woozy.

She remained on all fours and thrashed her way through the next couple of contractions with her head still buried in my lap. When they were over and she rocked back onto her heels, her face was sweaty and her pupils like pin-pricks. Three hours passed in the same way, with Zadie moaning, panting and sighing while her tummy rose and fell. Sometimes she clung to me but then seconds later she would groan and push me away. I tended to her as well as I could, rocking, patting, massaging and singing as she panted, groaned and yelped.

After another hour or so I felt a tempo change. Zadie's contractions seemed to have strengthened and she withdrew further into herself, becoming so intensely focused that I wasn't even sure she could hear me. I began to feel uneasy. I knew having a baby was natural, but not this young, not when she was still just a child herself. I tried hard to hide my fear but even with the calming presence of Suzanne, who really was marvellous, I couldn't shake the feeling.

Another contraction arrived on the tail of the one before, this time with seemingly no warning. Zadie flung her arms around my neck and hung there, her dark hair plastered flat to her scalp. Grateful for a draught from the window, I leaned against the high-backed chair and shook my head a few times, trying to keep myself awake enough to summon fresh encouragement. I wasn't absolutely sure that my words were reaching her, either that or my well-worn phrases – 'That's it, well done, sweetie!' – were wearing thin. Every so often, as Zadie gripped my hand and panted her way through the contraction, I would glance at Suzanne for reassurance. 'We're progressing nicely,' she regularly intoned in a sing-song voice while moving methodically around the room. I loved the way she said it, as if we were all in the same boat, but I wondered if any of the other women she tended in labour had reacted badly to the comment.

After another hour of regular contractions without much respite in between, Zadie became too weak to continue with her circuits and sank into bed. 'I can't stand this, Rosie,' she complained, her hair ebony against the stark white sheets, skin burnished. Moments later Suzanne strode purposely across the room and my heart sank.

'Oh no, please don't,' Zadie wailed as Suzanne closed the window.

'I'm sorry, sweetie. It's getting a bit cool in here and we have to keep it warm for the baby.'

'But what about me?!' Zadie cried out, her face tightening as another contraction rolled through her. It was the first time I had ever heard her raise her voice.

Suzanne shushed her briskly and suggested an internal examination instead, to see how close Zadie was to the second stage. It didn't strike me as much of an appealing trade-off, although thankfully Zadie, at that moment, was blissfully unaware of the fate awaiting her. Gasping on some gas and air, she clenched my fingers tightly, her eyes wide in horror as Suzanne carried out the task. The moment it was over and I saw the midwife's face as she pulled off her latex glove, I knew it wasn't good news. 'Two centimetres,' Suzanne announced in what sounded like an encouraging tone, though as she turned from Zadie's view she grimaced and raised her eyebrows at me.

Zadie, having read up on the stages of birth weeks earlier, wasn't easily duped, and she took it badly. 'I can't do it any more, Rosie,' she sobbed, laying her head against my chest.

Feeling helpless, I looked at Suzanne.

'Have something to help then, sweetie-pie,' Suzanne said. 'We can give you some Pethidine. It'll help take the edge off the pain. It's just a small injection, lots of people have it.'

Zadie looked at me. Her eyes were unfocused, her face flushed. 'Should I, Rosie?'

I stroked her damp hair back from her forehead. After she had told me that her family didn't approve of pain relief, and confused by the conflicting information on the internet, I had checked with Sofia to see if there was any religious basis for refusing help during labour. Sofia had told me that some Muslims objected to the use of narcotic pain relief but the general feeling among clerics was that the well-being of the patient was the most important priority. 'There's nothing wrong with accepting a little help, honey.'

Moments later Suzanne had drawn the Pethidine into a syringe and was injecting it into Zadie's hip. Even before the midwife had finished dabbing the jab site with a wad of cotton wool, Zadie began to react. The first thing I noticed was that her breaths were coming in little gasps. Then out of nowhere she went into a coughing fit that left her puce.

I looked back and forth between her and Suzanne, but the midwife was busy examining the monitor displaying Zadie's blood pressure and pulse. The numbers seemed to be running wildly, all over the place. Bright fluorescent strip lights snapped on overhead and I realised that Suzanne must have flicked a switch to power them up. Without the dimmed lighting the room was instantly transformed, no longer welcoming and homely but sanitised and clinical. Anxiety heightened my senses and I suddenly became aware of a pungent antiseptic smell that I hadn't noticed earlier. Acutely aware of a sharp change in Suzanne's demeanour, my hands shook as I poured Zadie some water and offered it to her, but she was wheezing too much to drink it. 'What's going on, Suzanne?' I said, trying to keep my voice steady.

'It's all right,' Suzanne said. Her tone was still sing-song but there was a brisk intensity to her movements. She ran her index finger over the printouts monitoring the baby's heartbeat, slipped an oxygen mask over Zadie's face, then calmly pressed a big red button on the wall above the bed. A loud bleep resonated along the corridor outside and a harsh beam of red light was projected in the space beneath the door.

Zadie's face drained of all colour and then she suddenly whipped off her mask and threw up on the sheet in front of her. 'There,' I said with cheery unease, rubbing her back and beginning to gather the sheet into a ball. 'You'll feel better now, isn't that right, Suzanne?'

But she didn't look better at all, and Suzanne, her concentration narrowed, didn't answer. It was then I noticed that Zadie's face was swollen. She began clawing at her throat. 'I can't breathe, Rosie,' she gasped, her eyes searching mine in panic. 'I'm going to die.'

'No you're not,' I said, trying to breathe away the tight band of anxiety around my own chest. I'm usually good at manufacturing an appearance of calm when I feel nothing of the sort, but my fear was beginning to fan into panic. I pulled myself upright and took a few long, calming breaths. 'You're just having a bit of a reaction to the medicine, that's all, sweetie.'

Seconds later a tall black man burst into the room. Suzanne began speaking immediately, passing on information in a calm but urgent tone. Dressed in a shirt and tie, with a stethoscope swaying around his neck, the consultant gave a curt nod in comprehension. I was relieved by his air of confidence, the way he strode towards us with absolute certainty of what needed to be done. Tipping the bed flat with a single touch, he leaned over Zadie, pressed a crooked forefinger to her brow and the pad of his thumb to her cheekbone and shone a light in her eyes. A blonde, young-looking doctor followed and the consultant barked an order at her, something technical that I didn't understand. Within moments it seemed as if the whole room was full of people. There were loud crashes as they whipped open drawers, pulling out tubes and rustling white packages with brisk competence.

Each moved deftly around the other and, through my terror, I marvelled at how they managed to keep so many plates spinning in such a pressurised situation. They seemed to know exactly what they were doing, moving around one another with an urgent, methodical calm. It was a perfect choreography that was both stunning and terrifying to watch. I noticed a steel tray being passed through a gap between the bodies surrounding the bed and a drip suddenly appeared in Zadie's arm. I found myself swept back, away from Zadie.

'Rosie!' Zadie croaked, gasping for breath.

'I'm right here, honey.'

'Don't leave me, Rosie.' There was utter panic in her voice now.

'I'm not going anywhere,' I called out. Instinct was shouting at me to go to her and pull her into a hug so that she would know she was loved and that she wasn't alone in all of this. I tried to touch her hand instead but I couldn't reach. 'I'm right beside you, honey.'

Raising myself on tiptoes, I tried to see past the sea of heads. The tall black doctor spoke quickly but precisely; most of what he said sounded like a different language. It was horrifying yet hypnotic and I couldn't tear my eyes away from the hospital bed. It must have been a few seconds before I realised that the gentle tug on my arm was Suzanne, drawing me away. 'Let's leave them to sort her out, Rosie,' she said, her voice soft but firm.

'Don't fight us, darling,' a disembodied voice said. There were now so many people in the room that I was losing track, although I recognised the accent as Irish. I kept swallowing to rid myself of the panic. Surely nothing bad can happen to her now, I thought, not after everything she'd already been through, as if her traumatic past meant a ransom had been paid providing immunity from future misery.

'Is she going to be all right?' I asked Suzanne, my voice quivering. By that point I had given up trying to put a brave face on it.

'She's in safe hands,' Suzanne said firmly, gently clasping my upper arms and ushering me back into the bright white corridor. 'I'm afraid we'll have to leave them to get on with it now.' She showed me to the relatives' room and assured me that she would let me know as soon as there was any news, but I was too tense to stay in one place. After a couple of minutes I slipped back into the corridor, in time to see some nurses wheeling a trolley swiftly around a bend and out of sight.

The air swirled with the smell of hospital food – boiled carrots, cabbage and roast chicken – so much so that my stomach rolled in protest. At least it was cooler though, I thought, as I headed towards the exit. Distantly, footsteps echoed and there was the sound of a telephone ringing. The cold, early morning air hit me with a rush and I stopped for a moment a few feet from the entrance, shivering. My coat was still in the delivery room, I realised, so I couldn't even text home to let them know what was going on.

'Mrs Lewis?' The consultant who had tended to Zadie in the delivery room was striding towards me down the corridor wearing a pale-blue smock top over wide-legged trousers of the same colour. When he reached me he shook my hand, patting my arm with his free hand. 'Mother and baby are fine. We had to perform an emergency caesarean but Zadie is conscious now and breathing for herself. We'll be taking her straight to the intensive care unit to keep a close eye on her.'

I pinched my eyes closed with relief. All the stress of the past 24 hours seemed to melt away, leaving me momentarily euphoric. I could feel all the colour and warmth returning to me. 'Thank you so much,' I said, barely able to meet his eye I was so in awe of him.

He smiled, squeezed my hand, then turned and walked away down the corridor. I watched him go, marvelling at his modest, down-to-earth manner and the fact that he had deigned to speak to me at all. Moments later, as the consultant's footsteps faded to a dull thud, my energy drained away. With my vision wavering, I leaned my head against the cool white wall and closed my eyes. It was all I could do to keep upright. Light-headed, I realised I had last eaten on Friday evening, which was what? I frowned. I couldn't even work out how long ago. Trying to summon the energy to hunt for a vending machine, I became aware of the sound of more footsteps. As they drew closer I turned to see a midwife with blonde hair and a blue uniform much like

Betrayed

Suzanne's was walking towards me, her head tilted, her arms cradling a tiny baby.

'Mrs Lewis?'

I nodded, wincing in the harsh light.

She smiled. 'Here we are, Nanny,' she said warmly, planting the tiny infant snugly in the crook of my arm. I looked down at the delicate sleeping face, so like Zadie's, the crescent of dark lashes so long that they rested on her cheeks. 'Boy? Girl?' I asked, realising that I hadn't even asked the consultant what sex the baby was. My eyes fixed on the little woollen hat that my neighbour had knitted for the baby and Zadie had insisted on packing; the midwives must have found it in her hospital bag.

'Girl. Five pounds six ounces.'

'And she's healthy?' I asked, subconsciously running my hands over her fingers.

'She scored 9 on the Apgar. She's absolutely fine. No adverse effects from Mum's reaction.'

I let out a sigh and thanked her with a brief smile before returning my attention to the baby. I stroked a tiny hand and her eyes fluttered open. She stared at me with a sort of wonder and I felt a deep clawing sensation in my stomach, almost as if I was afraid. Whether it was fear of what the future held for them or the realisation that they were both so vulnerable, I had no idea. I just knew it was there, a pressing feeling that was to stay with me through the weeks to come, however relieved I was that the birth and all its drama were behind us. I resolved to do all I could to make sure this little one would have the best possible chance of staying with her mother.

Zadie might be without her family but she had us, and I was going to make sure she had as much love and support as she needed to get her through.

Later that evening, after going home to give everyone the good news, I returned to the hospital, delighted to hear that Zadie had been transferred to a ward. The teenager looked colourless as she lay in bed, half-propped up against several white pillows. She was surrounded by tubes and there was a free-standing monitor beside her bed emitting a soft bleep.

Zadie's dark hair was clamped tightly to her head by the elastic of the oxygen mask on her face. I curled my fingers around her hand and leaned over her, careful not to dislodge the crocodile clip attached to her index finger. Her hand was cold, the skin flaky and dry. Her eyelids flickered and her long lashes seemed reluctant to part, clinging at the ends as she slowly opened her eyes. She blinked several times and frowned, swallowing hard.

'Hello, honey,' I said, smiling.

She parted her lips and tried to speak but all that came out was a croak, the oxygen mask misting up. She closed her eyes and shifted her weight on the pillow, angling her head up. Her mouth twitched again. I leaned in closer and gently eased the mask to her chin, my ear to her mouth. A sharp antiseptic tang rose to greet me. 'Where is it?' she asked, her eyes travelling over me, as if the baby was concealed beneath my coat.

'The baby? She's with the nurses outside. Would you like to see her?'

She shook her head and sank her head back to the pillow with a sigh. I nodded and replaced her mask, noticing the single tear running vertically from the corner of one of her eyes. Outside, there was the rattling of trolley wheels, the comforting, soft clomp of nurses' shoes.

'You've been through so much,' I said softly, brushing the hair from her face. 'You were so brave.'

She forced a smile but seemed distant somehow. I hoped it was a combination of the drugs and tiredness and not a reluctance to meet her baby. It wasn't as if I couldn't understand the turmoil she must feel. Her life had altered in ways she probably could never have imagined a year earlier – as well as the sense of loss at losing her family, what she had gained in its place was a huge burden of responsibility; a wonderful, precious burden but one that was bound to weigh heavily nonetheless – it was such a strange situation; happy and sad, all at the same time.

'Has Papa been told?' she asked quietly, her eyes averted. She picked at invisible threads on the white sheet beneath her fingers.

'I'm not sure, honey. I did call Peggy to let her know. Would you like me to find out?'

Seeing the hurt in her eyes as she glanced up made my own heart begin to ache. She shook her head slowly but I could see that she wasn't sure. After everything that had happened, she still wanted the comfort of a loving parent. It was amazing that she had enough capacity in her heart to forgive him and I wasn't sure that he deserved such devotion. I wondered whether he felt any regret when he had heard the news, whether he would feel loss knowing that he wouldn't hold his newborn grandchild in his arms. Filled with a sudden anger that I couldn't swallow down, I turned away from Zadie and started tidying the tall cabinet beside her bed.

'I think I would like to …' I heard her say as I swapped the position of a box of tissues with a lamp for no good reason. I turned towards her and she pulled the mask off, over her head. Still hissing faintly with wisps of white gas, it lodged itself in one of the gaps in the metal-framed headboard.

'What, honey?'

'I think I do want to see her,' she said quietly, 'but I'm scared.' Her chin trembled.

'I understand,' I said, grabbing her hand and giving it a squeeze. 'But I'll be right here beside you. One little look can't hurt you.'

A few minutes later a midwife with a greying bob, curled under at the ends, silently wheeled a transparent crib through the double doors. Giving me a half-wink, she turned and left us alone.

I pulled back the white sheet that was draped over her loosely swaddled form and gently lifted the baby up to my shoulder. Resting my flat palm on her back, my fingers formed a cradle to support her head and I laid her back in my arms. She yawned and looked up at me, her tiny mouth forming the shape of an 'O', her small fists resting, one on each cheek. I glanced towards Zadie who had stilled in quiet, anxious watchfulness.

'There. Go to Mama,' I whispered.

Zadie opened her arms awkwardly, holding them out in front of her like a child expecting a present. Leaning over,

I laid the baby, wrapped in a cellular blanket, in her arms. The teenager stared down, her anxious frown instantly replaced with a look of tenderness. Mesmerised, she took the little hand in her own and then leaned down, planting a soft kiss on the tiny fingertips. My heart filled at the sight, swelling in my chest.

'It feels strange to be called Mama. I don't feel like her mummy,' she said, her eyes fixed on the sleepy baby.

'Well, from where I'm standing you certainly look like it,' I said. 'You're handling her like an expert.'

'Really?' she asked, her eyes shiny with tears.

'Really, really,' I said, patting her on the shoulder. 'I'm so proud of you, Zadie.'

And that was it. Her shoulders slumped and the floodgates opened. She cried and cried, her tears rolling down her cheeks and onto the baby's soft hair. Easing the swaddled form from her arms, I laid her gently in the crib and took Zadie into my arms.

'I want to give her all the love that I never had,' she sobbed into my shoulder. Heartened, I stroked the back of her head, daring to nurse the hope that the worst was truly behind her.

It was chilly when I left the hospital that evening, only a little above freezing. Sofia had accompanied Nadeen to the hospital to meet her niece and, knowing that they would stay with her until the end of visiting hours, I didn't feel like I was abandoning her. Nadeen seemed to hold no bitterness towards her family and I was sure that her natural positivity and quiet determination would help to buffer

Zadie from the pain of being estranged from her other siblings and her father. Before I left I thanked Sofia for all she had done for us, and, as we hugged, Zadie made an announcement – she had decided to name her daughter Nailah, after her mother. Nadeen, cradling her niece in her arms, dissolved into happy tears.

As I drove home the image of Zadie cradling her daughter so lovingly stayed with me and I felt buoyed, optimistic. The streets seemed to shine with radiance as if they had been spring cleaned and then outlined with a black felt-tip. Our local shops shimmered with an unfamiliar glow, as if everything around us had been given the chance of a fresh start.

Zadie spent the next three nights in hospital and was finally discharged around lunchtime on the second Tuesday in November. She hobbled slowly to the car wearing the robe she had arrived in, although her hair was loose. It was the first time I had seen her outside of the house without a headscarf on and I wondered whether she had made a conscious decision to leave it off. Her face was creased with discomfort from the caesarean scar and I suspected that she was too uncomfortable to give much thought to anything else, especially something as irrelevant as clothing. She stared around her on the journey home as if she too was seeing everything for the first time. Sitting in the back of the car, she held her daughter's small hand in her own and gazed down at her with such tenderness; it was clear how much she loved her.

Peggy was her first visitor. She bustled into the living room, wheezing with the effort of carrying a wicker basket filled with bits and pieces for the baby. Her dedication brought a swell of admiration to my throat. It was one of those times when I understood why the British care system was so highly respected all over the world. Often, through high-profile cases that are reported in the media, we only hear the worst examples, but the way Zadie had been cared for, not only by social services but also the NHS, was exceptionally good.

After Peggy we received a steady stream of visitors throughout the day. Jenny, Liz and Rachel turned up unexpectedly, eager to catch a glimpse of the new baby. The neighbours popped in to see us, each of them bearing flowers or chocolates or little sleep suits for the baby. The newborn was passed around like a parcel, closely watched by Zadie who hovered in front of whoever was holding the precious package. She kneeled politely in front of our friends, ready as a safety net, should anyone be clumsy enough to drop her.

Towards the end of the afternoon Zadie began to wilt. She smiled politely and tried her best to chip in with the conversations going on around her – mainly revolving around our visitors' own experiences of childbirth – but her eyes became glassy and her voice slowed, almost to a slur. I remembered how tiring it was to entertain visitors after having a baby and so I tried to usher them out as graciously as I could, reluctant though they were to leave.

Later that evening I drew the curtains in Zadie's room and tucked her in, the baby asleep beside her in the Moses basket. Her eyes were heavy and she looked exhausted but she rejected my offer to keep the baby in with me so that she could get a full night's rest. Standing at the doorway, my eyes ran over the small soft toys that had been given as gifts throughout the day. Zadie had arranged them carefully on the shelves above the changing table, the Mother Goose quilt from my mum taking pride of place, hung up on the far wall near the crib.

The next few days seemed to pass in a blur. Megan was coming up to four months and could already roll onto her tummy and back again. I could no longer potter from room to room and rely on her being safe, so I couldn't turn my back, even for a second. She was so strong that she was already able to sit unaided for several seconds before sinking back onto a pile of cushions – something that caused her and Jamie no end of amusement.

Zadie, face puffy with hormone-induced tears, was mostly oblivious to all that was going on around her, submerged as she was in a struggle to establish breastfeeding. I could see by the panic in her eyes that Nailah's crying was upsetting her but to her credit she stuck with it, transferring the baby to all different positions, singing, bobbing up and down on the spot. Her dark eyes were shadowed with deep fatigue and, remembering my own struggles to feed Emily, I was full of admiration for her determination to keep trying. As a new mum I had read somewhere that babies born onto their mothers' tummy and left to their own devices managed to move their limbs enough to crawl towards the breast, latching on and feeding unaided. That small nugget of information had caused me no end of frustration at the time; it just wasn't as easy to pull off as it should have been.

Betrayed

At the end of a particularly long day about four days after leaving the hospital, Zadie came to me in the kitchen. The baby was screaming, her face ruddy with fury as she beat her small fists on Zadie's shoulder. 'Why won't she stop?' she asked tearfully, swaying back and forth with Nailah in her arms. Tears were rolling freely down her cheeks and her eyes were narrow, swollen with tiredness.

'She may be a little hungry,' I said, as gently as I could. The midwife who had called in to see Zadie earlier that day had been a little concerned the baby may be at risk of dehydrating. With a devotion I could hardly believe, Zadie had carefully sterilised a tiny spoon and was giving Nailah regular sips of water, but what she really needed was some milk. 'Maybe your milk isn't fully in yet.'

A cloud crossed her features, as if she felt she was responsible for the delay. 'It's nothing you've done,' I said, rubbing her shoulder. 'Meg said that there can be a bit of a delay after a caesarean but what you're giving her now is more important than milk.'

'The colostrum?' she asked.

'Yes. It will protect her from all sorts of things so it's wonderful she's had that. Tell you what, though. You might find your milk comes a bit quicker if you get some rest. Why don't you let me take over for a while?'

Zadie sagged in reluctant acceptance and handed the screaming baby to me. Nailah, the rascal, stopped crying almost immediately, probably because she could smell milk on Zadie. Instinct told her she wasn't going to get any out of me.

But Zadie took it personally. 'I don't think she likes me,' she choked, fresh tears rolling down her cheeks.

'Don't be daft, love. She's just a bit hungry. Babies are supposed to cry when they're hungry.'

'But formula milk is really bad for them. She already has a chance of something being wrong with her,' she sobbed miserably. I presumed she was talking about the dangers for a baby born from incest and I found myself running through the symptoms I had researched when I discovered that her brother was the father: genetic disorders, higher than usual infant mortality, reduced immune system function. The list went on, and so it wasn't surprising that Zadie, a new mum, should worry, especially with the proliferation of nightmare stories she had probably read on the internet. But it was clear that Nailah was absolutely perfect.

'I think it's about time we thought a bit about what might be good for you, as well as the baby. You matter too, honey.'

She looked at me and sobbed. 'But I will have failed her. I wanted to be the perfect mother.'

'Oh, honey. The perfect mother doesn't exist, however good our intentions. If truth be told, most of us just muddle through. At least, that's what I've spent the last 16 years doing,' I said, transferring the now sleeping baby into the crook of my other arm. 'Who was it who said that if you're not making mistakes you're not doing anything? Much of motherhood is discovering what doesn't work before you find out what does.' I laughed. 'Only don't tell social services I said that.'

She cocked an eyebrow. 'Really? Did you find it as hard as I do?'

'I was a mess when I had Emily. Didn't brush my teeth for the first three days, and it was a whole week before I got time to change my underwear.'

Zadie laughed through her tears.

'Honestly, I was terrified that something bad was going to happen to her. She seemed so tiny, too vulnerable. I almost wished her first few months away, just so she'd be more robust, safer. I was paranoid and *so* tense. I was probably a nightmare to live with at the time. And yet what I wouldn't give to bundle her up in a blanket and hold her in my arms now.'

Zadie smiled, wiping her eyes. 'I just never knew how hard it would be. No one ever says.'

'I know, honey, I know. When Emily was born I wondered why people didn't send cards saying, "Oh dear, you've had a baby, you're in for a year of hell." It's exhausting and frustrating and sometimes *so* monotonous.' I stroked her hair. 'But it's also just about the absolute best thing in the whole world. And they grow up so fast,' I said, surprised to find my own eyes damp. 'You have to try to savour every minute. And I'll help you all I can.'

As it was, the bottle did most of the work for us. The formula worked like a glass of sherry on my mother; she was flat out for the next five hours, and so was Zadie.

Des made us his last visit of the day. He seemed a little nervous as he offered his congratulations to Zadie, unusually deflated. Later, when Zadie had gone to bed and Emily and Jamie were watching television, we went into the dining room to talk. We sat at the table.

'I'm leaving at the end of the week, Rosie,' he said almost as soon as I had taken the seat opposite. His eyes were downcast, voice gravelly.

I felt a small stab of pain in my chest. My lips twitched with the effort of summoning a response. 'Oh,' was all I could say. I had been so busy that I had filed his plans in an unwanted information bubble at the back of my mind.

He was studying me closely, as if he was trying to work something out. After a moment his lips parted as if he was about to speak but then sealed shut again. I fidgeted, drawing horizontal lines across the tabletop with my fingernail. 'Right,' he said eventually, slapping his denim-covered knee. 'Pack up everyone's things. You're coming with me.'

I laughed, taking it as the joke I thought it was.

Des didn't smile. He reached across the table and scooped my hand up in his own, holding it with a firm grip. 'Or give me a reason to stay, Rosie.'

I glanced away, thinking about the way Des had always slotted so well into my ever-changing family, the banter going back and forth between him and the children, all of the laughter. It was probably only a second or two that his words hung in the air between us, but he was staring at me so anxiously that it felt like much longer. To see a man who was usually so comfortable in his own skin acting nervously was so endearing and for a split-second it was tempting to leave everything behind. I have always longed to go to the US, and the thought of starting somewhere new, with someone else to rely on other than myself, was more than a little appealing. But then, absurdly, I thought of the chicken in the bottom of the fridge that had to be used by the end of the week and the tea-towel marked with pasta sauce that I had left in the sink for a soak. And then the thought that trumped everything; I pictured Emily's forlorn expression at the breakfast table when Jamie had told me about their father's unexpected announcement.

My throat tightened around the words I wanted to say to him. I wasn't quite sure how to explain. I'm not even sure I understood myself.

'Right then,' he said softly when I didn't reply. His eyes lingered for a moment longer and then before I knew it the front door was open and he was walking down the path. I stood at the window watching as he climbed into his car, my fingers tapping on the glass, though too softly for him to hear. I wrestled the impulse to fly up the path after him. Don't be so ridiculous, Rosie, I told myself, you're not a teenager any more.

I let my hand fall and watched the mist from the warmth of my fingers shrink and slowly disappear.

That evening I felt a sort of ecstatic relief. I think that, though I felt a tug at my heart knowing that I might never see Des again, I was so glad and relieved to know that I had meant something to him. I supposed that it wasn't just children that craved a sense of belonging; everyone needed to feel wanted, and I felt a flicker of joy that Des's regard for me wasn't a figment of my imagination.

* * *

Zadie was wonderful with the baby. As the weeks went by she grew in confidence, some primal knowledge guiding her along so that she was able to soothe the baby effortlessly, with a hum under her breath, often even just a light touch on the head. If Nailah so much as squeaked Zadie was beside her in seconds, cooing, singing, rocking, singing lullabies. Quietly tenacious, she had managed to overcome her difficulties with feeding, and whenever we were home Nailah was breastfed. Too shy to feed her baby in public, we took bottles with us whenever we went out.

At our foster-carer support group I had heard of mother and baby placements going badly wrong. Foster placements were sometimes offered to expectant young parents to give them the opportunity to learn the skills needed to care for a young baby but sometimes young mums used their foster carers as on-site babysitters and went out clubbing, even before their milk came in. Zadie couldn't have been more different. She was so attentive that I barely got a look-in.

It was a joy to watch the two of them responding to each other, their bond strong against all the odds. Zadie had coped with all that life had thrown at her and came out fighting. I couldn't have been prouder. But there was another challenge that I felt she needed to confront, and when Nailah was eight weeks old, just a few days into the New Year of 2012, I felt the time had come to bring the subject up.

'You have a life full of possibilities ahead of you, Zadie,' I told her one afternoon, while she was leaning over Nailah, distracted from the task of changing the little one's nappy by blowing raspberries on her tummy, the pair of them giggling. I remembered what Sofia had said about some women living a life full of regret – I didn't want that for Zadie. Her life had changed immeasurably but that didn't have to mean that her dreams were now out of her grasp. 'I could look after Nailah for a few hours each day while you go to school,' I ventured. 'You'd soon catch up on what you've missed. You could still be a vet, if that's what you wanted.'

Zadie fastened the poppers of Nailah's vest and lifted her gently to her chest, her palm cradling the back of her head. She was wearing a pair of casual black trousers and a loose smock top, one of the outfits she had chosen online a couple of weeks earlier. Her robes were tucked away at the back of her drawer, although whenever we went out she still chose to wear her headscarf. She chewed her lip, then nuzzled the baby's neck. 'I love her too much to leave her, though.'

I smiled and knelt beside her. 'I know you do. But she'll be right here waiting for you when you get back, honey.'

Everyone needed an outlet, something to put their creative energies into, however much they loved their children. For me it was the hour I spent writing, late in the evening when the children had gone to bed. For someone as young as Zadie, a life outside of home was even more important, especially if she wanted to build a brighter future for her and Nailah, one where she was able to support both of them without relying on anyone else.

And so less than a fortnight later, as I stood at the front door, Megan in one arm and Nailah in the other, Zadie planted kisses on the tops of their heads and ventured off to school on her own. Deciding whether she should make her own way to school had been a difficult decision. As a parent, setting the goal posts is a tricky enough task; is it safe for them to sleep over at a new friend's house? Are they responsible enough to pop to the shops on their own? Would it be sensible or overprotective to refuse permission for them to meet with their friends at the local park?

As a foster carer, those decisions were usually complicated by all sorts of other factors. In the past, a child's social worker would shoulder the burden of making everyday decisions, but recent changes in practice meant that they were able to delegate their responsibility to the foster carer. In some ways the change was helpful; children were much less likely to miss out on school trips or sleepovers without the delays that come with waiting for the all clear from social services. Fortunately, Peggy was more than happy to discuss my plans for Zadie, particularly in the light of the teenager's background and previous concerns about her family. Together we decided that she was old enough to make her own way to school. She was 14 after all and it didn't seem fair to deny her the small freedoms that other children her age enjoyed. I drilled her on staying safe, as I did my own children, and bought her a mobile phone to take with her for extra peace of mind.

By mid-afternoon on her first day I bundled the babies up in coats and blankets and strapped them into the double pram, too eager to hear how her day had gone to stay at home and wait for her return. We took a slow walk to the park and, after giving Megan a few minutes in the swing, we made our way to the bus stop to meet Zadie.

Betrayed

One glance at her face as she stepped off the bus told me that I needn't have worried. Besides her excitement at seeing her baby daughter, there was an energy in her face that I had never seen before. As she lifted Nailah out of her pram and planted a dozen kisses on her face, I was certain, mistakenly, as it happened, that her struggles were finally over.

With just myself and the two babies at home, time slowed and the days seemed endless. It was ironic, then, that there was never a moment to get anything done. Within a week, the house was covered with a fine layer of dust. If I took too much notice I knew the disorder would have bothered me so I chose to ignore it, hoping that social workers wouldn't decide to swoop on the house to conduct one of their unannounced checks. Babies turn into toddlers in a flash, and I wanted to enjoy them; Megan was already crawling. Besides, I literally had no spare time. It was enough to keep up with the washing, shopping and cooking, and if I could fit in a hair wash every few days I was doing well. If ever I managed to co-ordinate Megan and Nailah's naps, which seemed a Herculean feat that was mostly beyond me, I tended to either catch up on writing my daily fostering diary or treat myself and join them.

It was when my mother visited, after the new arrangement had been in place for ten days or so, that I actually noticed how bad the situation was; in the living room every surface was covered with little clothes, cloth books and wooden toys, the flowers I had grabbed on my last whizz around the supermarket hanging mournfully from their vases. 'Oh my goodness, have you been burgled?!' Mum exclaimed, throwing her coat off and pulling up her sleeves, ready for action before she'd even reached the living room.

'I haven't had time,' I said lamely, a baby perched in the crook of each arm.

Mum tutted. 'Well, if you'd put them down for a minute you might find you get more done.'

'I was about to,' I said, 'but as soon as I do one of them wakes up.'

Her eyes swept over the sleeping pair and her expression softened. 'Ah, look at them,' she whispered, taking Megan from me in one smooth motion and settling herself on the sofa, the baby snuggled in the crook of her arm. 'Here we are,' she said, reaching out her spare arm. 'Give the little dot to me and you put the kettle on.'

I got more done in the next couple of hours while Mum nursed 'the twins' than I had all week.

Chapter 21

By the end of a gloriously warm March, Nailah was nearly five months old and thriving. Already sitting up, she would wiggle in excitement when any of us passed by but saved her open-mouthed smiles for her mummy. Megan, at almost nine months, was able to walk around the furniture and delighted Nailah by her very presence.

Zadie had managed to catch up on all she had missed in the curriculum by studying well into the evening and even continuing after giving the baby her dream feed at ten o'clock. How she managed it I couldn't say, especially since Nailah still fed through the night, every three or four hours.

It was the third week in April, just when I thought nothing could disrupt our happy, if a little unconventional, family, that things went horribly, drastically wrong.

The Easter holidays had passed quietly, unusually heavy winds and driving rain keeping us inside. At the beginning of the new term, Zadie walked away from us as we waited at the gate, turning when she reached the end of the road to raise her hand in a little wave. She scrunched her shoulders up, caressing the babies through the air with an affectionate smile.

And then she didn't come back.

The police sergeant arrived at 7 p.m., just after I had put Megan to bed. The worry hadn't really set in until after Emily and Jamie got in from school. The mobile I had bought for Zadie when she started travelling alone was switched off and she'd never been late before, but as I got tea ready I ran through all the reasonable scenarios: the battery was flat, her bus had broken down or perhaps one of her teachers had asked her to stay behind. It was only when I rang her school at just after 5 p.m. that I began to panic – the school receptionist, sounding quizzical but distracted, told me that Zadie had been absent all day.

Nailah, not due for a feed for another hour or so, was lying on the rug making contented noises. I sat nearby on the sofa, wringing my hands and trying my best to explain to the officer what Zadie was like.

'I hear what you're saying but I'm sure she just ran off,' the sergeant who had cheerfully introduced himself as Paul offered as he flicked through his notebook trying to find an empty page. Without the uniform he wouldn't have looked out of place in a gangster movie. He was a heavy-set man in his forties and the thin biro clutched between his meaty fingers looked in danger of snapping under the pressure. There was a kindness behind his cragginess but he just didn't seem to appreciate the gravity of the situation. 'We get this sort of thing all the time, believe me. She'll turn up in a day or two. Lots of kids go AWOL from care.'

Beside him on the sofa, I pressed my lips together and swallowed down a rush of irritation. His response wasn't really, on the face of it, all that unreasonable. Zadie had form for running away and, to an outsider, a 14-year-old girl with a baby of her own meant a likely rebel. 'There's no way she would leave the baby,' I said quietly, almost to myself. It was at that moment that it really sank in. Zadie had been taken. I closed my eyes, the realisation making my stomach churn and my throat narrow.

When I looked up he was staring at me with concern, the professional façade gone from his face. He touched me on the shoulder. 'You all right, love?'

'She's been snatched,' I said, my mouth parched as the certainty settled itself heavily on my chest. 'I'm sure of it. They've taken her.'

And then I explained everything, as quickly as I could: Zadie's own fears, disclosed to me months earlier, before Nailah's birth. My visit to Sofia and her stark warnings that the family would seek to remove the source of their shame. Paul listened carefully, scribbling intermittently and taking a note of Sofia's contact details so that he could gather some more background information.

Reassuringly, before I'd finished talking he held up his hand to stop me, removing his airwave radio from his jacket pocket. There was a crackle as he fiddled with one of the dials and then he raised it to his lips. 'Control? I need an urgent welfare check at …,' he flicked back a few pages in his notebook and then read out Zadie's home address.

'Try not to worry,' he said as he stowed the radio back into his pocket, although his own expression was now grave. 'A squad car is on its way to check the home address and I'll organise a warrant for the morning. We'll search the house, the garage and all the associated premises. No stone unturned, Mrs Lewis.'

I nodded, eager for him to leave and get on with the job of finding her. Sofia's warning about the girls who went missing, never to be found again, kept playing over and over in my mind, and suddenly I felt so light-headed that I closed my eyes, praying it wasn't already too late.

My nausea faded a little as he snapped his notebook shut and made a move to pick up his black briefcase. 'Are you sure you're all right? You look very pale.'

'Yes, I'll be OK,' I said, scooping Nailah up and resting her on my hip. My nausea had faded a little with the knowledge that the police had already taken some action, but as soon as I closed the door on the sergeant it surged again. I laid the baby down on the rug in the middle of the floor and ran to the bathroom, throwing up in the sink. Panting and gasping, I hurried back to the lounge and sat beside Nailah, patting my mouth with a tissue.

With each hour that passed my panic increased. It was a relief to tuck Nailah into her crib that evening, though she was tetchy, reluctant to take her bottle, perhaps because my trembling fingers offered anything but comfort. It was almost as if she could sense the danger her mother was in.

Running my eyes around the half-light of Zadie's bedroom, my eyes fell on one of her headscarves, neatly folded on the top of her dresser. Reaching for it, I let it unfurl and then ran my fingers over and over the soft material wishing it were a talisman so that I could conjure her back. Aware of a pain in my throat, I wrapped it around Nailah, easing one of the corners into her curled fist. After stroking her head for a couple of minutes her eyelids began to flicker and she rolled onto her side, her small hand nestled beneath her chin. Securing more blankets around her, I began to hum one of the songs Zadie used to settle her, realising that her young mother could be halfway across the world by now, perhaps even already married. I shuddered, imagining the possibility that we might always be left wondering what had happened to her. Worst of all and so ironically, since it was the last thing Zadie would ever have wanted, little Nailah would grow up without the love of her own mother.

Downstairs all was quiet but there was tension in the air. Emily sat staring into space as Jamie leaned over the back of the sofa, watching out of the window. And some people say that foster carers do what they do for the money. I looked at the concern on their faces and felt the tremble in my own fingers, the nerve pulsing above my right eye. No one could possibly need money this badly.

We sat quietly during that first evening, trying to distract ourselves from the worry by playing card games, though without any of our usual banter. At midnight I managed to persuade Emily and Jamie to go to bed, but without their company the restlessness really kicked in.

I wandered aimlessly from room to room, my eyes scanning the furniture, our books, trying to find some task I could settle myself to. Uncomfortable wherever I went, and faintly claustrophobic, I grabbed a blanket from the sofa and draped it across my shoulders, then walked to the front door and opened it. The air was crisp, sharp with a tang of frost. Taking a deep breath I sighed and sat down on the top step. A late evening mist was lowering itself over the hedges that bordered the houses opposite ours, stars glittering in the cloudless sky. Somewhere in the distance a dog began barking. Leaning my head against the door frame, I shivered and wrapped the blanket closer around myself, hoping that wherever Zadie was, she was tucked up warm.

For the rest of the night I sat on the sofa, my eyes flicking from the phone balanced on the armrest to the clock above the fireplace and then back again. Every so often my head would nod to my chest, only to jerk up at the tiniest noise. Peggy rang every few hours for an update, her voice thick with tiredness. By 4 a.m., as I relayed the latest message from Sergeant Nicholls, that there was no trace of Zadie at her family's address, I was beginning to lose hope that we would ever hear anything from her again. The officer had reassured me that everything that could be done was being done – Sofia had been contacted and was working alongside the team to provide invaluable cultural knowledge and, I was pleased to hear, the local Islamic community leaders were on board to support the search. 'We've not run out of ideas yet, love,' Paul had said, but I could tell by Peggy's hesitant tone, as I relayed his words, that she was as fearful as I was.

Saying goodbye to Peggy, I lowered my mobile to the coffee table in slow motion, reluctant to let it go. I thought of Zadie's gentle kindness and humour, her timidity and the well of sadness underneath it all. Resting my head in cupped hands, I steered my anxiety towards anger. She didn't deserve any of this, I raged, but then, what child did? Didn't it always come down to that same basic fact – every child deserved to be cherished. It was difficult to accept that there were times when, however hard outsiders may try to help, some children were always going to slip through the net.

In the morning, after persuading Emily and Jamie that the best thing they could do was keep to their usual routine and go to school, I tried my best to fill my head with mundane thoughts; what to cook for dinner, what games I could invent that Megan and Nailah might enjoy. It didn't really matter what I did, I told myself, falling back on my trusted philosophy when everything seemed to be going wrong, as long as I was busy enough to keep the jitters at bay. Trouble was, my renegade stomach was having none of it, and every time I stopped for breath the awful churning would start up again.

After lunch and with still no word from Sergeant Nicholls, I strapped Nailah and Megan into their pram and set off for the shops. Every now and then I stopped, having imagined that my mobile was ringing, only to check and be confronted with the same blank screen. I passed several people I knew along the way and we exchanged nods and smiles. 'Yes, I'm fine, thank you,' I said several times over, wondering as I walked away why we all feel the need to keep up such a pretence.

By late afternoon I was so drained that I had already laid out Nailah and Megan's sleep suits, willing for 7 p.m. to come. Megan, on the cusp of taking her first steps, loved nothing more than holding onto my hands and pottering around, helping me with whatever task I was doing, but with my nerves so frayed it was difficult to muster the energy to involve her. Usually so happy and generous with her smiles, she had spent the last couple of days studying me with a worried frown, no doubt wondering what had gone wrong. It was as if the whole house had gone into mourning.

Emily and Jamie tore down the path together at just gone 4 o'clock, their faces eager and hopeful. I greeted them with a small shake of the head and they grimaced, their shoulders sinking as they dropped their bags slowly to the floor.

That night I dozed fitfully on the sofa again. I couldn't go to bed: it would have felt like an abandonment of Zadie. Fully dressed, I arranged some pillows in an upside down 'V' and leaned against them, keeping my mobile close to my side. As my eyelids began to flicker I hoped with all my heart that, wherever Zadie was, she was confident that, no matter what, I would do my best for Nailah. And at least I was sure of one thing; whatever she was doing, she would know in her heart that we were all rooting for her.

Each morning I woke with a sweeping roll in my stomach and a tight feeling in my chest. I tried to remain hopeful, remembering what Sergeant Nicholls had said about leaving no stone unturned in the hunt for Zadie, but with the arrival of May, after a week of no positive news, it was becoming increasingly difficult to visualise a happy ending to it all.

A week after her disappearance, Emily got up, pensive and tired looking. I made her a cup of tea and then left her watching Megan. It was a little after half past six and Nailah was still asleep. I reckoned on little more than five or ten minutes before she woke so I undressed quickly and stepped into the shower. Even before I had rinsed the shampoo from my hair I heard heavy footsteps thumping up the stairs, Jamie shouting as he came. My heart flew into my mouth.

'Mum! You've missed a call,' Jamie shouted through the door.

'Pass it through,' I said breathlessly as I stood dripping over the bath mat. Leaning over, I unlocked the door, opened it a crack and snatched the phone as soon as Jamie slipped it through the gap. From Zadie's room I could hear a weak cry – Nailah was waking up. Fumbling to unlock the keypad, I scrolled down to 'Missed calls', my pulse rising when I saw the words 'Private number'. A faint blue light in the top right-hand corner of the screen was flashing – someone had left me a message.

Hurrying into the bedroom, I picked Nailah up then laid her down on Zadie's bed. She beamed up at me as I sat beside her, cooing and tickling her tummy while dialling to pick up the voice message with my free hand. Jamie, standing in the doorway, started to say something but I waved my hand to shush him, frowning as I listened to the message.

'I don't believe it,' I said as I turned to Jamie, the phone still clamped to my ear even though Sergeant Nicholls's recorded voice had fallen silent. 'My spoons set off the bleeper! Zadie's been found at the airport.'

After a check-up at the local hospital, Sergeant Nicholls dropped Zadie home. When we heard the squad car pull up on the drive I rushed to pick Nailah up and then Jamie, Emily and I ran to the front door. Zadie looked pale and drawn as she climbed out of the back of the panda car. She was dressed in a robe that was crumpled and much too small, her feet and ankles visible below the uneven hem and the cuffs barely touching her wrists. Her old rucksack rested on her shoulder, the base covered in dark watermarks, as if at some point it had rested in a puddle.

She turned, her eyes lighting up as soon as she caught sight of us. Gathering her robe up in her hands, she charged towards us and, taking Nailah gently into her arms, she planted rapid kisses all over her soft hair. The three of us encircled them in a group hug and then Zadie and the others went into the house, Emily and Jamie firing rapid questions at her, as if she'd just returned from a holiday. I hung back to have a quiet word with Sergeant Nicholls. Eyes shining, he was leaning over the open driver's door, his craggy, square jaw softened in a tender smile.

'So, what exactly happened?' I asked in a hushed tone when the others had disappeared from view.

He walked around the door and perched on the boot, crossing his feet at the ankles and folding his bulky arms. 'Well, it seems they'd been planning their little operation for weeks. Zadie was moved around after she was snatched to avoid detection and when their fake passports were ready she was escorted to the airport by an uncle and cousin. We found flight tickets on them for Egypt but Zadie was held up at the body scanner; she kept setting the alarm off. When security staff took her aside she told them she had been kidnapped.' He levelled his gaze, smiling. 'I have to say, Rosie, those spoons were a stroke of genius. How did you ...'

I cut him short with a hand brushed through the air. 'I can't take the credit for that, I'm afraid. I was following advice from Sofia.'

'Ahhh.' He lifted his chin. 'Well, Sofia quite probably saved that girl's life.'

We fell silent for a moment and I wondered whether his mind was marvelling at the sheer randomness of life, as mine was. Decisions made in a heartbeat had the potency to ripple outwards, changing the course of a whole lifetime. If Sofia hadn't taken the time to talk to me, Zadie might not even be here. It was a disturbing thought, and as I thanked Paul and walked back into the house I resolved to make the most of every day and put all the petty worries that sometimes got me down firmly aside.

One evening, about three weeks after Zadie had returned to us, Sergeant Nicholls rang. At first when I heard his voice he sounded so jovial that I thought he was just making a courtesy call to make sure all was well with Zadie or to update us on the prosecution of the family members who had snatched Zadie and tried to smuggle her out of the country. As I listened to what he had to say I sank down on the sofa, my free hand rising to cover my cheek. 'I don't believe it,' I half-whispered. Emily, Jamie and Zadie migrated from their seats to gather round, their faces full of concern.

After thanking the police officer, I lowered my phone to the cushion beside me and looked at Zadie. Her expression was grave, no doubt wondering what else could possibly go wrong for her.

'Zadie,' I said, reaching out to grip her hands, holding them tight. 'You're not going to believe this, darling. They've found your mum.'

Her eyes grew wide. She let out a breath. 'Really?' she asked, a stream of tears rolling down her face.

'Really,' I replied, smiling through my own mist of tears.

And then the two of us were laughing and crying all at once. Behind us, Emily and Jamie raised their hands in a high five.

It took a while to decide on a meeting place for the reunion. Nailah Hassan was more than welcome in our home but I worried that she might feel a little intimidated by the prospect of meeting her daughters after so many years in the house of a stranger. Peggy had suggested the neutral territory of a local café but the event was so momentous that it seemed fitting to choose a grand setting; somewhere with enough nooks and crannies for me to drift into the background and allow the family some privacy.

We eventually agreed on Chatsworth House in Derbyshire, one of Emily's suggestions. The stately home was a bit of a trek from us but the journey was straightforward, and Nailah, having flown into East Midlands Airport from Egypt, was staying in a B&B in nearby Chesterfield.

And so early one Friday morning at the beginning of June we left the babies in the care of my mother and set off for Derbyshire. Zadie and Nadeen sat quietly in the back of the car, each so absorbed in their own thoughts that they barely uttered a word during the whole two-hour journey. As we neared our meeting place the roads narrowed, the trees arched overhead shading us from the emerging sun. Surrounded by parkland and nestled between low, rocky hills and the River Derwent, Chatsworth House was stunning.

We arrived with plenty of time to spare and so ambled slowly through the heather moorland leading to formal gardens. Cows dipped their heads in a distant meadow and a pair of squirrels scrambled down the trunk of a nearby tree, the bark crackling under their claws. Down on the grass they raised themselves up on their hind legs, craned their necks and then, as if startled by an inaudible noise, simultaneously darted beneath some neatly clipped bushes. All of these things I pointed out to the girls and they bobbed their heads in acknowledgement, both too far away to respond with any more than a vague smile. When we reached the Emperor Fountain, our pre-arranged meeting place, the two sisters stood motionless, each holding the other's trembling hand.

A roux of pine and freshly dug earth clung to the light breeze and I breathed it in deeply, trying to reign in my own nervous protectiveness – I had no idea what their mother would be like and they had both been through so much; I hoped the reunion would be all they expected it to be. In the distance I could see a woman walking towards us. She was wearing a long black skirt and a plain dark top but her head was uncovered so, assuming that Nailah would be wearing a headscarf, I quickly dismissed her, my eyes scanning the landscape for other possibilities.

But then I noticed a movement behind me; a stiffening in Nadeen's posture, a quickly inhaled breath from Zadie. The girls released their hands and froze, watching as the woman in the long skirt quickened her step. When she was about ten feet away she stopped and stared, raising her hand to shield her eyes from the sun. Her other hand flew to her mouth and she began to shake. I found myself holding my breath as I glanced back at the girls, the agony of anticipation so intense on their young faces.

'Girls?' the woman said in a querulous voice, the word sounding like a question, as if she couldn't quite believe they were really there in front of her.

Nadeen held out her free hand and smiled, offering a bridge across all the years that they had been separated. Zadie laughed a little hysterically and followed suit. Their mother flew to them, locking them both in a tight embrace. She was talking between sobs, her foreign words tumbling into their hair. Every so often she pulled away, cupping each of their faces in a trembling hand.

Tears were pouring down Zadie's cheeks. 'I've missed you, Mama.'

The three of them closed arms around each other and I circled, first a few feet away and then further, keeping them within my sight. After a few minutes Nailah pulled away from her daughters and reached her hand out towards me. Zadie and Nadeen turned to look at me, smiling through their tears. I crossed the path and walked towards them. When I reached the group Nailah took hold of my hand and kissed it, repeating soft-sounding words over and over as she enclosed it between her palms.

Zadie's departure was as her arrival had been – quiet and understated. It was July, just four weeks after the reunion with her mother, when we packed up her and little Nailah's things and carried them downstairs to the hall. Nadeen, who had just turned 18, was staying in a small flat above a women's centre in east London, working as their administrator to cover the cost of her rent. After checking with them, she invited Zadie to join her.

Their mother, Nailah, hoping that asylum would be granted by the British government, was also staying in the flat and was more than happy to help out, promising to look after the baby so that her youngest daughter could continue her education. There were the usual nerves in the air on the morning before Zadie's departure, each of us dreading the moment of saying goodbye. I think the babies sensed from our subdued moods that changes were afoot; their usual excited babble was muted, their expressions quizzical.

Even Peggy seemed reserved when she arrived at just after 10 a.m. to pick Zadie up. There was no booming greeting or impatient chivvying, just a brief, sympathetic glance thrown in my direction. Emily and Jamie helped Peggy and me as we loaded the cases into the boot of her car, Zadie keeping an eye on the babies as they tumbled around the living-room floor. With everything in place, I strapped Megan into her buggy and wheeled her one-handed onto the drive, Nailah balanced on my hip. Peggy smiled at me, nodded to Emily and Jamie and then climbed into the driver's seat with a creak from her hip and a small groan, leaving us to our goodbyes. Emily, already weeping, threw her arms around Zadie in a bear hug and stole my usual line, reminding her that we could be contacted by email, phone or text (at any time, day or night!).

When they pulled apart Emily covered her face with her hands, softly sobbing. Zadie brushed her eyes on her fore-arm then turned shyly to Jamie. He jogged awkwardly on the spot for a moment and then held his arms out at a stiff angle. They leaned towards each other, touched opposite shoulders and then straightened, both laughing and exchanging bashful glances.

Watching from behind, I leaned down to brush a kiss on little Nailah's perfect brow. She gazed up at me, smiling quizzically. 'Goodbye, my little angel,' I whispered, strok-ing her soft cheek. Zadie walked over and stood in front of me, her arms outstretched. Twisting Nailah around, I planted her into her mother's loving arms with a little pinch in my chest.

I looked at Zadie. 'You look after yourself,' I said, my voice cracking as I squeezed her arm.

'Oh, Rosie,' she cried, bursting into tears. 'How can I ever thank you?'

'You have nothing to thank me for,' I said, my eyes mist-ing over as I pulled her into a sideways-on cuddle. 'Just look after each other,' I said, planting a kiss first on Nailah's and then on Zadie's head.

Knowing how happy the family were to be reunited would make it easier not to dwell on the loss of Zadie, I was certain of that, but as I tipped Megan's buggy up the steps and followed Emily and Jamie back into the house I knew that we would all miss her gentle presence.

About a week after Zadie had moved on I accepted another placement and it was as I prepared our fostering room for the new arrival that I felt the teenager's absence most keenly. A lump rose to my throat as I moved around the space, my thoughts drifting to the special moments we'd shared and of new beginnings and hope for the future. One of the most important skills foster carers have to learn is the ability to shape themselves around their constantly changing family. By opening our home and hearts to another child, I was trying to move on in the best way I could.

Epilogue

Towards the end of November 2013 the British government granted Nailah Hassan refugee status, allowing her to stay in the UK. Zadie, a regular visitor to our home, told me that her mother was relieved and delighted by the news. I hoped that being part of her granddaughter's life and watching her grow might go some way to compensating for the years Nailah had missed out on being with her own daughters.

The family live in a small flat in east London but, with little Nailah starting nursery, all three women are now in paid employment and saving for a place of their own. Zadie continues to study in the evenings, still nursing the hope of working with animals one day. Wherever the family eventually settle and whatever they do, I am confident that they have freed themselves from the shackles of the past, their future promising to be a lot brighter than the life they had left behind.

ROSIE LEWIS

Trapped

The terrifying
true story of a
young girl's secret
world of abuse

The Terrifying True Story of
a Secret World of Abuse

Phoebe, an autistic nine-year-old girl, is taken into
care when a chance comment to one of her teachers
alerts the authorities. After several shocking incidents
of self-harming and threats to kill, experienced foster
carer Rosie Lewis begins to suspect that there is
much more to Phoebe's horrific past than she
could ever have imagined.

TRAPPED

AVAILABLE AS E-BOOK ONLY

An abandoned baby girl

Rosie is called to look after a new baby, born to an addict mother on a freezing cold December night, and to care for her until she can meet her forever family.

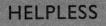

HELPLESS

Toddler Charlie is found after falling from a second-floor window

Once he is taken into care, Rosie helps terrified Charlie open up and uncovers his traumatic past.

A SMALL BOY'S CRY

ROSIE LEWIS

Two More Sleeps

A true short story

Found beneath a bench, seemingly alone

Angell comes into the home and heart of foster carer Rosie Lewis. Will Angell be destined to spend the rest of her childhood in care or will her mother return for her?

TWO MORE SLEEPS

eNewsletter

Moving Memoirs

Stories of hope, courage and the power of love…

If you loved this book, then you will love our Moving Memoirs eNewsletter

Sign up to…

- Be the first to hear about new books

- Get sneak previews from your favourite authors

- Read exclusive interviews

- Be entered into our monthly prize draw to win one of our latest releases before it's even hit the shops!

Sign up at

www.moving-memoirs.com